QUEER/TONGZHI CHINA

GENDERING ASIA

A Series on Gender Intersections

Gendering Asia is a well-established and exciting series addressing the ways in which power and constructions of gender, sex, sexuality and the body intersect with one another and pervade contemporary Asian societies. The series invites discussion of how people shape their identities as females or males and, at the same time, become shaped by the very societies in which they live. The series is concerned with the region as a whole in order to capture the wide range of understandings and practices that are found in East, Southeast and South Asian societies with respect to gendered roles and relations in various social, political, religious, and economic contexts. As a multidisciplinary series, *Gendering Asia* explores theoretical, empirical and methodological issues in the social sciences.

Series Editors: Wil Burghoorn, Gothenburg University and Cecilia Milwertz, NIAS (contact details at: http://www.niaspress.dk).

1. *Working and Mothering in Asia. Images, Ideologies and Identities*, edited by Theresa W. Devasahayam and Brenda S.A. Yeoh

2. *Making Fields of Merit. Buddhist Female Ascetics and Gendered Orders in Thailand*, by Monica Lindberg Falk

3. *Gender Politics in Asia. Women Manoeuvring within Dominant Gender Orders*, edited by Wil Burghoorn, Kazuki Iwanaga, Cecilia Milwertz and Qi Wang

4. *Lost Goddesses. The Denial of Female Power in Cambodian History*, by Trudy Jacobsen

5 *Gendered Inequalities in Asia. Configuring, Contesting and Recognizing Women and Men*, edited by Helle Rydstrøm

6. *Submitting to God. Women and Islam in Urban Malaysia*, by Sylva Frisk

7. *The Authority of Influence. Women and Power in Burmese History*, by Jessica Harriden

8. *Beyond the Singapore Girl. Discourses of Gender and Nation in Singapore*, by Chris Hudson

9. *Vietnam's New Middle Classes: Gender, Career, City* by Catherine Earl

10. *Gendered Entanglements: Revisiting Gender in Rapidly Changing Asia*, edited by Ragnhild Lund, Philippe Doneys and Bernadette P. Resurrección

11. *Queer/Tongzhi China: New Perspectives on Research, Activism and Media Cultures*, edited by Elisabeth L. Engebretsen and William F. Schroeder (with Hongwei Bao)

12. *Cultivating Gender. Meanings of Place and Work in Rural Vietnam*, by Cecilia Bergstedt

NIAS Press is the autonomous publishing arm of NIAS – Nordic Institute of Asian Studies, a research institute located at the University of Copenhagen. NIAS is partially funded by the governments of Denmark, Finland, Iceland, Norway and Sweden via the Nordic Council of Ministers, and works to encourage and support Asian studies in the Nordic countries. In so doing, NIAS has been publishing books since 1969, with more than two hundred titles produced in the past few years.

UNIVERSITY OF COPENHAGEN

norden

Nordic Council of Ministers

QUEER/TONGZHI CHINA

CHINA

New Perspectives on Research, Activism and Media Cultures

edited by

Elisabeth L. Engebretsen
and William F. Schroeder

with Hongwei Bao

Nordic Institute of Asian Studies
Gendering Asia series, no. 11

First published in 2015 by NIAS Press
NIAS – Nordic Institute of Asian Studies
Øster Farimagsgade 5, 1353 Copenhagen K, Denmark
Tel: +45 3532 9501 • Fax: +45 3532 9549
E-mail: books@nias.ku.dk • Online: www.niaspress.dk

A CIP catalogue record for this book is available from the British Library

ISBN: 978-87-7694-153-6 (hbk)
ISBN: 978-87-7694-155-0 (pbk)

Typeset in Arno Pro 12/14.4
Typesetting by Lene Jakobsen

Cover art by Hoover Hoo and Ma Xiaoqi. Model: Toni.

Printed and bound in Great Britain
by Marston Book Services Limited, Oxfordshire

Contents

Acknowledgements

This volume originates from the conference panel 'Queer Theory in/ and China', organized for the 4th Sino-Nordic Gender and Women's Studies Conference in Aalborg, Denmark, 25–27 October 2011, and the workshop with the same title held at the University of Copenhagen on 28 October 2011. We are grateful for the generous funding and support from NIAS and the Ford Foundation, which enabled several China-based activists, film-makers and academics to attend these events. Most of the contributing essays were developed out of the panel itself and film screenings and debates that followed the Aalborg and Copenhagen events. In addition, the editors invited other activists and academics who work on these issues to write chapters that complement the existing papers and to add diversity to the collection. Many of our contributors have also been involved in workshops and activities sponsored by the Queer China Working Group, a diverse group of international scholars, artists and activists who first met in 2012 at the Europe–China LGBTQ Exchange, hosted in Manchester, UK.

The editors wish in particular to thank Hongwei Bao, who first took the initiative to organize the Nordic workshop and conference panel back in 2011 and has been an integral part of a range of international networks that study queer China. This volume would not exist without his foundational work.

Thanks are due also to the two anonymous reviewers who offered constructive suggestions and insights that helped strengthen the overall quality and clarity of the volume. Gerald Jackson at NIAS Press has actively supported the publication of this volume since we first tried to sell him our idea back in Copenhagen in 2011, and we express our gratitude for his positive interest in adding a queer volume such as ours to the NIAS Press catalogue. We would also like to thank David Stuligross for his close and patient copyediting, which has helped make the book as polished as it is.

Our deepest thanks, however, go to all the contributors who have enthusiastically and patiently collaborated with us and each other across geographical terrains, academic fields, different languages and various queer practices and politics to generate the conversations that have become this volume. We hope they feel the book conveys accurately and fairly the extensive range of debates and realities that they observe in their work, and that *Queer/Tongzhi China* may inspire similar projects and future recordings.

Note on Language

Throughout this volume personal names, whether Chinese or other, have been presented forename before surname, though Chinese-character renderings of course remain as original. Some exceptions exist for well-known Chinese names, where we use the conventional Chinese method of writing names with surname first, for example Li Yinhe or Cui Zi'en. The pinyin transcription system is used throughout for Chinese words and phrases, and Chinese script has been added in most texts, depending on the wishes of the authors.

Most contributors to this volume do not speak or write English as their first language and some texts were originally written in Chinese, before being translated into English for inclusion in the book. The process of negotiating translations, meanings, and nuances alongside demands for linguistic accuracy and academic standards in English-language publishing has been one of the most challenging yet inspiring aspects of working on this project. We trust that remaining linguistic quirkiness and approximations of meanings contribute usefully to the overall theme of queerness, broadly defined.

About the Authors

Hongwei Bao 包宏伟

Hongwei Bao is Assistant Professor in Media Studies at the University of Nottingham, UK. His research focuses primarily on queer film, alternative media and LGBT activism in mainland China. He has published articles in *Cultural Studies*, *Health, Culture and Society*, *Culture Unbound: Journal for Current Cultural Research* and *Interventions: International Journal of Postcolonial Studies*.

Stijn Deklerck 涂建平

After finishing his law studies in Belgium, Stijn Deklerck moved to China where he studied Chinese language and Chinese law. He proceeded to research human rights conceptions in China's civil society, engaging in fieldwork at several grassroots organizations that work on HIV/AIDS, disability and LGBT issues. Throughout his research activities, Dr Deklerck increasingly involved himself as an activist and a producer of socially engaging films. He produced the documentaries *I Want to Grow Old in China* and *The Silk Road of Pop* with the film collaborative Smoke Signal Projects. In 2007, he was involved in setting up the Chinese LGBT webcast *Queer Comrades* and became its full-time producer in 2009. Since 2010, he has worked as administrative director at the Beijing Gender Health Education Institute, a Chinese NGO organizing various LGBT awareness-raising initiatives. In 2015, Dr Deklerck received his PhD with the thesis *Queer Comrades - A Visual Ethnographic Study of Activism in China's Contemporary LGBT Movement* from the University of Leuven (Belgium), where he teaches a course on modern Chinese law.

Elisabeth L. Engebretsen 殷利

Elisabeth L. Engebretsen is Senior Lecturer at the Centre for Gender Research, University of Oslo, Norway. She is the author of *Queer*

Women in Urban China: An Ethnography (Routledge 2013), which was awarded a Ruth Benedict Honorable Mention in 2014 by the American Anthropological Association's Association for Queer Anthropology. Dr Engebretsen holds a PhD in Anthropology from the London School of Economics (2008) and has previously held academic positions in the USA, Canada, Finland, the Netherlands and China. In 2013, she co-founded the European Network for Queer Anthropology.

Popo Fan 范坡坡

Popo Fan is a queer film maker, writer and activist. Born in 1985, he graduated from the Beijing Film Academy. He published *Happy Together: Complete Record of a Hundred Queer Films* (Beifang Wenyi Press, 2007). Fan's documentary works include *New Beijing, New Marriage, Mama Rainbow* and *The VaChina Monologues,* among others. He has participated in international film festivals in Taipei, Copenhagen, Los Angeles, Mumbai and other cities. In 2012 he received the Prism Prize at the 22nd Hong Kong Lesbian and Gay Film Festival. He is now a committee member in the Beijing Queer Film Festival and a board member at the Beijing LGBT Center.

Xiaoxing Fu 富晓星

Xiaoxing Fu lectures in anthropology at the School of Sociology and Population Studies, Renmin University of China, Beijing. Her major research fields include visual anthropology, medical anthropology, sexuality and gender. Dr Fu's monograph 《空间，文化，表演：东北A 市男同性恋的人类学观察》[*Space, culture, performance: An anthropological study of gay male communitites in A city in China's north-east*] was published in 2012 by Guangming Ribao Publishers.

Ana Huang 黄阿娜

Ana Huang received her BA in Studies of Women, Gender and Sexuality from Harvard University. She is a PhD Candidate in Cultural Anthropology at Duke University. Her undergraduate thesis on gender roles in Chinese *lala* culture won the Thomas Hoopes Prize for distinguished scholarship at Harvard. She has served in leadership positions in China's queer feminist movement for several years.

Lucetta Yip Lo Kam 金曄路

Lucetta Yip Lo Kam is Assistant Professor in the Department of

Humanities and Creative Writing at Hong Kong Baptist University. She teaches gender and sexuality studies, media and popular culture, and creative writing. Her research interests are gender and sexuality in Chinese societies, *tongzhi* communities and activism in China, and Hong Kong Studies. She is the author of *Shanghai Lalas: Female* Tongzhi *Communities and Politics in Urban China* (Hong Kong University Press, 2013; Chinese edition 2015) and *Lunar Desires: Her First Same-sex Love in Her Own Words* (《月亮的騷動——她她的初戀故 事：我們的自述》, Cultural Act Up Press, 2001). Her work has appeared in *As Normal as Possible: Negotiating Gender and Sexuality in Mainland China and Hong Kong, Querying Marriage-Family Continuum* ("置疑婚姻家庭連續體"), *Journal of Local Discourse* (《本土論述》), *AsiaPacifiQueer: Rethinking Gender and Sexuality in the Asia-Pacific* and *Journal of Lesbian Studies*.

William F. Schroeder 许志伟

William F. Schroeder is Lecturer in Chinese Studies at the University of Manchester. He received his PhD in Sociocultural Anthropology at the University of Virginia in the United States in 2010. His research has focused on leisure practices in the queer community in Beijing and draws on queer, play, affect, and kinship theories. Dr Schroeder's work has appeared in *GLQ* (Duke University Press) and edited volumes and blogs. He is a co-founder of the Queer China Working Group, an international collaboration of artists, activists, and scholars concerned with the queer PRC, and is co-editor of Manchester University Press's book series "Alternative Sinology".

Qian Wang 王黔

Qian Wang earned his PhD from the Institute of Popular Music, the University of Liverpool, UK, and did his post-doctoral research at the Department of Sociology, Tsinghua University, Beijing. He is currently a lecturer at the School of Literature and Journalism, Yibin University, Sichuan. His research is mainly focused on Chinese popular music and its cultural scene. He examines the redevelopment and transformation of Chinese popular music since the economic and political reform in 1979, analysing its intertwined relationship with industrial progress and the stratification of Chinese society. Dr Wang also writes about politics, mass communication, gender and sexuality. He is the author of *The Crisis of Chinese Rock Music in the Middle 1990s*.

Wei Wei 魏伟

Wei Wei is Associate Professor of Sociology at East China Normal University, Shanghai. His research and teaching interests include gender/sexuality, urban space, social movement and qualitative methods. Dr Wei is the author of 《公开：当代成都同志空间的形成和变迁》(*Going Public: The Production and Transformation of Queer Spaces in Contemporary Chengdu, China*, Sanlian Shudian, 2012), an urban ethnography of a local gay community and activism in mainland China. His upcoming book, *Queering Chinese Society: Urban Space, Popular Culture and Social Policy*, takes a cross-disciplinary approach to the study of contemporary Chinese society from a queer perspective.

Jiangang Wei 魏建刚

Jiangang Wei was born and raised in Xinjiang, China. After finishing his acting studies at the Xinjiang Arts Institute and the Shanghai Drama Academy, he moved to Beijing where he starred in some of the first Chinese LGBT-themed movies. He founded the LGBT Webcast *Queer Comrades* in 2007 and directed more than 50 webcast episodes and documentaries for the program. Wei's documentaries *Comrades, you've worked hard!* (2010), *The Cream of the Queer Crop* (2010) and *Cures that Kill* (2011) have been shown at film festivals around the world. In 2010, Wei became the executive director of the Beijing Gender Health Education Institute and founded several large-scale annual events in this capacity, including the China Rainbow Media Awards, the China AIDS Walk and the China LGBT Community Leader Conference. In 2013, Wei was awarded the International Vanguard Award by the Los Angeles LGBT Center for his LGBT rights work.

Yanrui Xu 徐艳蕊

Yanrui Xu is Associate Professor of Communication at Ningbo Institute of Technology, Zhejiang University. She is the author of *Media and Gender: Femininity, Masculinity and the Formulation of Gender in Media* (Zhejiang University Press, 2014) and *Contemporary Feminist Literary Criticism in China 1980s–2000s* (Guangxi Normal University Press 2008). She has published research on women's literature and queer culture. Dr Xu is also a BL novelist, and her stories have appeared in Chinese BL magazines and literature websites such as *Jinjiang, Lucifer Club* and *My Fresh Net*.

Ling Yang 杨玲

Ling Yang is Assistant Professor of Chinese at Xiamen University. She is the author of *Entertaining the Transitional Era: Super Girl Fandom and the Consumption of Popular Culture* (China Social Sciences Press, 2012), and the co-editor of *Fan Cultures: A Reader* (Peking University Press, 2009). Dr Yang has published on contemporary Chinese fan culture, web literature and youth fiction.

CHAPTER 1

Introduction

Queer/Tongzhi China

Elisabeth L. Engebretsen and William F. Schroeder

Almost four decades of post-Mao economic reforms and social change in the People's Republic of China (henceforth 'China') have made sexual and gender diversity more visible and have drawn attention to a host of related issues there. Politically orthodox concepts of uniformity and the stifling fear of social difference have receded, allowing the diverse lifeways and voices of Others increasingly to be able to find arenas for expression, communities of support and even mainstream sympathy – if not legal protection and recognition. Especially since the turn of the millennium, academic research, activist initiatives, and media coverage are addressing the diversity of people identifying, or at least feeling an affinity with, non-normative sexual and gender subject positions. However, scholarship addressing Chinese gender and sexual diversity from a social-science and humanities perspective remains limited by a complex reality that involves factors such as political and academic censorship, stubbornly conformist social and moral norms, and continued authoritarian governance, as well as ongoing challenges that non-Chinese academics face when conducting empirical research.

Nevertheless, *Queer/Tongzhi China* brings together some of the most exciting, original and cutting-edge work being conducted on these topics today. The work that appears here is not limited strictly to academic research, allowing us to acknowledge the crucial roles of activism, the media and popular culture in establishing this field of knowledge. The book as a whole, and each chapter specifically, firmly places queer China in the context of contemporary (East) Asian regional and global flows of queer politics, culture and academic research. It contributes new and important insights to the broad interdisciplinary field of transnational queer, gender and sexuality studies that as a body of work seeks to challenge the theoretical and political prominence of western scholarship and to build a critical vocabulary for addressing the experiences, aspirations and bodies of knowledge that shape both human diversity and similitude.

The chapters here exhibit an exciting tableau of ongoing and very recent projects from a new generation of scholars, activists and scholar-activists, complementing the results of research conducted mainly in the 1990s (see, for example, Rofel 2007; Sang 2003), or in other Chinese societies, including the overseas Chinese diaspora (for example Kong 2011; H. Huang 2011). The book contains original essays by some of the most prolific and prominent queer activists in China today, placing their writing alongside work by emergent and established scholars from a variety of disciplines and backgrounds, including anthropology, cultural and media studies, Chinese studies, literature and sociology. The book thus offers unique perspectives in more than one way. First, it presents primary accounts of the creative and multi-faceted strategies that activists and community organizers have developed to disseminate queer ideas and develop queer communities. These efforts range from organising film festivals and cultural events, to creating new media platforms online and in print, collaborating with transnational groups and individuals, and producing documentary archives. Second, in addition to accounts produced by cultural actors themselves, the book draws on empirical research into everyday queer/*tongzhi* lives, offering a rich record not only of established community and activist perspectives, but also of voices that originate outside this core.

The book as a whole thus constitutes an entry into the historical archives of queer/*tongzhi* life in the very broadest sense: we are concerned with people who live such lives, those who research them, and those who do both and much more. The volume is then perhaps a recording more than a record. Like a recording that is static from one perspective and dynamic from another – having captured something but remaining alive in the interpretations and thought-worlds of those who engage with it – *Queer/Tongzhi China* breathes as it speaks, in different ways than standard mono-ethnographies or social-scientific documentaries of queer life ordinarily could. Part of the reason it can do this is that the volume includes such a variety of contributions and contributors.

Perhaps the most direct consequence of this diversity is that *Queer/Tongzhi China* does not advance one particular theory or one particular viewpoint and is in fact sometimes at odds with itself. Nonetheless, some identifiable themes come together despite what may seem like a contrapuntal flow. For this reason, we recommend listening to the book like a long-play album: the chapters are works in themselves, but the collection is a statement about a particular era and movement. Both the whole and the parts are richer because of variations that emerge when each perspective is considered in relationship to the others. Another way to understand this volume might be to read it as queer China improvisation. In that vaunted way that classic jazz aspires to perfect a balance between highly individualistic experimentation and collective variation on a theme, this book has come together as a result of committed individuals' enthusiasm for identifying and assessing, from their own points of view, what is important to take account of when discussing 'queer/ *tongzhi* China' as a concept. Improvisational solos are judged not necessarily for their accomplishment – although one recognizes virtuosity when it happens – but for their becoming, and recordings of great moments are seen by connoisseurs as episodes in the emerging careers of their creators. Listeners appreciate confident experimentalism as much as any aspect of definitive tone. Certainly, the pieces in this volume all demonstrate a kind of virtuosity; each author, based on a wealth of experience, makes a statement worthy of contemplation. But each also represents a moment in the becoming of a contemporary queer China scholar, activist or artist who has by no means finished a career and in most cases is just beginning one. Thus, our collection gathers a rare ensemble and showcases work that does not ordinarily get picked up because of language barriers, difficulty of access to publishing outlets, censorship and hegemonic structures of global queer theory production.

As editors, we are delighted to introduce this ensemble and prepare the reader for the broad repertoire of rhythms and soundscapes that echo through the volume to create an audibility that Hongwei Bao (chapter 3) identifies as so important to the study of queer/*tongzhi* China. We choose to offer some liner notes that draw out common themes and set a context but that leave the uniqueness of each work to speak for itself.

Notes on Themes

Readers will notice a consistent tension in treatments of the question of belonging, often expressed through a concern with the inside and the outside, being and not being. Similarly, contributors collectively wonder about definitional status, identificatory stasis and role assumption regarding every kind of subject position – from researcher, to *tongzhi*, to gay to queer to *T* to *P* to Chinese to western to artist to activist to citizen. Most are looking for ways to avoid lingering on the question of whether something *is* or *is not* and instead occupy themselves and their work with expressing how their informants, or indeed they themselves, have avoided getting trapped by definitions (usually quite as a matter of course). One of the most satisfying aspects of these expressions is the way that they seem to emerge without cajoling from the experiences and encounters of the people whose lives are being detailed. On reading these accounts, one does not feel that they aim to be manifestos or follow any specific politics or ideology. Rather, they derive, in the best sense of the word, from the empirical.

Rejecting China as Exception: Queer Studies and/in China

One of the best examples of the beautiful messiness of empirical storytelling emerges from the very history of the study of queer/*tongzhi* China and the ongoing debate about the usefulness and translatability even of the concept of 'queer' itself. The appearance of the term *ku'er* (酷儿, 'queer') in China is a recent one, and the word was at first confined to academic and cosmopolitan activist communities. *Tongzhi* (同志, 'comrade') enjoyed a more colloquial but still in-group use early on, later becoming more widely known as a term of art to refer to sexual and gender non-normativity. The inevitable contestation, critique and even rejection of terminology will be familiar to any student of language and culture, and it is not necessary here to go into theoretical detail on the matter. Suffice it to say that emerging Chinese discourses on sexual and gender diversity, identity politics and research have come to include what are ostensibly queer perspectives, if one defines the concept broadly to include any challenge to non-normative sexual and gender epistemology, but that are uniquely *tongzhi* just the same.

The term *tongzhi* is best defined not as a word but a debate that encompasses a multitude of dimensions and subjectivities across different social, political, cultural, economic, regional and philosophical landscapes. The word itself has a complex and ancient history in Chinese, having taken on its modern political character in the late 19th and early 20th centuries. It came to designate people with common

4

outlooks on social and political change and was associated with rebelliousness during its use in anti-Qing uprisings at the end of the imperial period, continuing to be used by both Nationalists and Communists. After 1949, the term took on the socialist character of 'comrade' that the English term also carries because of its implementation as a preferred non-hierarchical form of address. It was used throughout the Maoist period in mainland China as an everyday appellation and is still used as a formal way of introducing people, especially in public ceremonies. Most queer scholars agree that its current use, similar to the English 'queer' without the pejorative connotations, comes from Hong Kong activists' ironic appropriation of the term in the late 1980s or early 1990s. Perhaps one of the best ways of describing what *tongzhi* means is to say that it is a 自称 (*zicheng*), or way of calling oneself and people one assumes are like oneself, which usually implies sexual or gender non-normativity or an affinity with the political and social movements surrounding these ideas. This use incorporates all the older senses of revolutionary uprising, shared political spirit and egalitarianism, but specifies a frame of reference related to gender and sexuality. Now commonly understood throughout the Chinese-speaking world in its newer sense, the word occupies a provocative but still deceptively polysemous status. Young urban mainlanders, for example, might first associate the term with sexual identity projects and movements. Yet as recently as 2013, one of the editors was asked by a twenty-something salesperson at a gift shop in Beijing whether the item to be wrapped would be given to a 男同志 (*nan tongzhi*) or a 女同志 (*nü tongzhi*), meaning in context very pragmatically but politely and simply whether the thing was for a man or a woman. We therefore can only approximate a gloss, but refer readers to the growing body of relevant publications discussing the term (Chiang and Heinrich 2014; Engebretsen 2013; Liu and Rofel 2010; Chou 2000; Wong 2004, 2005; Schroeder 2012).

The present volume is, we suggest, itself a meditation on the multiple meanings and uses of *tongzhi*, alongside other terms and concepts such as queer, *ku'er*, gay, homosexual, lesbian, trans and so on, as well as the diverse practices of social activism that stretch beyond single-issue identity politics. This is one of the reasons the book's title appears as it does. The choice to juxtapose 'queer' and '*tongzhi*' evokes both the unevenness and the variety of flows of practice, politics and discourses related to sexuality, gender, identity, nationality and temporality. *Queer/ Tongzhi China* intends to leave open a conceptual space for the multiple ways that these and related concepts are appropriated in the book as a whole, and in the work the chapters reference. The closing chapter recounts Cui Zi'en's philosophies on the 'queer'/*tongzhi* debate specifically and could actually be consulted as a starting point, but only with the understanding that *tongzhi* means many things to many people and is by far not the only way to designate one's queerness.

Ideas about sexual and gender non-normativity that emerged under the rubric 'queer theory' were introduced in China at the turn of the new millennium. From renowned sociologist Li Yinhe's translation of *Queer Theory* (*Ku'er Lilun*, published in 2000) to the ever more popular use of the term *ku'er* in China's LGBT community (e.g., 酷儿电影 *ku'er dianying*, 'queer film', and 酷儿艺术 *ku'er yishu*, 'queer art'), the term 'queer' – and the paradigm of non-normativity associated with this term – have been appropriated more and more widely in Chinese discourses and have helped shape emerging activist and academic work. However, queer theory is also being put under careful scrutiny and critique. It has been rejected by some as unfit and inappropriate for Chinese culture, politics and society, even as it has been embraced by others. With this in mind, we ask provocatively: What do queer subject positions and politics look like in contemporary China? How do perspectives on gender and sexual diversity informed by global flows of queer theory fit into a Chinese framework, if there is one? What, specifically, could a Chinese cultural and political perspective add to existing debates on global queerness and transnational sexuality and gender studies? What new synergies, or contours of future lifeworlds, are possibly emerging from the range of explorations of queerness – beyond identity projects in and of themselves? Can one consider scholarly attention itself to be a (mostly) subtle challenge to a dominant social cartography that bounds proper, respectable, appropriate ways of being?

The argument that queer theory – as an anti-identitarian strand of scholarship developed in the early 1990s and building on the post-Stonewall lesbian/gay movement in North America – does not fit the Chinese cultural and historical context has been made most famously by Hong Kong activist–scholar Chou Wah-shan (2000) and US-based Chinese gay activist Damien Lu (2011). Chou argues that cultural and political logics differ profoundly between China and the generic 'West'. In Chinese societies, he explains, same-sex desiring women and men organize their lives in a socio-centric way based on Confucian family values that are at odds with western individualism. Chou suggests that China's cultural traditions are essentially non-homophobic and characterized by a tacit tolerance for same-sex practices but one should not conflate these practices with the identity-based concept of 'homosexuality' or an imagination of the 'homosexual person'. According to this logic, sexuality defined by personal identity and 'coming out' is superfluous to extant sensibilities and therefore retains an air of cultural impropriety. 'Homosexuality', then, is an inherently western construct and the discourses surrounding it are identity-based, directly confrontational and individually selfish. Lu, who is influential in US–mainland funding and activist-training circles, echoes the rejection of western queer theory models but promotes a locally specific identity-based politics in China. He argues in a recently published online article that, because queer theory does not fit the Chinese context, activists should advocate a specifically Chinese politics that does not attempt to deconstruct the local identity on which a movement should be based (Lu 2011). His article has triggered heated and ongoing debate in China's *tongzhi* communities.

Such views, however, have also provoked an astute critique from scholars of Chinese societies who work centrally on queer theory, including Petrus Liu in his essay 'Why does queer theory need China?' (2010), Ding Naifei and Liu Jen-peng in their essay 'Reticent Poetics, Queer Politics' (2005) and Hans Huang in his recent book *Queer Politics and Sexual Modernity in Taiwan* (2011). They argue forcefully against a nostalgic and Sino-centric view of exceptional Chinese sexual culture and history, encouraging us not to see China as categorically different. Their critiques place the politics of violence and normalization at the centre of the analysis. For example, Huang and Ding & Liu warn against Chou's argument that the Chinese convention of tacitly tolerating sexual and gender variety in fact could mask a homophobia that perpetrates significant violence against queer people. The Sino-centric view, they argue, reproduces harmful power inequalities, whereby heteronormativity and social-familial conformity figure as morally good, respectable and worthy of maintaining (see also Kam 2012: 93ff). Petrus Liu counters the Sino-centric view in a different way when he writes: 'The possibility of practicing queer theory in Chinese contexts demonstrates that critical attention to local knowledges and concerns does not immediately constitute a categorical rejection of "the queer"; rather, it shows that what is "queer" is constantly expanded, supplemented, and revised by what is "Chinese"' (2010: 297). Moreover, 'our critical task in the coming years is to transform the signifier of "China" into a useful set of queer tools' (316).

We might add to this discussion that, in everyday uses, *tongzhi* and *ku'er* are not always rigidly separate in meaning and are sometimes used interchangeably. Rarely is any one of us able to police his or her language with ultimate critical effectiveness, nor are our interlocutors consistently able to process the subtleties of our linguistic choices. When confronted with competing interpretations, the editors have not privileged any one definition or name. Readers will notice, for example, that *tongzhi* can be characterized as an in-group term used by the LGBT community (Deklerck and Wei, chapter 2), as a male-gendered subject position equivalent to gay (Wei, chapter 11), as a concept that conveys certain activist ambitions (Engebretsen, chapter 6), as a sexual minority community (Kam, chapter 10) and as an expansive group of like-minded people with any variety of sexual orientations (Fan, chapter 5). Appropriating the concept 'queer/*tongzhi*' – using an English and a Chinese term, each with a complex history and contested interpretations regarding sexual politics – indexes this volume's conscious approach to the politics of language, terminology and translation. This use highlights the necessarily symbiotic relationship between languages, identifications and positionalities, politics, locations and theories.

Against these multiple understandings and theoretical backdrops, through discussions of emerging forms of what might be called 'queerness' in a specifically but never monolithically 'Chinese' context, this volume attempts to lay bare the complicated processes of knowledge production and the tense but productive intersections between activism and academic work in and on China. The tension brought to light here will be familiar to those who know debates in western queer theory about the relationship between political activism – which has its own internal divisions between accommodationist and radical strands – and research that seeks to represent or reflect the breadth of lifeways that could fall under the 'queer' rubric. Same-sex marriage debates often bring out strong views related to this tension. Chinese debates are similar in their tacking between polarities, and marriage is just as contested and just as sought after in Chinese queer communities as elsewhere. Yet the roots of the relevant debates emerge from different historical ground and evolve in unpredictable ways. Documenting each culturally specific path is a useful corrective against the temptation to imagine that all queer movements dance to the same, over-produced global soundtrack. In this sense, *Queer/Tongzhi China* engages the complex issues involved in positioning 'nativist' research, critical reflexivity and the production of sexual identities and politics in regional and global nexuses of power. Translation is one important nexus, and one that we, as both editors and non-native Chinese speakers, have struggled with. We have the privilege of naming and labelling, which always carries risks of confusion and discursive violence. As editors with a certain Anglophonic academic privilege, we face the additional risk of subconsciously inserting elements of our own queer narratives, despite our best intentions. Whereas we cannot solve such fundamental shortcomings in our editorship, we can at least address a key factor in marginalization by bringing voices that otherwise are not heard because of language barriers and lack of publishing opportunities to the cacophonous Anglophone discussion itself. We mean for our volume to contribute towards the process of critically thinking about the politics of global queer activism and academic practice. Perhaps at minimum, the essays' wonderful diversity, and their resulting ability to probe the multiple contexts where queer perspectives on gender and sexuality develop, will show some of the innovative ways that marginalized subjects strive to find strategies for creating a home, shaping local practice and social views and, at the same time, engaging the geopolitics of recognition, community and belonging.

We have a profound hope that these essays will portray Chinese queer life not simply as exceptional – as a different set of practices and cultures than those with which readers may be familiar – but as a site where familiar though never simply identical or perfectly overlapping vocabularies of shared practice, desire, ideology and politics might also develop. A central point emerging from the essays in this volume – spanning as they do a large part of the post-Mao period and several provinces across the vast country – is the need to rethink and reflect on the units and objects of analysis with which we all work, including such notions as the local, the regional and the Chinese. As Ara Wilson argues in her important essay 'Queering Asia', '[understanding] the intra-Asian formation of queer Asian lives calls for attention to a plurality of differentiated flows and circuits' (2006: 19). The cases presented here confirm initial impressions that, in addition to intra-Asian circuits, contemporary queer/*tongzhi* activists and academics participate not only rather consciously in a global discourse, but also that their global presence feels appropriate and obvious.

Doing research in China

The climate for independent and empirical research on sexual and gender minorities in China remains complex and difficult. That this book has come to life at all is a triumph of individual and collective perseverance. We are especially proud that a distinctively new generation of voices is joining the performance, represented perhaps best by Xiaoxing Fu and Wei Wei, whose Chinese-language monographs were recently published in the mainland after much delay (Fu 2012; Wei 2012). Yanrui Xu and Ling Yang as well as Qian Wang, who all contribute to this volume, also do productive work in Chinese academic settings. These and the other few Chinese scholars who openly work on queer/*tongzhi* issues find their publishing and teaching practices heavily scrutinized and censored, making day-to-day academic work – and ability to engage in long-term research projects – extremely challenging. Similarly, the situation of queer activism in present-day China remains fraught, with the central and municipal governments exercising control on a whim. It is not a coincidence that the heavily arbitrated platforms of film and online media appear as some of the most crucial places for activism in China. This volume boasts four first-person reports (Fan, Deklerck/Wei, Fan/Cui, Bao) that vividly describe ways political censorship and proactive self-censorship continue to shape activist practices.

Scholars and activists based in non-Chinese settings have persevered and improvised in their own ways to gain access to and create dialogue with their Chinese peers. Through dialogue and cooperative research methods, each identifies and interrogates central tensions: the pressure to conform, the dynamics of the local and the global, and contestations about belonging and identity. Careful, ethnographic descriptions help to clarify when and how local historical moments converge with broader processes identified in the literature on 'global sexualities' – as well as when and how they do not converge. These scholars and scholar-activists draw on key insights, such as those by Inderpal Grewal and Karen Caplan, regarding the necessity to 'examine complicities as well as resistances in order to create the possibility for critique and change' (2001: 675). Grewal and Caplan – and implicitly all the contributors to this volume – argue for the importance of interdisciplinary work that addresses the movements between and co-existence among discourses and experiences from across different global locations. These arguments are highlighted explicitly in the themes particular contributions engage, including the globalization of sexual identities and the tension between the local and the global (Bao, Huang, Engebretsen); the translation of theories and research practice (Kam, Schroeder); and the localization of queer politics, most significantly in the universality of the term 'queer' or the cultural specificity of the term *tongzhi* (Cui, Fan, Wei/Deklerck, Wang).

We now present the work of our contributors, who are situated quite differently from one another but have surmounted a host of obstacles to demonstrate the range of their voices, inspired by their variously activist or academic affiliations, different nationalities and citizenships and multiple or interdisciplinary allegiances.

Chapter Overview

The book is not divided into strictly organized and separate parts as such, but various clusters connect with each other in ways that speak across the specifics of location, discipline and author perspective. Together, they help interpret and interrogate the volume's crucial concept-metaphor, queer/*tongzhi* China, not by offering static definitions or experiences ready to be captured and held still in and across time and location, but by providing figurative indicators of always evolving positions, modes of thought, being and knowledge.

Demonstrating the importance of film, art and web-based communication in establishing community and activism centred on queer/*tongzhi* identity and discourse in China's particular socio-political climate, one cluster is concerned with queer activism read through media platforms, including production and dissemination of documentary film, webcast, and digital video. Some of the most influential Chinese producers of such media write here about their experiences and objectives, as well as the contents of their work and their reflections on how these media practices relate to queer/*tongzhi* activist politics. In his chapter on independent filmmaking, Popo Fan discusses why Chinese filmmakers and activists appropriate film and film festivals differently than their western counterparts. Fan details the restraints and censorship resulting from dominant politics in the country today, and how these hamper the establishment of lasting public platforms and avenues for dissemination of minority voices, especially in film.

In one way or another, all chapters in the book touch upon the creative ways in which queer/*tongzhi* Chinese demonstrate a strategic sensitivity to official politics and customary social norms and apply this knowledge as they try to establish community, discourse and platforms. These efforts are meaningful on several levels, even if they may not be permanent or publicly visible as such. Stijn Deklerck and Jiangang Wei, for example, document the first years of what has become a phenomenally successful, bilingual webcast series: *Queer Comrades*. As both authors have been intimately involved with the webcast since its inception, they are uniquely situated to provide vivid details about its rationale, its politics, its relationship with established global queer politics and culture, and also the ways in which the webcast has developed local and global audiences and support despite facing shifting official censorship and the challenge of having scant resources.

Hongwei Bao builds on the importance of the digital in his astute analysis of the prominent filmmaker and activist Cui Zi'en's pivotal documentary film and queer-historical archive, *Queer China, 'Comrade' China'* (2008). Bao uses Cui's own theory of 'DV activism' (digital video activism) to comment on the importance of building visual archives as part of queer/*tongzhi* theory building and movement development. Film-maker and activist Popo Fan's intimate interview with Cui Zi'en provides a 'hearing' of the prominent queer figure's recollections of his career as a director, activist, community leader, and public intellectual. The prevalent theme of inside/outside is detected in the way Cui Zi'en considers whether he would categorize himself as a queer director, a world cinema artist, an individual, a commentator, or any number of other subject positions, and his responses can be seen as an extended musing over artistic and activist belonging.

Continuing the discussion of queer media from the perspective of online literature, Ling Yang and Yanrui Xu's chapter on the popular genre of web literature explores 'boy love' (BL) readers' habits and dispositions. In their ethnographic assessment of this textual genre, the authors position themselves as commentators on the cross-cultural state of feminist literary theory as they situate the gender-bending practices of a group that forces a reconsideration of 'queer' boundaries. Another provocative study of popular culture is Qian Wang's careful look at popular music in China, in which he considers the questions of potential and actual queer performance and performativity. Wang subtly imagines what the stakes might be for a queer Chinese researcher who takes seriously the shenanigans of pop artists and fame-seekers that otherwise could be dismissed as vapid or inconsequential in scholarship. He situates an entire history of the explosion of Chinese pop media and its queering capacity while, at the same time, reflecting on how a researcher from the queer periphery who works on the fringes of Chinese academia could gain professional respect and carry on in the future.

The volume also contains notably empirical, situated research and analysis that traverses cultural studies, anthropology and the blurred activist/academic dynamic that continually emerges in the book's soundtrack. In her 'On the Surface: "*T*" and Transgender Identity in Chinese *Lala* Culture', Ana Huang addresses the question of gender using ethnographic examples from recent work among *lala* women, specifically considering transgender and lesbian/queer cutting-edge perspectives and theories. Huang provocatively posits a way to reorganize thinking around gender by removing the focus entirely from sex-based theories, proposing instead a culturally informed and ultimately queer way of looking at the malleable gender performances of contemporary *lala* non-normativity.

Xiaoxing Fu's and Wei Wei's chapters both contribute intriguing spatial perspectives to the volume. Their ethnographic studies offer unique empirical data on sexual and gender diversity in China beyond the relatively cosmopolitan coastal areas. In her chapter on gay men's community development in the northeastern city of Shenyang, Fu delineates the relationship between space and identity through changing times of social and economic development. She addresses these pertinent issues through a uniquely local yet dialogic and communicative piece that makes a powerful contribution to the archive. Fu's discussion of 'Men's Street' suggests that space has been used in Chinese queer communities with far more aplomb and for far longer than most scholars and activists have imagined. Wei's 'Queer Organizing and HIV/AIDS Activism: An Ethnographic Study of a Local *Tongzhi* Organization in Chengdu' offers readers yet another perspective on the situation of queer knowledge production, this time in central China. He also explicitly and implicitly documents his own challenging journey as an activist/scholar doing work on *tongzhi* issues in contemporary China.

Lucetta Kam and William Schroeder add reflexive and methodological aspects to the discussion in their chapters: both specifically consider challenges involved in conducting empirical research on queer communities in China. Kam explores her relationship to the field and the people she meets there, openly considering how her status as a native Shanghainese expatriate who grew up in Hong Kong does and does not affect her ethnography of *lala* life. She considers in now classic, but also humanistic, style how her position provides access to a research cohort but also casts her outside. This self-ethnographic contribution places Kam together with others in the volume who consider their own careers and trajectories, but who at the same time tell the reader something important about what it means to produce *tongzhi* knowledge in the 21st century. Schroeder's essay on 'Research, Activism and Activist Research in *Tongzhi* China' details similar concerns as the previous chapter, but narrates his position as a non-Chinese researcher on the kinds of approaches and sensibilities one must take account of when conducting and framing queer China scholarship. He reflects on disciplinary imperatives and cultural translatability to underscore the complexity of looking at the question of activism and its sometimes major role in knowledge production, suggesting that there is more than one way to consider the queer Chinese 'movement'. Elisabeth Engebretsen's chapter on queer grassroots activism in postmillennial China situates local activist cultural practice and political specificity in broader interdisciplinary and transnational context, thus relativizing (and yet showing what is particular about) Chinese queer/*tongzhi* cultures and activism. Through the conceptual lens of the central ideological and political principles of 'pride' and 'visibility' in minority rights movements, Engebretsen considers the question of what counts as activism from the perspective of community-internal and -external rifts and connections. She reveals along the way a necessary but delicate meta-balance among reflexivity, intercultural belonging, and scholarship by clearing the path in work concerning queer/*tongzhi* China for both orthodox and heterodox approaches to queer social change.

We hope readers who take a few moments to listen to these chapters find themselves stimulated the first time but encouraged to listen again. We can imagine a lot of people with interests in sexuality and gender theory, China, the politics and experiences of non-normativity, or simply language might find themselves nodding their heads to our queer syncopations. But we also hope to provoke a debate about how to understand each of the issues that is raised in this volume, challenging people with notes that could sound odd or feel unexpected but that still deliver a memorable musicality. As many of our contributors suggest, both implicitly and explicitly, it is in the echo of a thing, its memory, its recollection, that sensing movement is possible. And so, on reading, listening, and doing those things again, we become moved.

References

Chiang, Howard, and Ari L. Heinrich, eds (2014) *Queer Sinophone Cultures.* London: Routledge.

Chou, Wah-shan (2000) *Tongzhi: Politics of Same-Sex Eroticism in Chinese Societies.* London: Routledge.

Engebretsen, Elisabeth L. (2013) *Queer Women in Urban China: An Ethnography.* London: Routledge.

Fu, Xiaoxing (2012). 空间，文化 表演： 东北A市男同性恋群体的人类学观察 (Kongjian, Wenhua, Biaoyan: Dongbei A shi Nantongxinglian Qunti de R enleixue Guancha.) [Space, Culture, Performance: An Anthropological Study of Gay Men's Communities in A City in China's Northeast]. Beijing: Guangming Ribao Chubanshe.

Huang, Hans Tao-Ming (2011) *Queer Politics and Sexual Modernity in Taiwan.* Hong Kong: Hong Kong University Press.

Grewal, Inderpal and Caren Kaplan (2001) Global Identities: Theorizing Transnational Studies of Sexuality. *GLQ,* 7(4): 663–679.

Kam, Lucetta Yip Lo (2012) *Shanghai Lalas: Female Tongzhi Communities and Politics in Urban China*. Hong Kong University Press.

Kong, Travis (2011) *Chinese Male Homosexualities: Memba, tongzhi and golden boy*. London: Routledge.

Li Yinhe, ed. and trans.(2000) 酷儿理论 西方90年代性思潮 [Ku'er Lilun: Xifang 90 niandai xing si chao; Queer Theory: Western sexual thought in the 1990s]. Beijing: Shishi Publishers.

Liu, Petrus (2010) Why does Queer Theory need China? *positions: east asia cultures critique* vol. 18, no. 2, pp. 291–320.

Liu, Petrus and Lisa Rofel (2010) Beyond the Strai(gh)ts: Transnationalism and Queer Chinese Politics, *positions: east asia cultures critique* vol. 18, no. 2, pp. 281–289.

Lu, Damien (2011) 什么是酷儿理论？ 它与同志运动有什么关系? [Shenme shi ku'er lilun? Ta yu tongzhi yundong you shenme guanxi? 'What is Queer Theory? What does it have to do with China's gay liberation movement?'] http://www.lestalk.org/bbs/forum.php?mod=redirect&tid=1694&goto=lastpost (first posted June 1, 2011; first accessed June 20, 2011)

Ma, Jingwu (2003) From 'Long Yang' and 'Dui Shi' to Tongzhi: Homosexuality in China, *Journal of Gay and Lesbian Psychotherapy*, vol. 7, nos 1–2, pp. 117–143.

Rofel, Lisa (2007) *Desiring China: Experiments in neoliberalism, sexuality, and public culture*. Durham, NC: Duke University Press.

Rofel, Lisa (2012) Grassroots Activism: Non-normative sexual politics in post-socialist China. In Wanning Sun and Yingjie Guo (eds) *Unequal China: The political economy and cultural politics of inequality in China*, 154–167. New York: Routledge.

Sang, Deborah Tze-lan (2003) *The Emerging Lesbian: Female same-sex desire in modern China*. University of Chicago Press.

Schroeder, William F. (2012) On Cowboys and Aliens: Affective History and Queer Becoming in Contemporary China, *GLQ*, vol. 18, no. 4, pp. 425–452.

Wan, Yanhai (2001) Becoming a Gay Activist in Contemporary China. In Gerard Sullivan and Peter A. Jackson (eds), *Gay and Lesbian Asia: Culture, identity, community*. pp. 47–64. New York: Harrington Park Press.

Wei, Wei (2012) *Gongkai: Dangdai Chengdu 'tongzhi' kongjian de xingcheng he bianqian* [Going Public: The production and transformation of queer spaces in contemporary Chengdu, China] Shanghai: Shanghai Sanlian Shudian.

Wilson, Ara (2006) 'Queering Asia', *Intersections: Gender, history and culture in the Asian context*, Issue 14 (Nov.) http://intersections.anu.edu.au/issue14/wilson.html

Wong, Andrew D. (2004) Language, Cultural Authenticity, and the *Tóngzhì* Movement, *Texas Linguistics Forum (Proceedings of the Twelfth Annual Symposium about Language and Society)*, vol. 48, pp. 209–215.

Wong, Andrew D. (2005) The Reappropriation of Tongzhi, *Language in Society*, vol. 34, no. 5, pp. 763–793.

CHAPTER 2

Queer Online Media and the Building of China's LGBT Community

Stijn Deklerck and Xiaogang Wei

The first mainland Chinese gay websites came into life at the end of the 20th century. In an environment where gay gathering places almost exclusively consisted of public toilets, bathhouses and parks, which were often swept by the police, websites were mainly developed as safe platforms for interpersonal communication and mutual support. Since then, queer online media in mainland China (China hereafter) have come a long way. China now has hundreds of LGBT (lesbian, gay, bisexual, transgender) websites and the internet is the main action arena for the LGBT movement. While still fulfilling their role as communication platforms, queer online media have also taken up the role of spreading information and reporting on LGBT issues. They have become the major medium for the creation and dissemination of LGBT culture.

In this chapter, we discuss the importance of webcasts as a queer media tool in China. We do this by focusing our presentation on our own experiences while producing the queer community webcast 'Queer Comrades'.[1] While the use of webcasts is still a relatively recent phenomenon in China's queer community, webcasts like Queer Comrades play an important role in the LGBT identity construction and community building in China today.

Founded in 2007, Queer Comrades is an independent LGBT webcast that aims to document queer culture and to raise public awareness of LGBT issues in China. In the following pages, we provide an introduction to Queer Comrades, illustrate our development as an online queer

---

1.   All 'Queer Comrades' videos are available online at www.queercomrades.com. For more information, please write us at info@queercomrades.com.

18

video media institution in China, and discuss the importance of Queer Comrades in constructing LGBT identity and LGBT community building in China today. In a conclusion, we discuss the 'queerness' of Queer Comrades by giving a short reflection on the impact of queer theory on our activities.

About 'Queer Comrades'

Queer Comrades is China's only independent, long running LGBT webcast. We produce and broadcast online videos on important developments and issues in the Chinese and global LGBT movement. Our mission is to document queer culture in all its aspects in order to raise public awareness.

We aim to inform both the LGBT and the non-LGBT members of Chinese society in a relaxed and unrestrained way on the various aspects of queer culture by sending out empowering images of queer life. We strive to provide well-researched, informative, entertaining and positive insights into queer culture. We do not spend time justifying homosexuality; instead, we choose to increase the visibility of the LGBT community and appreciate its intricacies both inside and outside China.

We produce Queer Comrades because we find that there is an overall lack of information about LGBT issues in China. The mainstream media either ignores LGBT issues or reports with a negative slant. Almost no sexual education addresses LGBT issues and it is generally difficult to encounter accurate information about LGBT in China. It is even harder to find positive representations of LGBT people in the mainstream media and in Chinese society in general. LGBT people are often talked about and represented as mentally unstable, as victims and as second-class citizens.

With our webcast, we show empowering LGBT images: our audience sees people who are not ashamed of their sexual orientation, people who are proud of who they are, people who talk openly about issues that our audience members might be struggling with themselves. We create a forum beyond taboos, a forum where people can gain positive insights into LGBT culture.

Online broadcasting allows us to reach a wide audience of both LGBT and non-LGBT people. We also broadcast on the internet because it is a relatively free media space in China. Chinese authorities regulate and monitor the internet much less vigilantly than TV, radio and print media. Nevertheless, LGBT websites are regularly blocked or closed down and we are continually cautious of government intervention. While we discuss LGBT rights issues in both direct and indirect ways, we focus on the communication of positive, energetic and empowering LGBT information (*how we can make things better*) and try to avoid negative and blameful content (*what the Chinese government is doing wrong*).

Evolution of the Webcast

Season 1

The first season of Queer Comrades ran under the English name 'Queer As Folk Beijing' and the Chinese name 同志亦凡人 *tongzhi yi fanren*. Its eleven weekly talk shows were broadcast between April and June 2007. We produced this first season on a very limited budget. We mainly relied on our group of LGBT contacts; we borrowed filming and editing material from friends and we engaged a team of volunteers to realize this first webcast season. The webcast was founded by Chinese national Xiaogang Wei and Chinese-born American national Steven Jiang. The volunteer group also included both Chinese and foreign nationals including Stijn Deklerck; he acted as a 'distant producer', securing funds and consulting on the programming.

Each of the half-hour episodes featured one or more guests, who were invited to the Queer Comrades studio to discuss a particular issue affecting the lives of the queer community in China. In addition, every episode featured an 'on location' segment that included interviews with experts and street surveys. We broadcast the show on five major mainstream video websites (Sina, Liu Jian Fang, Tudou, Wo Le, Youtube). The programmes were promoted through blogs, fan pages and outreach via other social networking forums. Viewer response was tremendous: by the beginning of 2008, the season amassed close to one million hits.

During this first season, we faced two content-related struggles. First, our choice of topic depended very much on the interests and expertise of the guests who accepted our invitation. In the beginning, identifying guests was a challenge. One of our major goals with the webcast is to show people who are out and proud about their sexual and gender identity. China did not have a well-developed 'out community' in 2007. Further, we sought individuals who were comfortable about being out not only with their friends and acquaintances but also with potentially millions of unknown – and possibly unsympathetic – internet viewers. This was a tall order. We therefore worked with the people we knew, including foreigners residing in Beijing and Chinese people who had studied overseas. Guests were given considerable freedom to shape content of the shows they appeared on; we discussed the issues that were closest to their hearts. During the first season, we also worked with several straight people who voiced their understanding of and support for the LGBT community; they did not perceive the same risks and potential social costs of being open and on camera.

Second, we were concerned about the reactions of the Chinese government to our programmes. We understood that we could not accomplish any of our goals if we were shut down, but since webcasts like ours were completely new, nobody had a clear idea about where the permissible boundary might be. We chose to focus on less sensitive topics and generally avoided direct political comments on Chinese society.

Our content approach during the first season is exemplified by our very first episode: 'Fag Hags'.[2] We invited Helen Feng, a musician and former TV host, to our studio to talk about her relationship with the LGBT community. Our 'on location' segment included interviews with people on Beijing streets about their knowledge of homosexuality and homosexuals.

Season 2

The second season of Queer Comrades, 24 talk show episodes in all, was broadcast every two weeks between March 2008 and February 2009. We received limited funding for the production of the second season, which allowed us to purchase some basic equipment and hire two full-time employees: Xiaogang Wei (host/director) and Guan Shengsheng (camerawoman/editor). We also started to operate as a project under the non-governmental organization, Beijing Gender Health Education Institute. Though he still co-presented a number of episodes, Steven Jiang ultimately resigned as co-host of the programme. He was replaced by Liang Ma, who had built up extensive work experience at Beijing

---

2.   The video can be viewed at http://www.queercomrades.com/en/videos/queer-comrades-videos/talk-shows/fag-hags/

Picture 2.1: Queer Comrades talk show studio
Copyright: (c) Queer Comrades

Tongxing Working Group, an NGO that focuses on HIV/AIDS prevention among Men who have Sex with Men (MSM). Stijn Deklerck stayed
on as a volunteer 'distant producer' and all other tasks were also taken up
by a number of volunteers. By the end of its second season in February
2009, Queer Comrades had gathered a total of more than six million hits
for its programmes.

Though it was still difficult in 2008 to find LGBT people to appear
openly in our videos, we had more time and resources to plan our
content. We focused on bringing a range of LGBT issues to the fore
and diversifying our programming, producing both 'light' content
(gay travelling, love at a distance, fruit flies) and more 'serious' content
(homophobia, body and gender). We produced videos featuring a large
selection of China's pioneer LGBT activists, including filmmaker Cui
Zi'en, artist Shi Tou and gay activist scholar Xing Xing. We diversified
our on-location segments by making short reports on LGBT events,
like the public celebration of a gay wedding in Beijing and LGBT

conferences, workshops and training sessions. As we did not encounter government interference with our webcast throughout our first season, we grew bolder with our programming during our second season. We pushed the boundaries, and included programs on sensitive topics such as male sex workers working illegally in China.

Our big breakthrough in popularity came when we broadcast the episode 'Lesbian Toy Story', dedicated to lesbian sex (toys).[3] Literally millions of people watched this episode. We planned that episode because we knew it would generate a lot of attention to our webcast. We did not act upon this obvious interest from our audience by planning more sex-related episodes however; rather, we steered public attention towards other episodes treating topics more in line with our broader goals for the webcast.

Season 3 and Onwards

At the start of the third season, we changed our English name to 'Queer Comrades' while our Chinese name stayed the same. Our third season started in April 2009 and is still ongoing. We gradually received more extended funding throughout our third season, which allowed us to expand our programming and hire extra personnel. Xiaogang stayed on as director/host and Stijn became our full-time producer. Xiaogang and Stijn remain in these respective positions as this volume goes to press. The other full-time, part-time and volunteer positions were taken up by a variety of Chinese and foreign nationals throughout the years.

During the third season, our programmes continued their evolution toward productions that were more emotionally engaging. Initially, we broadcast monthly with subsequent episodes appearing every three months. Our programmes gradually evolved from talk shows into documentaries, where we interview a wider array of people on a particular subject and give the audience more opportunity to identify with the interviewees. At the time of writing (January 2015), we produced 31 shows with an average length of 50 minutes in our third season.

In addition, we started to produce video news items. With these news items, we now have a separate vehicle to report on the actions of the LGBT movement in China and to advertise important LGBT events

---

3.   The video can be viewed at http://www.queercomrades.com/en/videos/queer-comrades-videos/talk-shows/lesbian-toy-story/

to the Chinese public. We also use news items to report on important global LGBT events and to communicate short messages of a more entertaining nature. In total, we have produced more than 200 news items of 3 to 5 minutes each.

By now, Queer Comrades has gathered more than 20 million hits for its programmes broadcast on mainstream video websites. During this season, we have also created our own website, www.queercomrades.com. It provides viewers with easy access to all talk show episodes, news items, blog articles and public events produced by Queer Comrades. It also features audience-generated LGBT video and other content. The Queer Comrades website went online on 1 January 2010. At the time of writing, it has already amassed more than 20 million hits, averaging almost 15,000 every day.

Since the beginning of our third season, finding LGBT people willing to appear on camera has not been the problem it was. We even noticed that appearing on Queer Comrades has become a matter of pride and we have received multiple requests to appear in our videos. This change has given us the confidence to plan the content of our videos more firmly, allowing us to focus on issues that we felt were important to communicate to the Chinese society and moving away from building our videos around the individuals who agreed to appear on film. By producing video news items, we have also felt less inclined to integrate longer pieces on current LGBT events in China into our webcast episodes. Rather, our longer webcast episodes are thematic, focusing on what we perceive as important LGBT information for the Chinese society.

We focused on issues affecting the LGBT-community worldwide, such as homosexuality and religion, and homosexuality and ageing. We also attracted funding to report on international LGBT events – such as the Outgames 2009, the Gay Games 2010, and the ILGA Asia Conference 2010 – and discuss their relevance for Chinese society. In other programmes, we explored poignant LGBT problems in Chinese society, including homosexuality and mental health, sexual education in China, and bullying. In a sense, we have been able to place ourselves more firmly as part of the LGBT movement in China, gradually veering into politically sensitive areas (cancelling of the Mr. Gay China 2010 event, queer activism in China).

同志他他他她她她 ...
The Cream of the Queer Crop

Picture 2.2: The Cream of the Queer Crop
Copyright: (c) Queer Comrades

Our webcast episode 'Cures that Kill'[4] reflects our choice for a more proactive stance regarding the discussion of pressing LGBT issues in China. The episode is concerned with exposing the misconceptions about LGBT by large parts of Chinese society, and the mental health profession in particular. It points out the dangers involved with treating homosexuality as a mental disorder and shows the advantages of treating LGBT people with respect and acceptance. The documentary was screened at an event organized for mental health professionals in Beijing, and it now forms part of an ongoing programme to educate mental health professionals on LGBT issues.

More Than a Webcast

While the webcast still forms the basis of all Queer Comrades activities, we have gradually evolved into an institution that plays a larger media and educational role in Chinese society.

An Independent Webcast for All

In its production and programming, Queer Comrades has always sought a balance between developing and maintaining an audience for its programmes and accomplishing its advocacy goals. We want people

---

4.   The video can be viewed at http://www.queercomrades.com/en/videos/queer-comrades-videos/queer-comrades-documentaries/cures-that-kill-1/

to be interested in our programmes and continue watching them. We aim to address the whole spectrum of Chinese people – from people completely ignorant of LGBT issues to activists well versed in everything LGBT and everyone else falling in between. At the same time, we do not want our desire to reach a sizeable audience to compromise our goal to provide well-researched, informative and positive insights into queer culture, and to advocate for issues we feel are important.

In practice, this has resulted in a huge range of programming. We create episodes and news items that, while raising public awareness, are more entertaining or popular in nature due to the subject matter and/or the tone of the programme. These are meant to lure many new viewers toward our videos. We combine these with programmes of a more serious nature that more directly aim to advocate certain positions. While some videos might be more specifically geared towards certain (LGBT or non-LGBT) population groups, we take care to explain and repeat basic information, ensuring that everyone can understand what our videos are about.

Our overall strategy lies in finding an 'in' with audience members from different walks of life through one or more Queer Comrades videos, who then potentially will click through our other webcast videos, thereby learning about different issues occupying the current Chinese LGBT movement. In this process, we have always put more emphasis on content and less on artistic qualities, though we have increasingly put more effort on improving the filmic qualities of our videos throughout our third season. As such, in developing our webcast, we have been mainly guided by our mission to document queer culture in all its aspects in order to raise public awareness on LGBT matters. Staying true to that mission has meant that we are not yet commercially viable. We have avoided becoming a slave to our audience numbers and of tactics that would make our webcast more commercially viable.

Commercially, it would probably be wiser for Queer Comrades to zoom in on a specific audience group and develop money-earning strategies specifically geared towards this group. Considering the commercial reality of today's Chinese LGBT-related market, this would mean focusing specifically on the male gay population. Currently, the businesses most likely to invest in advertising and/or promotion on LGBT websites are gay entertainment businesses, most of which are directed specifically towards gay men. To date, the LGBT-related websites succeeding in earning a revenue are geared towards this demographic. They feature a variety of ads for spas, dating services, gay clubs and other businesses geared towards the male gay population. In addition, they often have some dating service or similar attached to their website. While most are strictly commercially oriented, some also manage to combine community service activities with other, more commercial goals.

As we wish to remain a welcoming platform for all members of the LGBT and non-LGBT community, we have always refrained from considering those commercially more viable options. We still hope to capitalize on our considerable audience numbers, yet we hope to find funding with mainstream businesses not specifically geared towards LGBT or non-LGBT people but which are willing to advertise their commitment towards the LGBT cause publicly. More than exploring viable financial ways in which to run our webcast, our search for mainstream sponsors has become part of our activism. Their support would further the cause of raising public awareness on LGBT matters throughout society at large.

Queer Comrades has been able to steer its independent course through public funding coming from foreign institutions focused on supporting projects related to sexuality, reproductive health, and/or LGBT rights. With Chinese government funding currently unavailable the large majority of LGBT projects, and mainstream companies still largely unwilling to commit to public LGBT support, foreign funds currently remain our prime means of subsistence.

A Queer Media Institution

During more than eight years of producing and broadcasting, we have established ourselves as a queer media institution and an important partner in the Chinese LGBT movement. We continue to fill an important gap with our broadcasts, as mainstream media still pay scant attention to LGBT-related issues and events.

We have noticed that, when the mainstream Chinese media choose to cover LGBT events – like for example the forced cancellation of the 2010 Mr. Gay China Pageant, which received huge coverage – they borrow footage from our shows. Though we would like them to acknowledge us as full media partners (the footage was broadcast by the mainstream media without any mention of Queer Comrades), we do feel that this is

Picture 2.3: Organizer Ben Zhang faces media after cancellation of Mister Gay China Pageant

Copyright: (c) Queer Comrades

a positive development and we hope we can expand cooperation with mainstream media.

An Audiovisual Information and Support Centre

We have also been building out our role as an audiovisual information and support centre for the LGBT movement in China. We have helped numerous LGBT and HIV/AIDS NGOs both inside and outside of Beijing to record, advertise and report on their events and activities in China. Together with the other members of our audience, NGOs are also invited to broadcast their videos and advertise their events on our Queer Comrades website. All our filmed material, even the footage not used for our programmes, has been collected in our archive of LGBT-related audio-visual material in China, thereby creating a visual memory of all things queer in China. This archive is open to researchers and NGOs, who have often used our videos for their research and educational purposes.

Bringing Queer Imagery to Society

While we still are mainly online-based, increasingly we have engaged ourselves in the organization of public events that bring queer imagery to the (offline) Chinese public. To give some examples, we co-organized the China Queer Film Tour, which brings queer movies to live audiences throughout China; we co-organize the Beijing Queer Film Festival; we have distributed our HIV/AIDS programmes to audiences that have difficulties getting online; and we have organized IDAHO Media Events.

Educational Activities

One important part of our offline strategy has been to organize and co-organize LGBT educational classes that use our videos. Our two main audiences have been university students at various Chinese universities and mental health professionals. Class audiences react very well to the videos, which form an excellent opening for educational activities such as discussions, lectures or panel sessions.

Global LGBT Movement

Since the founding of our webcast, we have worked to bring important issues and events of the global LGBT movement to the Chinese public. We noticed that the global LGBT community was very interested in what was happening in China and, from the second season onwards, we started subtitling all of our videos in both Chinese and English. This has helped us tremendously in linking up and cooperating with the LGBT movement in other countries. We have shown our videos at numerous LGBT film festivals around the world, and we are working together with different international organizations on human rights, LGBT and other issues.

Constructing Identity and Community

Looking back on almost a decade of online queer media activities, one can see different themes emerging in our programmes regarding the construction of LGBT identity and community. Though it is hard to tell how these elements have concretely influenced China's LGBT culture, we hereby list them while estimating the contribution they have (had) on the construction of identity and community.

Visual LGBT Identity

LGBT issues and people continue to be largely invisible in the Chinese mainstream media. Chinese LGBT film production, and the LGBT visual identity, has increasingly developed since the end of the last century, yet it largely retains an 'underground' quality, reaching only a limited audience. We have created an online queer media institution, largely etched on traditional Chinese television standards, to counter the lack of LGBT representation in the mainstream media and the distribution restrictions set on LGBT films. We believe that by doing so, we have succeeded in further developing the LGBT *visual identity* and in disseminating it to a wider Chinese public.

Whereas we believe that the visual LGBT presence generated by our online queer media activities has been of importance to a diverse audience, we have received particularly positive feedback from the internet-savvy and visually inclined younger LGBT generation in China. Many have stated that they spent their high school years watching, and identifying with, every Queer Comrades episode.

Coming Out

In China, *coming out* as an LGBT person remains challenging, and the large majority of Chinese LGBTs are 'in the closet'. In our videos, however, we have always shown people who are willing to talk openly about their sexuality, gender identity and sexual identity. Our audience observes people who talk openly about issues that our audience members might be struggling with.

Rather than using face-covering mosaics or other masking tools to film people who do not want to appear openly on camera, we have always opted not to engage them as filming partners, thereby respecting their privacy. We made one exception during our second season, when filming male sex workers illegally working in China, since their open appearance on our webcast might have resulted in criminal proceedings.

Our refusal to use masking tools stems from the fact that the Chinese mainstream media often utilize these tools when interviewing LGBT people. While we recognize the privacy rights of these interviewees and their choice to remain incognito on camera, we have always felt that this attaches a sense of shame and taboo to the LGBT identity. It also does not fit well with our goal to disseminate the visual aspects of LGBT identity.

It is for this reason that Queer Comrades has always promoted a very 'out' LGBT identity. During our first two seasons, we did so mainly through the choice of our featured characters. In the third season, and particularly during our episodes dealing with topics of coming out and activism, we have also become vocal in encouraging our viewers to consider more openness regarding their own sexuality and sexual orientation.

Diversity and Unity

In our content and our featured guests, we portray a *diverse LGBT identity*. We focus on Lesbian, Gay, Bisexual and Transgender aspects of such identity and feature people of all ages, backgrounds, religions, social strata, educational levels, homesteads, etc. While doing so, we seek to steer away from a divided identity. Admittedly, it has been hard to focus our attention equally on all different groups in the LGBT community. Some episodes could be considered largely gay while others might deal strictly with lesbian issues. Nonetheless, Queer Comrades has always tried to inspire a sense of unity, emphasizing solidarity and connectedness among all community members.

We also apply this 'diverse but not divided' approach to promote a global LGBT identity. By featuring foreign guests in our videos, by covering international LGBT events, by illustrating LGBT issues in foreign countries, and by following Chinese LGBT delegations abroad, we try to illustrate that the Chinese LGBT community is a part of the global LGBT community and that there is a common movement.

A Positive Approach

In our webcast, we focus on sharing *positive insights* and on how to make things better. We highlight the kinds of problems the LGBT community encounters in China, but at the same time, we also focus on how people are making this better, how our audience can contribute to create a solution for these problems, and so on. As such, we emphasize a positive LGBT identity, an empowered LGBT identity, one that encourages people to work through the issues they are facing and to celebrate themselves and their lives.

Our choice to accentuate the positive is also politically motivated. Throughout our experiences in Chinese civil society, we have noticed that the communication of positive, energetic and empowering information is less likely to attract negative government attention than negative and blameful content.

Activism

Especially since the start of our third season of production, we have sought to instill a sense of responsibility in our viewers and convey the importance of *activism*: they have to act if they want things to get better. Especially when showing specific LGBT-related problems, LGBT community activities and events (domestic and international) and LGBT

你如此坚强
STRONG

INTERNATIONAL DAY
AGAINST HOMOPHOBIA & TRANSPHOBIA
國際不再恐同日

一部反对暴力对待性少数人群的纪录片
A DOCUMENTARY AGAINST VIOLENCE TOWARDS LGBT PEOPLE

Picture 2.4: Strong
Copyright: (c) Queer Comrades

campaigns, we have become increasingly vocal in calling out our viewers to actively contribute to the LGBT movement and help in solving the problems that the LGBT community continues to be confronted with. This choice to promote activism is also connected to our emphasis on an LGBT identity that is both 'out' and positive. Queer Comrades aims to empower people to stand up for themselves and actively find solutions to the issues and problems they are dealing with in their lives.

LGBT Community
Finally, Queer Comrades has been steadily developing in our role as an audiovisual information and support centre for China's *LGBT community*.

This has been achieved not only by helping numerous LGBT and HIV/AIDS NGOs to record, advertise and report on their events and activities in China but also by steadily creating a visual archive of all things queer in China that is open to researchers and organizations. In this sense, we consider Queer Comrades to be an active part of the LGBT community, and we aim to instil this sense of community in our audience.

Conclusion: How 'Queer' is Queer Comrades?

The Chinese name of Queer Comrades, (同志亦凡人 *tongzhi yi fanren*), does not refer to the term 'queer' (酷儿 *ku'er*). In literal translation from Chinese, the webcast title reads 'Comrades (as well) as Ordinary Persons'. Whereas the English name of our webcast refers to 'queer' – whatever is at odds with the normal, the legitimate, the dominant – the Chinese webcast name refers to a sense of normalization. This reflects the situation in which the Queer Comrades webcast operates in China.

On the one hand, by nature of our institution, by nature of the content we produce and broadcast, by nature of the cause we strive for, we are at odds with the dominant heteronormative society in China. Still, we also find strength in being the 'other', in recognizing that it strategically unites us as a community. On the other hand, we do want Chinese society to know more about us, to understand us and to accept us as ordinary and equal people.

The idea that we might be able to accomplish a change of the status quo not by aiming for normalization consisting of toleration or equal status, but by following the more 'queer' idea of challenging the sexual order and categorization embedded in all of our social institutions, is slowly finding resonance with LGBT activists in China. Queer Comrades, too, has been increasingly influenced by queer thought during the course of its development. Whereas our early webcasts presented a clear hope for normalization, tolerance and equality with respect to 'Chinese mainstream society', our ideas have evolved along a queerer path that aims to challenge labels altogether.

While we do reflect and report on queer ideas, use them and increasingly challenge our viewers to question dominant ideas about categorization of gender and sexuality, Queer Comrades does not make an explicit point of emphasizing queer theory or queer struggles in the programmes. One reason for this is the fact that such a standpoint could be interpreted as a political activity by the Chinese authorities and might trigger obtrusive negative attention to our activities. Another reason is that an emphasis on queer theory and politics would in all likelihood lead to confusion for audience members who are in the process of getting a basic grip on sexual diversity; most Chinese LGBT and other people are still firmly imbibed within the normative conception that 'normal' heterosexual society is the ultimate decision-maker when it comes to tolerating 'abnormal' sexual minorities. As evidenced by the discussion in this chapter, we therefore still make use of LGBT identity labels. By giving these labels a diverse, positive, active and open connotation, Queer Comrades is ultimately inviting the entire Chinese society to celebrate themselves and each other for who they are.

Authors' Note

We would like to thank Elisabeth Engebretsen, Bao Hongwei and William Schroeder for their scholarly support and supportive editing. The discussions we had in the framework of the international research network they established continue to inspire us in our daily work. We furthermore thank our fellow contributors to this book and all of our Queer China Working Group members for their valuable input. This article is dedicated to all of the Queer Comrades staff members, volunteers, funders, partners, audience members, talk show guests, documentary characters, fans, guest directors and contributors who worked with us throughout the years on documenting queer culture and raising public awareness. We would especially like to thank Steven Jiang, co-founder of Queer Comrades; all the volunteers who helped us during our crucial first broadcasting season; and the Ford Foundation, for supporting our webcast from our beginning years up until today.

CHAPTER 3

Digital Video Activism
Narrating History and Memory in Queer China, 'Comrade' China

Hongwei Bao

> To articulate the past historically does not mean to recognize it 'the way it really was' (Ranke). It means to seize hold of a memory as it flashes up at a moment of danger.
>
> Walter Benjamin, *Theses on the Philosophy of History*

With the song 'make the world full of love' (*rang shijie chongman ai* 让世界充满爱), the curtain dropped for the premiere of Cui Zi'en's 2008 documentary *Queer China, 'Comrade' China* (Zhi tongzhi, 誌同志, *Queer China* hereafter). The lights were turned on, showing a simply-equipped auditorium with approximately one hundred people seated inside. The audience burst into applause. Their eyes followed a colourfully dressed and slightly androgynous-looking man walking up to the platform. Another person (Zhu Rikun 朱日坤) standing at the podium introduced the man as Cui Zi'en (崔子恩 hereafter Cuizi 崔子), the director of the film.[1] Holding the microphone, Cuizi began his speech with a routine list

---

1. In this chapter, I use Cuizi 崔子, which is the director's preferred way of being addressed, to refer to Cui Zi'en 崔子恩. For the other Chinese names used in this text, I follow the Chinese protocol; that is, surnames first, and followed by given names.

    The films Cuizi has directed include *Enter the Clowns* 丑角登场 (2002), *The Old Testament* 旧约 (2002), *Feeding Boys, Ayaya* 啊呀呀，去哺乳 (2003), *Keep Cool and Don't Blush* 脸不变色心不跳 (2003), *Night Scene* 夜景 (2003), *An Interior View of Death* 死亡的内景 (2004), *The Narrow Path* 雾语 (2004), *Shitou and That Nana* 石头和那个娜娜 (2004), *Star Appeal* 星星相吸惜 (2004), *My Fair Son* 我如花似玉的儿子 (2005), *WC* 呼呼哈嘿 (2005), *Withered in a Blooming Season* 少年草花黄 (2005), *Refrain* 副歌 (2006) and *Queer China,*

of acknowledgements. He had hardly finished reading the list when he began to sob. A young woman, lesbian filmmaker Shitou (石头), walked up to the front, placed her arms around him and hugged him. All of the audience, myself included, were moved by the scene.[2]

A few days later, when I met Cuizi in a small cafe near the Beijing Film Academy on a sunny winter afternoon, he recalled the moment when he shed tears and described his feelings: 'I feel that history unfolds itself in front of my eyes. There are too many historical events, feelings and connections, both on and off the screen; they have been lit up by the film.'

'History is what hurts', writes Frederic Jameson (1981: 102). For Cuizi, history did not so much hurt as it conjured up nostalgic sentiments and traumatic memories. Recollecting, reassembling, narrating, and sharing of the history of China's LGBT (Lesbian, Gay, Bisexual, Transgender) movement through the medium of digital video and the performative practice of film screening contribute to the continuous construction of *tongzhi* (同志 lit. comrade, meaning gay or queer) identity and queer spaces in China.[3]

In this chapter, through critical analysis of Cuizi's *Queer China*, in tandem with my ethnography at queer film screenings in China, I discuss the construction of *tongzhi* identity and queer spaces through what Cuizi terms 'digital video activism' (*yingxiang xingdong* 影像行动). Digital video activism, as a means of community engagement advocated by Chinese queer film directors and activists, encourages people to rethink film as art, media, technology and institution, and its relation to identity formation, community building and social movements. I also

---

Comrade China 誌同志(2008). He was both director and scriptwriter for most of the films mentioned above

2. This was the premiere of Cui Zi'en's 2008 documentary *Queer China*, a two-hour-long documentary about LGBT movement in China, screened at the Songzhuang Art Gallery, Beijing, on 25 November 2008. Following its screening throughout China and the world, the film has gained considerable popularity, mostly on university campuses and within LGBT communities. It also won the audience award for best documentary at the 2009 Torino LGBT film festival.

3. *Tongzhi* ('comrade') is the Chinese term for gay, LGBT or queer, depending on the specific context. It used to be a common form of address in the communist era and was appropriated by LGBT activists to refer to LGBT people in Hong Kong and Taiwan respectively in 1989 and 1992 (Chou 2000; S. Lim 2006, 11). The term has since gained popularity in the Chinese-speaking world. Cuizi's film *Queer China* is titled *Zhi tongzhi* in Chinese, meaning 'Documenting [the History of] the Comrades'.

consider *tongzhi* politics practiced by Cuizi and other queer filmmakers in China as localized and creative queer politics which might challenge the dominant Euro-American-centric form of queer politics.

Narrating Histories and Memories

Queer China, a two-hour documentary film, explores China's LGBT movement in the period from the 1980s to 2008.[4] The film is divided into nine parts, each covering topics relevant to homosexuality in China: from academic research to political activism, from medical cases to legal discussions, from public media representation to queer film production, from 'coming out' stories to a booming pink economy. It traces some watershed events in China's LGBT history, including 'firsts' such as the first academic publication on homosexuality, titled *Their World* (*Tamen de shijie* 他们的世界) (Y. Li and Wang 1992); the first queer film, *East Palace, West Palace* (*Donggong xigong* 东宫西宫) (Y. Zhang 1996); the first LGBT journal, *Friend Exchange* (*Pengyou tongxin* 朋友通信) (B. Zhang 1998); the 1997 repeal of 'hooliganism' (*liumang zui* 流氓罪, the legal code under which homosexuality had been prosecuted) from the Criminal Law; and the acknowledgement that ego-syntonic homosexuality is not a mental illness in the third edition of *Chinese Classification of Mental Disorder* (CCMD–3, 中国精神疾病分类方案与诊断标准第三版) in 2001. Based upon approximately thirty interviews with academic researchers, medical professionals, LGBT activists and ordinary gays and lesbians, the film represents a 'Who's Who' in China's LGBT history from the 1980s to 2008.

The film's narrative is chronological: it is linear, unidirectional and progressive.[5] The interviewees all agree that the 1970s and 1980s were an age of 'darkness'; people were ignorant about homosexuality and society treated LGBT people unjustly. The end of the film shows the success of some LGBT events such as queer film festivals and society's

---

4. The film has two versions: a one-hour version and a two-hour version. In most screenings, the one-hour version is used. The screening discussed in this article is the two-hour version.

5. This author's understanding of history has been informed by post-structualist historiography and, in particular, by Michel Foucault's notion of 'genealogy', which accounts for 'the constitution of knowledges, discourses, domains of objects, and so on, without having to make reference to a subject which is either in transcendental relation to the field of events or runs in its empty sameness throughout the course of history.' (2003: 306).

increasing acceptance of LGBT issues. The film's chapter titles, such as 'From Pitch Black to Light Grey', 'From Knowing to Knowledge' and 'From Slow Motion to Fast Forwarding', clearly indicate a historical teleology. In the narrative, the past is of necessity portrayed as grim; the precarious present inevitably points to a bright future. Most important of all, the narrative implies an assumption historical irreversibility: tragedies of the past are never to be repeated. In addition, individual agency is highlighted. People can combat unjust social structures with their strong will, a voluntarism that was at the core of the Maoist revolution. Practices that point to progress are naturally justified; others, which may impede progress, are invariably condemned. The belief shared by many people in China that the country is becoming a more open society empowers LGBT activists and ordinary gay people alike in their pursuit of social justice and sexual freedom.

Those who wish to criticise the film would have no dearth of opportunity. Cuizi's linear and progressive history seems to reduce the complexities and ambiguities of the LGBT experience into a purposeful simplistic narrative. One audience member complained to me that the film was too 'academic'. The early stage of China's LGBT movement seems to have drawn primarily on sociological and medical research and it consists mainly of interviews with leading academics in the field. Besides, the documentary showcases 'talking heads' of the LGBT celebrities, which 'clearly function to make "queerness" visible or audible to the viewer' but also 'underline the fact that the act of documentary inscription is not neutral, but moulded by the subjectivity of the director' (Robinson 2012: 123). Ordinary gay people's lives seem to have been overlooked by these 'expert' voices. A further shortcoming is that most of the LGBT people represented are male. Most events take place in urban settings, with the voices of lesbians and other sexual minorities marginalized, as are those of people from the country's provincial and rural regions and of some ethnic minorities. In addition, there are important omissions in the film due to the director's own preoccupations and possible bias. For example, the political activism of Wu Chunsheng, Chou Wah-Shan and Wan Yanhai, the early lesbian activism led by Susie Jolly and He Xiaopei in Beijing, together with Liu Dalin, and Lu Longguang's sociological and medical research in the 1990s (Liu and Lu 2005) should have received more attention. The fact that the film is imbued with a romantic and nostalgic atmosphere, especially the representation of previous film festivals, renders some scenes poetic rather than providing a realistic account of the past.

But Cuizi's history cannot be dismissed simply because of its linear and progressive narrative. It represents way of writing an alternative history that counters and subverts the official narratives of history in mainland China. For decades, the Chinese government has been silent about LGBT issues. Ordinary people have been ill-informed about the existence of homosexuality, to such an extent that many people had never heard of homosexuality in China. Most consider homosexuality to be 'Western decadence' or a 'feudal remnant' that is incompatible with the country's socialist system (Evans 1997: 207; Hinsch 1990: 163). In the early 1950s, homosexuality, together with prostitution and polygamy, was effectively 'eradicated' from the socialist public discourse. People who engaged in such practices were 'transformed' into 'socialist new people' by the Maoist regime. While a few scant records of same-sex intimacies in the Maoist era have survived, most scholars agree that an important part of the LGBT history has been lost (Guo 2007; Sang 2003; Zhou 2009). In a way, LGBT people have become 'spectres' (*youling* 幽灵) hovering over contemporary Chinese society (R. Wan 1990: 103).

Around the 1990s, medical and sociological research into homosexuality began to appear in mainland China (Fang 1995; Y. Li and Wang 1992; B. Zhang 1994). This was concomitant with Chinese LGBT activists' efforts to organize community events and raise LGBT consciousness (X. He 2002; Y. Wan, 2001). The discovery of HIV/AIDS in China in 1985 brought LGBT issues to the public attention and soon the Chinese government began to acknowledge the existence of LGBT groups and the importance of HIV/AIDS prevention programmes. Although the link between LGBT identities and public health discourse stigmatized LGBT communities, more and more LGBT NGOs have been established with the help of transnational capital and the Chinese government (X. He 2006; Jones 2007; D. Li 2004). By the late 1990s, the increasing popularity of the Internet provided a venue for LGBT people to meet each other and to build an online community (Cristini 2003; Ho 2010). The decriminalization of homosexuality in 1997 ushered discussions of homosexuality into the public discourse. Meanwhile, China's 'open-up' (*kaifang* 开放) policy and market economy also opened up a 'pink economy' in China, evident in the increasing numbers of LGBT commercial venues appearing in the major Chinese cities (Farrer 2002; Ho 2010; Rofel 1999b; Rofel 2007). Transnational media and popular culture engendered more open attitudes toward gender and sexuality in the urban youth (Farrer 2002; Farrer 2006; Ho 2010; Martin et al. 2003; Rofel 2007; Wei 2008). Despite this, the surveillance of the nation state and the influence of Confucian notions of family and kinship continued to shape Chinese LGBT identities in important ways (Chou 2000; Engebretsen 2005; Engebretsen 2008; Ho 2010; Rofel 2007).

In many ways, Cuizi is rediscovering (and 'recovering') LGBT histories that had been excluded from mainstream historical narratives dominated by the nation state and by heteronormative logic. The state apparatus had constructed its own particular version of history and remained silent about alternative histories. Cuizi, along with his colleagues, 'rescue[s] history from the nation' (Duara 1995). By interviewing people who experienced China's LGBT movement over the past three decades, Cuizi tries to uncover memories that may enrich the dominant historical narratives. When a national history tries to homogenize people's memories, remembering the past and uncovering forgotten histories can be an act of subaltern politics. As historians and anthropologists (Halbwachs and Coser 1992; Hershatter 2002; Nora 1996; Rofel 1999b) remind us, remembering and forgetting are not as natural as they appear to be. Selective memory is often constructed by dominant narratives and, at times, challenges these narratives. In the process of negotiating competing discourses in an attempt to make sense of a contingent world and to make sense of one's subject position within it, people construct memories that change the ways others understand history. Two widespread forms of memory include nostalgia and trauma.

Nostalgia and Trauma

Nostalgia is often considered a romanticized rendition of the past by people who situate themselves in the present. As a strategy of representation, nostalgia 'persists as a longing, structured through narrative, for the authenticity of absolute presence and the origin of lived experience; it reflects a wish to close the gap between experience and its mediation in language' (Rofel 1999a: 135–136). Nostalgia is necessarily inauthentic. By portraying the past as utopian and nearly perfect, nostalgia serves as a type of popular cultural criticism that conveys people's dissatisfaction with the present without spelling out explicitly the reasons behind this dissatisfaction.

By using historical footage and old songs, Cuizi successfully creates a nostalgic effect. The nostalgic event, which seems utopian when placed in the context of frustrations in later years, was the first China Queer Film Festival, held in 2001 on the campus of Peking University, one of the most prestigious and liberal universities in China. Although it only lasted three days, shorter than originally planned due to pressure from the university authorities and police, many people still hold fond memories of it. Li Yu, a female film director who attended the festival, recalled: 'I will never forget the experience at Peking University. I did not mind the size of the festival or the number of participants. People understood my film; that is all I care about' (Cui 2009b). Yang Yang, an organizer of the film festival, recalled: 'the event attracted a large number of people. The auditorium had a seating capacity of 300 people. It was packed on every screening. The last night, when we showed *Lan Yu*, people stood in the aisles and leaned against the walls. More than 30 journalists from Chinese and international media reported the event' (Cui 2009b).

Due to the pressure and intervention from the Peking University Youth League, the first queer film festival could hardly be called a great success. However, it does not render the interviewees' accounts less authentic. Their 'sweet' memories should not be seen simply as a faithful statement about the past. They should also be read in juxtaposition to the second queer film festival, which was banned by the venue provider in association with Peking University's publicity administration before it opened, and to the third and fourth queer film festivals, which could only be held on the outskirts of Beijing due to the interventions from Beijing municipality's publicity, public security and business licencing administrations.[6] By remembering the past in particular ways, the

---

6. Holding a queer film festival at Peking University, one of the most liberal universities in China, is symbolic due to the unique position of Peking University in modern Chinese history and in China's enlightenment movement. Many audience members have complained about the venues for the Third (2007) and Fourth (2009) queer film festivals, the Songzhuang Art Centre and Fanhall cinema, both of which are located in Songzhuang modern art district in the eastern suburbs of Beijing, a two-hour subway journey combined with bus ride from the city centre. This prevented many people from attending the festivals. The location change

interviewees expressed their regrets about not being able to hold the event on university campuses and their anger towards the government's restrictions of free expressions of gender, sexuality and artistic forms.

Memories of the past are sometimes traumatic: this was evident in the narrations of the second queer film festival, which was scheduled to open on 22 April 2005 at the Centennial Hall of Peking University. Ten minutes before the opening ceremony, when all the preparation work had been completed, the administration of Peking University's Centennial Hall to allow the screening to go ahead. The festival organizers had to apologize to the audience and cancel the three-day festival. They found a temporary screening venue, a small art gallery in the 798 Modern Art District in the northeastern suburb of Beijing, which they could use, but only for a few hours on the following evening. A small audience, together with the organizers, attended the event. Their feelings were a blend of disappointment, anger and fear.[7]

In *Queer China*, Cuizi uses a montage of old photos from the event, dubbing them with Tian Zhen's melancholic song *Perseverance* (*zhizhuo* 执着) to evoke the atmosphere. Yang Yang remarked when she was interviewed in the film:

> I graduated from Beida [Peking University]. I used to study at Beida. I was very much sentimentally attached to the university, at least at that time. When it came to the second queer film festival, I wished that it could still be held at Beida. In my mind, Beida was the most liberal and the most avant-garde place in China. After the failure of the second queer film festival, I felt that Beida had died, at least in my mind. (Cui 2009b)

---

was due in part to a lack of support from venue providers in the city centre. Zhu Rikun, the venue provider at Songzhuang, has been very supportive of queer films. The third queer film festival was a part of the Beijing Independent Film Festival organized by the Li Xianting Film Fund and the Songzhuang Art Centre. Another common complaint from the audience was the poor publicity surrounding the event. The festival programs only went online and through group emails and mobile phone messages a few days before the opening ceremony. Festival organizers explained that they did this deliberately to avoid government intervention. See Y. Yang and Fan (2009). See also Wei Wei's chapter in this volume.

7. For an account of past queer film festivals, see Y. Yang and Fan (2009) and Cui (2009b).

The failure of the second queer film festival constitutes a traumatic memory in Chinese LGBT history, traumatic not only because of the failure of the festival but also due to a general disillusionment with the prospects of liberal democracy in China, a popular sentiment since the Tian'anmen Student Protest in 1989. Fifteen years after that traumatic historical event, with China's entry into the global economy and with the pervasive influence of transnational neoliberalism in Chinese society, LGBT people in China found, to their great disappointment, 'our country and our universities are homophobic to such an extent that they cannot ever tolerate a beautiful film festival' (BGLFF 2009).

Recalling traumatic memories and voicing them, i.e. 'telling bitterness' (*suku* 诉苦), has a long tradition in modern China. In the Yan'an period (1935–1947) and during the early Maoist era, the rural poor were mobilized by the Communist Party through attending public meetings and were instructed to recall and tell their sufferings of the past (Hershatter 2002). 'Telling bitterness' provided an effective means for the so-called 'subaltern class' to make sense of history and social change and to construct their identities in response to the demands of the new political regime. It 'provided a means of interpellation; it led people to conceive of themselves as new kinds of subjects, as subaltern subjects' (Rofel 1999a: 138). Telling bitterness is not simply a linguistic practice; it is also performative. It constructs narrators and audience as certain subjects. But this does not necessarily make 'telling bitterness' equivalent to the penetration of 'ideology' or 'false consciousness'. To be sure, 'speaking bitterness' is also a 'technology of the self' (Foucault 1988); it can serve as resistance to certain dominant narratives of history. The incoherence, ambiguity and contradictions in the 'bitter' stories may disrupt the seamlessness of history and dominant narratives.

Cuizi's film can be seen as a form of 'telling bitterness'. In his interviews, many people talked about the suppression of LGBT people by the Chinese government and by Chinese society at large. They also expressed their relief that such days are never to return and that tomorrow will be better. This effectively constructs a 'repressive' narrative, which often leads to a 'liberatory' narrative. Michel Foucault questions the 'speaker's benefit' hidden in such narratives, 'It seems to me that the essential thing is […] the existence in our era of a discourse in which sex, the revelation of truth, the overturning of global laws, the proclamation of a new day to come, and the promise of a certain felicity are linked together' (1990: 7). Seen in this light, the narratives in this film are far more complicated than they first appear to be.

The responses of the audience are also more complicated than they first appear. Having experienced the frustrations of the second, third, fourth and fifth festivals, people who saw Cuizi's film were emotionally ready to feel nostalgic about the relative success of the first festival. Cuizi's film provided a vehicle to release emotions that society and government had created.

It would, however, be reductive to conclude that the narrative of LGBT history has been made and manipulated by LGBT activists in China. Admittedly, many people, from LGBT activists to queer studies scholars, from government officials to ordinary gay people, have participated in the process of 'incitement to discourse'. It seems that talking about sex in opposition to the state has brought transgressive pleasure to more than one party. It is in the process of talking about sex and sexuality and transgressing imagined boundaries that *tongzhi* identity is brought into existence. *Queer China* and queer film festivals are but small components of a complex social machine that produces sex, sexualities and subjects in contemporary China.

Cuizi and His Queer Films

It is important to situate *Queer China* in Cuizi's life trajectory in order to understand why he constructs China's LGBT history in particular ways. As a queer film director, producer, screenwriter, critic, novelist and outspoken queer activist, Cuizi is among the best known names in China's LGBT communities. His life story to a large extent parallels the history of post-Mao China's (1978–present) LGBT movement. In 1991, while working as a teacher lecturing in screenwriting at the Beijing Film Academy, China's lyceum for film professionals, he came out as gay. For this reason, the school authority imposed a punitive 'administrative penalty' (*xingzheng chufa* 行政处罚) on Cuizi.[8]

---

8. 'Administrative penalty' (*xingzheng chufa* 行政处罚) is a type of non-judicial punishment enforced by the work units (*danwei* 单位) to which one is assigned. In the case of Cuizi, it includes a low academic title with little hope of promotion, a low salary, deprivation of the university-provided accommodation on the school campus, and deprivation of the right to lecture for ten years. Cuizi also mentioned

In 1997, Cuizi published his first queer novel, titled *The Pink Lips* (*Taose zuichun* 桃色嘴唇). In 1999, he was screenwriter and actor for *Man Man Woman Woman* (or *Men and Women, Nannan nünü* 男男女女), one of the earliest queer films made in mainland China.[9] The film won the FIPRESCI (International Federation of Film Critics) award at the Locarno International Film Festival in 1999. From 1999 to date, he has published approximately twenty queer novels and six academic monographs on literary and film criticism. His novel, *My Uncle's Secular Life* (*Jiujiu de renjian yanhuo* 舅舅的人间烟火), won the 2001 Radio Literature Award in Germany. Cuizi is also a prolific filmmaker, with about twenty films to his credit; he worked on most of these films as screenwriter, director and sometimes producer. His films are not publicly released in mainland China. Most of them are shown at film festivals and in LGBT community screenings.

Cuizi's novels and films differ sharply in style. While he utilizes sophisticated language and writing styles in his novels, his films often appear 'amateurish'. They feature incoherent storylines, monotonous narratives, long takes, hand-held cameras, and ambient sound – a style akin to Italian neorealism and *cinéma vérité*.[10] He often makes films on small budgets within a short period of time. His access to digital video cameras, amateur actors and actresses, and editing equipment at Beijing Film Academy, where he works, along with the kind help and generous volunteer work of his friends and fans, enables him to produce low-budget films. Cuizi seems to be more radical than many of his peer filmmakers in China in terms of cinematic techniques and aesthetics: his films are extremely slow and 'anti-aesthetic'. Watching his *Man Man Woman Woman* (1999) reminded Chinese film critic Chris Berry of 'post-Stonewall, earnest talking heads documentaries and depressing, low-budget, realist dramas' (2004: 195). Cuizi, however, justifies himself

that the school authority ordered him to go to hospital so that he would be diagnosed as a 'pathologized homosexual', one who should not enjoy the responsibilities and rights (*wu zeren nengli* 无责任能力) of a 'normal' citizen. Cuizi points out in *Queer China* that the most common 'penalties' that gays and lesbians face in mainland China is not assault from the police but the 'administrative penalties' enforced by their work units.

9. Another English translation of the film title is *Men and Women*.

10. Cuizi observes that his style changed abruptly and dramatically after *Queer China*. See Fan Popo's interview with Cuizi in this volume.

by characterizing his films as 'zero rhetoric' (*ling xiuci* 零修辞), which he describes as a radical departure from literary techniques and conventions:

> I hope to make a brand new type of films, films without rhetoric. When Zhu Rikun asked me why I chose to make films, I told him that this is a way for me to break away from the language and rhetoric that I have been familiar with since my childhood. I have finally found a way to give up that language and to create something new with a different type of language: unsophisticated language. The new language points to a new life. Sophisticated language only conceals, romanticizes and aestheticizes social realities. It makes us sound literary and artistic, but not strong. (Quoted in Jia'ni 2008)

Films, especially digital video films, provided Cuizi with a means of breaking away from established artistic conventions. This was not simply a matter of aesthetics, but something intrinsically political:

> In the past two years, I have changed my mind about film-making. I don't think that I can create art for art's sake any more. Nor do I think that art can be free from politics. I have begun to relate art to politics and to the liberation or suppression of certain groups of people. I have debunked the boundaries between art and politics. The best art works should be those that can influence and liberate the oppressed, instead of those displayed in museums or art galleries to satisfy the needs of the bourgeoisie and those who have time and money. (Quoted in K. Zhao 2009: 18–19)

Cuizi's film philosophy can be best understood through Walter Benjamin's writings on works of art in the age of mechanical reproduction. For Benjamin, new media and modern technologies such as photography and films have broken the myth of the 'aura' that characterized old forms of art such as painting. Painting is based on a belief in tradition and authenticity as well as on ritualistic performative practices; it is often manipulated by the ruling class to create illusions among the masses. New reproductive art and technology, on the other hand, keeps the audience distracted and reflexive of their subordinate positions, thus giving rise to subaltern consciousness and mass politics (2007 [1968]: 217–242).

Benjamin's discussion of new art forms in relation to fresh aesthetical experience and alternative forms of politics is pertinent to my discussion of independent films and *tongzhi* politics in China. Digital videos have made it possible for LGBT people to create their own films despite the state monopoly and censorship of mainstream and commercial film production. Through events such as film screening and queer film festivals, Chinese LGBT community is constructing its own public culture. A queer 'counterpublic', as Michael Warner (2002: 80) would say, is emerging in mainland China through the LGBT community's engagement with media. Stephanie Hemelryk Donald (1999) warns against being too celebratory when speaking about a 'public sphere' and 'civil society' in China. Her notion of 'public secrets' helps us to think beyond the public/ private dichotomy and the roles that films play in the construction of civility in China. Along with Mayfair Mei-Hui Yang (1999), I have reason to believe that the performativity of queer films and queer film festivals can bring a queer 'public sphere' into existence in China.

Digital Video Activism

Since 2001, Cuizi and other Chinese queer filmmakers and activists have been organizing queer film festivals. There have been six such events thus far, together with numerous nationwide 'Travelling Queer Independent Film Festivals' (*ku'er duli yingxiang xunhui zhan* 酷儿独立影像巡回展). Directors have screened their films in various cities across China. There have been numerous queer film screenings, including 'festivals', at LGBT venues and on university campuses. These festivals, generally organized by the same group of individuals, have changed names over the years, from Beijing Homosexual Film Festival (*Beijing tongxinglian dianyingjie* 北京同性恋电影节) in 2001 and 2003 to Beijing Queer Film Exhibition (*Beijing ku'er yingzhan* 北京酷儿影展) in 2007 and 2009. Both changes, from 'homosexual' to 'queer' and from 'festival' to 'exhibition', demand an explanation; both are components of Cuizi's digital video activism.

Cuizi's idea of activism is, in part, to have films seen by as many people as possible. The activism is the screenings, the ideas communicated in the films, and the community forged among audience members – with film among the focal points that brings this community together. Both rhetorical changes – homosexual to queer and festival to exhibition – were self-conscious attempts to 'package' events in a way that would allow activism to happen; that is, in a way that would allow films to be shown and viewed in public. 'Homosexual' has a well-known and negative connotation; its use immediately raised a red flag. 'Queer,' on the other hand, was an unknown idea. 'Unknown' is better than 'provocative'. Similarly, the word 'festival' has a specific political connotation in the Chinese context. 'Exhibition' has no such connotation and, indeed, fits into a longstanding Chinese narrative that respects learning. In addition to demonstrating political sensitivity, both labels are also honest. The events *did* emphasise queerness and they *were* festive exhibitions.

The change from homosexual to queer suggests a conscious departure from gay identity politics to queer politics. The film festival encompasses a wide range of topics regarding gender and sexuality: homosexuality, heterosexuality, transgenderism, sadomasochism, as well as other fluid gender identities and non-identities. The term 'queer', in Chinese context, is not generally considered a political identity, not to mention that most straight people (government officials included) have no idea of what it implies. The term *tongxinglian* (同性恋 gay / homosexual / LGBT), on the other hand, is not only often related to pathological and legal discourses but to human rights (*renquan* 人权) discourses as well. Terms such as 'human rights', 'democracy' (*minzhu* 民主) and 'freedom' (*ziyou* 自由) have become so heavily loaded with Cold War rhetoric and a China / West dichotomy that LGBT activists in China know only too well that it is better not to invoke these abstract and elusive concepts in their practice of political activism.

'Film exhibition', as opposed to 'film festival', denotes a more pragmatic attitude on the part of the organizers. According to Cuizi, the new name 'film exhibition' sounds more academic and artistic. It also sounds less politically sensitive, which is an important consideration in China.[11]

---

11. In early 2008, China's state media administration, *Guojia guangbo dianying dianshi zongju* 国家广播电影电视总局, stipulated that media contents involving homosexuality, pornography and violence cannot be shown in public media in China Delate the reference.The first travelling queer film festival (*ku'er yingxiang xunhuizhan* 酷儿影像巡回展) started in response to the regulation. Some young Chinese queer film directors, including Fan Popo and Shitou, showed eighteen queer films in twelve cities from 2008 to early 2009. They also wore a T-shirt with the characters 'we want to see queer films' (*women yao kan tongxinglian dianying* 我们要看同性恋电影) printed on it (Fan 2009). The second round of travelling queer film festival started in Beijing in October 2009. (See Popo Fan's chapter in this book.)

'Film festivals' are always considered as state-sanctioned events with considerable symbolic power in China. Any organization or individual, mostly associated with the art community, can hold an exhibition without necessarily posing a threat to the state power. Filmmakers who want to highlight the artistic features (*yishuxing* 艺术性) of the festival choose Songzhuang, a modern art precinct in an eastern suburb of Beijing, as the festival venue. The Third and Fourth Queer Film Festivals invited scholars engaged in queer film studies to hold forums or seminars (*ku'er dianying luntan* 酷儿电影论坛) to emphasize the festival's academic dimension (*xueshuxing* 学术性). In June 2009, queer film scholars and directors from Hong Kong, Taiwan and mainland China were invited to participate in three panel discussions.

The notion of 'film exhibition' also expresses a philosophy of art that is less hierarchical and more diverse than the elitist and institutionalized 'film festival'. 'The film exhibition neither assesses films nor offer awards. We don't think that we can compare films as the Olympics Games do to athletes.' (Cui 2008: 2) Indeed, if the 'Olympic Games' represent an arborescent, polarised and hierarchical social order, the 'film exhibition' opens up a decentred, fragmentary and rhizomatic political imaginary and a 'non-fascist' mode of existence (Deleuze & Guattari 1988).

In an interview, Cuizi summarized the type of queer activism that uses digital video films as digital video activism, explaining the task as follows: 'We do not think that we should advocate and promote those so-called standard, artistically refined and excellent films. We call for acting with digital videos and changing the world' (Cui 2009a). He attributes a 'soft' and 'flexible' texture to films and juxtaposes this quality with the 'hard' and 'stiff' (*yingxingde* 硬性的) world. 'It is convenient and direct to connect films to the hard times and to change the society' (Cui 2009a).

Cuizi's description of the media effect evokes the impact of films on the audience in Benjamin's writing: 'the enlargement of a snapshot does not simply render more precise what in any case was visible, though unclear: it reveals entirely new structural transformations of the subject' (2007 [1968]: 236). Both Cuizi and Benjamin attach importance to the making of new subjectivities, and hence a new public, through film viewing. If, as Benedict Anderson (1983) suggests, identities and communities are necessarily 'imagined', then a particular type of Chinese gay identity and community has been 'imagined' through watching queer films, through sharing memories and trauma, and through affective communication in the queer public sphere.

Tongzhi Politics and Queer Audibility

Digital video activism as *tongzhi* politics challenges the 'global queering' thesis (Altman 2001) or 'gay internationalism' (Massad 2007), which asserts not only an ahistorical gay identity all over the world but also advocates a universal gay identity politics, irrespective of social and cultural differences. Queer films and queer film festivals in China refuse to be named 'politics' or 'political'. They are often self-labelled as academic and artistic activities. The fact that they are being held in modern art centres and avant-garde cinemas is consistent with these labels. Digital video activism, unlike the Stonewall type of gay liberation movement in the West, does not advocate 'coming out' politics. It avoids public confrontation with the government and the police. In addition, it avoids mentioning politically sensitive topics such as democracy and human rights. However, this does not render digital video activism less political. The screen provides LGBT participants with an opportunity to imagine their identities and communities. The festival venue provides people with a 'heterotopia' (Foucault 1986), a way of constructing a 'queer space' in which LGBT people conduct affective communication. Political activism takes place at the simply equipped screening venue and in the mundane practices of film watching. The impact of such activism is hardly known. Yet, several audience members that I have interviewed expressed their confidence in a better future for LGBT people in China. Many LGBT people have lent their support for Cuizi and other queer film directors on *tongzhi* websites. Increasing numbers of people are experimenting on making films with digital cameras and taking an active part in queer film festivals as filmmakers.

Cuizi illustrates the impact of media on people and society through his 'sound' and 'echo' metaphors:

> This is called 'making sounds' (*fasheng* 发声). Echoes (*huixiang* 回响) always follow sounds. The effects of sounds differ on walls. Walls in China are particularly good at absorbing sounds. However, there are still echoes and there are still people who can hear the echoes. Sounds act like sparks of fire. They make burning flames as they accumulate. Sounds do not disappear completely as if they were in a complete vacuum.

> Sounds always have some effects on the society. [Queer] films and film festivals are channels to transmit sounds. The sounds echo in a society. We may not hear the sounds immediately; they may still be far away from us. However, we can hear the echoes. From the first [queer film festival] to date, we have heard the echoes and these echoes cannot be underestimated. (2009a)

Cuizi's 'making sounds' metaphor reminds of the late Lu Xun's (2009: 19) 'iron house' (*tie wuzi* 铁屋子) metaphor . Lu Xun was one of the most influential writers in 20th-century China. In his 'Preface' to *Outcry* (*Nahan zixu* 呐喊自序) written in 1922, Lu Xun compared the early 20th-century China to an 'iron house' where all the people inside fall asleep and risk being suffocated to death without being aware of their situation. Lu Xun wondered whether he, or enlightenment thinkers like himself, should 'make sounds' and 'wake up' the Chinese people. He seemed to be quite hesitant about making sounds and at times ambivalent about what sounds to make. He finally decided that writing is the best way to 'make sounds' and to 'wake people up'. In a similar vein, Cuizi, adopting the approach of an enlightenment thinker and social activist, considers media an important way of enlightening people. However, Cuizi seems more determined than Lu Xun in his 'sound-making' practice. While Lu Xun hesitates to make sounds and ponders slowly on the effect of the sound-making practice, Cuizi resolutely raises the slogan of digital video activism and engages in making queer films and organizing queer film festivals.

'Making sounds', or 'queer audibility', is an alternative way of thinking about queer politics from the dominant paradigm of 'queer visibility', which often privileges representation and by extension raises questions of who represents whom and whether the representation is sufficient and justified. Digital video activism affects Chinese society by making sounds and producing echoes. Sounds and echoes are not individualistic; they are intersubjective and effectively connect actors, media and the audience without privileging each actor. They recognize the importance of media and the heterogeneity of media effects; they are historically sensitive and context specific and refuse to impose a single criterion; instead of being rigid and top-down 'strategies', they are flexible and bottom-up 'tactics' (de Certeau 2011 [1984]: 34); they are not repetition of the same but repetitions with differences. It is through the metaphor of sounds and echoes that alternative imaginaries of queer politics become possible.

Author's Note

Many people have contributed to the creation of this chapter. They include Professor Catherine Driscoll, Dr Gavin Brown, Professor Stephanie Hemelryk Donald, Dr Elisabeth Engebretsen, Dr Anja Kanngieser, Dr Cecilia Milwertz, Dr Tina Schilbach, Dr William Schroeder and Professor Mayfair Mei-Hui Yang. I thank the two anonymous reviewers and David Stuligross for their insightful comments and suggestions. I also thank Cuizi, Fan Popo and other Chinese queer filmmakers and activists for their kind help during my fieldwork in China, and for their enduring friendship, genuine trust and support.

References

Altman, D. (2001) *Global Sex*. Chicago: University of Chicago Press.

Anderson, B. (1983) *Imagined Communities: reflections on the origin and spread of nationalism*. London: Verso.

Benjamin, W. (2007 [1968]) *Illuminations*. Ed. H. Arendt, trans. H. Zohn. New York: Schocken.

Berry, C. (2004) 'The Sacred, the Profane and the Domestic in Cui Zi'en's Cinema'. *Positions*, vol. 12, no. 1, pp. 195–201.

BGLFF (2009) 'Di'erjie Beijing tongxinglian dianyingjie fangying anpai' [The second Beijing gay and lesbian film festival programme]. http://fanhall. com/group/thread/3056.html, accessed 1 November 2009.

Chou, W. (2000) *Tongzhi: Politics of same-sex eroticism in Chinese societies*. New York: Haworth Press.

Cristini, R. (2003) 'Gay Literature from China: In search of a happy ending'. *International Institute for Asian Studies Newsletter*, vol. 31, no. 27, p.27.

Cui, Z. (2008) 'Yingzhong suiyue: zhici tongxinglian dianying luntan' [Times of light and image: a forum on queer films]. *No. 3 Beijing queer film festival program*, Beijing.

——— (2009a) 'Yong yingxiang xingdong, gaizao shijie' [Acting with digital videos and changing the world]. http://channel.pybk.com/life/rwjl/2009-08-18/19950.html, accessed 1 November 2009

——— (2009b) *Zhi Tongzhi* [Queer China, 'Comrade China']. Beijing: Cuizi DV Studio.

De Certeau, M. (2011 [1988]) *The Practice of Everyday Life*. Trans. Steven Rendall. Oakland, CA: University of California Press.

Deleuze, G., and F. Guattari (1988) *A Thousand Plateaus: Capitalism and schizophrenia*. London: Athlone Press.

Donald, S. (1999) *Public Secrets, Public Spaces: Cinema and Civility in China*. Lanham, MD: Rowman & Littlefield.

Duara, P. (1995) *Rescuing History from the Nation: Questioning narratives of modern China*. Chicago: University of Chicago Press.

Engebretsen, E. (2005) 'Lesbian Identity and Community Projects in Beijing: Notes from the field on studying and theorising same-sex cultures in the age of globalisation'. Paper presented at the Permanent Archive of Sexualities, Genders, and Rights in Asia: 1st International Conference of Asian Queer Studies. http://bangkok2005.anu.edu.au/papers/Engbretsen.pdf, accessed 28 April 2010.

——— (2008) 'Queer Ethnography in Theory and Practice: Reflections on studying sexual globalisation and women's queer activism in Beijing'. *Graduate Journal of Social Science,* vol. 5, no. 2, pp. 88–116.

Evans, H. (1997) *Women and Sexuality in China: Dominant discourses of female sexuality and gender since 1949*. Cambridge: Polity Press.

Fan, P. (2009) 'Zou xiaqu: ji diyijie ku'er duli yingxiang xunhuizhan' [Walk on: The first travelling queer film festival]. *Dian* [Gayspot], vol 9, pp. 24–25.

Fang, G. (1995) *Tongxinglian zai zhongguo* [Homosexuality in China] Changchun: Jilin Renmin Chubanshe.

Farrer, J. (2002) *Opening Up: Youth sex culture and market reform in Shanghai*. Chicago: University of Chicago Press.

——— (2006) 'Sexual Citizenship and the Politics of Sexual Story-telling among Chinese Youth', in E. Jeffreys (ed.), *Sex and Sexuality in China*. New York: Routledge, pp. 102–123.

Foucault, M. (1986) 'Of Other Spaces', *Diacritics,* vol. 16, pp. 22–27.

——— (1988) *Technologies of the Self: a Seminar with Michel Foucault*. Amherst: University of Massachusetts Press.

——— (1990) *The History of Sexuality, Volume I: An Introduction*. London: Penguin.

Guo, X. (2007) *Zhongguo fa shiye xiade tongxinglian* [Homosexuality in the gaze of Chinese law]. Beijing: Zhishi Chanquan Shubanshe.

Halbwachs, M. and L. A. Coser (1992) *On Collective Memory*. Chicago: University of Chicago Press.

He, X. (2002) 'Birthday in Beijing; Women tongzhi organising in the 1990s' China'. *International Institute for Asian Studies Newsletter,* vol. 29, no. 10, p.10.

He, X. (2006) '*I am AIDS': living with the epidemic in China*. Unpublished Unpublished Ph.D. Thesis, University of Westminster.

Hershatter, G. (2002) 'The Gender of Memory: Rural Chinese women and the 1950s'. *Signs: Journal of Women in Culture and Society,* vol. 28, no. 1, pp. 43–70.

Hinsch, B. (1990). *Passions of the Cut Sleeve: The male homosexual tradition in China*. Berkeley: University of California Press.

Ho, L. (2010) *Gay and Lesbian Subculture in Urban China*. London and New York: Routledge.

Jameson, F. (1981) *The Political Unconscious: Narrative as a socially symbolic act*. Ithaca, NY: Cornell University Press.

Jia'ni. (2008) 'Beijing Independent Film Festival Queer Forum'. http://www.cinenotes.org/?cat=4&paged=2, accessed 1 November 2009.

Jones, R. (2007) 'Imagined Comrades and Imaginary Protections: Identity, community and sexual risk among men who have sex with men in China'. *Journal of Homosexuality,* vol. 53, no. 3, pp. 83–115.

Li, D. (2004) *Aizibing zai zhongguo: falv pinggu yu shishi fenxi* [HIV/AIDS in China: legal assessment and factual analysis]. Beijing: Shehui Kexue Wenxian Chubanshe.

Li, Y. and X. Wang (1992) *Tamen de shijie: zhongguo nan tongxinglian qunluo toushi* [Their world: a perspective on China's male homosexual community]. Hong Kong: Cosmos Books Limited.

Lim, S. H. (2006) *Celluloid Comrades: Representations of male homosexuality in contemporary Chinese cinemas*. Honolulu: University of Hawaii Press.

Liu, D., and L. Lu. (2005) *Zhongguo tong xing lian yan* jiu [Studies on Chinese homosexuality]. Beijing: Zhongguo she hui chu ban she.

Lu, X. (2009) *The Real Story of Ah-Q and Other Tales of China: The complete fiction of Lu Xun*. London: Penguin Books.

Martin, F., Berry, C., & Yue, A. (2003) *Mobile Cultures: New media in queer Asia*. Durham ; London: Duke University Press.

Massad, J. A. (2007) *Desiring Arabs*. Chicago, IL and London: The University of Chicago Press.

Nora, P. (1996) *Realms of Memory: Rethinking the French Past.* New York: Columbia University Press.

Robinson, L. (2012) *Independent Chinese Documentary: From the studio to the street.* New York: Palgrave Macmillan.

Rofel, L. (1999a) *Other Modernities: Gendered yearnings in China after socialism.* Berkeley: University of California Press.

———(1999b) 'Qualities of Desire: Imagining gay identities in China'. *GLQ,* vol. 5, no. 4, pp. 451–474.

———(2007) *Desiring China: Experiments in neoliberalism, sexuality, and public culture.* Durham: Duke University Press.

Sang, T.-I. D. (2003) *The Emerging Lesbian: Female same-sex desire in modern China.* Chicago and London: The University of Chicago Press.

Wan, R. (1990) 'Xing'ai zai da bianzou' [Great changes in sexual love], in F. Chen (ed.), *Xingbing zai zhongguo* [Sexual diseases in China], Beijing: Beijing Shijie Wenyi Chubanshe, pp. 101–132.

Wan, Y. (2001) 'Becoming a Gay Activist in Contemporary China', in G. Sullivan and P. Jackson (eds), *Gay and Lesbian Asian: Culture, identity, community,* New York: Harrington Park Press, pp. 47–64.

Warner, M. (2002) *Publics and Counterpublics.* New York and Cambridge, MA: Zone Books.

Wei, W. (2008) 'Resistance in Dreaming: A study of Chinese online boy's love fandom'. Paper presented at the Annual Meeting of the International Communication Association. Montreal, Quebec, Canada, 22 May.

Yang, M. (1999) *Spaces of Their Own: Women's public sphere in transnational China.* Minneapolis: University of Minnesota Press.

Yang, Y. and P. Fan (2009) 'Bejing tongzhi yingzhan shihua' [History of the Beijing queer film festival]. *Dian* [Gay spot] vol. 9, pp. 21–23.

Zhang, B. (1994) *Tongxing'ai* [Same-sex love]. Jinan: Shandong Kexue Jichu Chubanshe.

———(1998) *Pengyou tongxin* [Friend exchange]. Qingdao: Qingdao Daxue Yixueyuan Fushu Yiyuan Xing Jiankang Zhongxin.

Zhang, Y. (1996) *East Palace, West Palace (Donggong xigong)* Amazon Entertainment/Cean Films/Quelqu'un d'Autre Productions.

Zhao, K. (2009) 'Zhuanfang Cui Zi'en: Zhongguo de tongxinglian dianying hai chuyu zifa qi' [Interviews with Cui Zi'en: Chinese queer films are still in their initial stages]. *Dian* [Gay Spot], vol. 9, pp. 18–19.

Zhou, D. (2009) *Aiyue yu guixun: Zhongguo xiandaixing zhong tongxing yuwang de fali xiangxiang* [Love and discipline: juridical imaginations of same-sex desires in Chinese modernity]. Guilin: Guangxi Shifan Daxue Chubanshe. Thittt.

CHAPTER 4

Research, Activism, and Activist Research in Tongzhi China

William F. Schroeder

During a 2012 workshop on queer mobilization, I asked my colleagues from the People's Republic of China (PRC, or China) about their visions of a concept that is revered by Euro-American scholars across many disciplines and especially queer studies: activism.[1] Having known many queer people in the United States and Europe who specifically identify as activists and who have considered making careers out of such work, I have frequently wondered what those who dedicate their lives to the *tongzhi* cause in China might think of the concept, especially because of the political and social obstacles that make activism of the kinds scholars tend to take for granted extremely difficult there. My question, posed in Mandarin, fell rather flat, however, for reasons I did not immediately discern.[2] I have since come to learn that the translation of 'activist' I was using – 积极分子 (*jiji fenzi*), a term I had learned in a university language class many years earlier – does not have entirely positive connotations for mainlanders.[3] Instead, the preferred terms seem usually

---

1. I asked these questions at the 'Europe–China LGBTQ Exchange', which several of the contributors to this volume attended, hosted by the Queer China Working Group in Manchester, UK, 23–25 March 2012.

2. The definition of activism did not at the time seem to me to require much context, especially considering accounts like Wan Yanhai's 'Becoming a gay activist in contemporary China' (2001), which uses the English term in a straightforward way to describe the author's community-organizing and AIDS outreach work.

3. After a 2014 panel in Beijing on which I spoke concerning 行动主义 (*xingdong zhuyi*), or 'activism' in the sense I had originally meant in 2012 of turning cause-oriented activities into a movement or ideology – and after having learned a lot more in the intervening years about the ways 'activists' in China describe their work – I received a specific definition of *jiji fenzi* from a mainland informant. I was told that *jiji fenzi* is a 被动名词 (*beidong mingci*), or 'passive noun'. The Chinese

to be 行动者 (*xingdongzhe*) or 活动家 (*huodongjia*). In addition, not everyone in the room had the same kind of occupation – some were professors, some were filmmakers, some ran community organizations, and some were artists (indeed some were many of these things at the same time). And in any case, many activists would modestly reject the label, wishing instead that the spotlight be placed on the issues with which they are engaged.

Whatever the reason for my colleagues' demurral, the fact remained that no one immediately answered my questions about the definition of activism, so I turned to the people I assumed would be most likely to think of themselves in this way, directing my gaze toward those who had set up their own community centres or who worked with various foundations to fund work that benefitted the *tongzhi* community. Still, almost everyone refused the label, saying they did not think of them-selves as activists and had started doing what they do out of a feeling of necessity or filling a gap: providing information or a space for talk, for example, in a homophobic atmosphere that did not allow for such things.[4] If indeed their reasons for doing what they do were practical,

---

Communist Party (CCP) uses it specifically to refer to recruitees who are at a certain stage on the way to becoming full-fledged members. In particular, the *jiji fenzi* stage is one of focused training before a candidate is given the designation 预备党员 (*yubei dangyuan*), or probationary party member. My informant further added that this word is used as a way of enticing people to enter into the applica-tion registers, as if to be known as a kind of zealot would give people a status they craved, but also as a way of controlling the ranks. At the same time, many people could perceive an emptiness in this so-called zealotry, because of the widely held notion that party membership is simply a means to social and economic advance-ment rather than a commitment to the ideals of socialism. Moreover – and this is perhaps key for the arguments in this chapter – the moniker *jiji fenzi* is not one that these 'activists' or zealots themselves choose, but one that is bestowed on them. Neither is it a stable or long-term designation, but rather a position my informant likened to being a pawn in the CCP's political game. For these reasons, and possibly also for *jiji fenzi*'s connotation of zealotry – near-blind devotion to a cause rather than studied and open-minded participation in a movement – the participants in the 2012 event had trouble interpreting my question.

4. The one person who admitted to thinking of himself as a *jiji fenzi* said he had never considered the work he did in China to be activism until he witnessed violent homophobic reactions to queer organizing in Eastern Europe. This need for countering violence became a clarion call for him, even though homosexuality does not often provoke threats of physical harm in mainland China.

my colleagues are nevertheless extremely brave for drawing attention to themselves at all, because fickle authorities could at any moment deem the work organizers do too sensitive for public consumption or too subversive to be tolerated. This precariousness makes career devotion to the *tongzhi* cause exceedingly rare.

The awkwardness of my questions that day reminded me that, as an American researcher of queer China, I am presented with a host of difficulties – among others, how to recognize activism, and then how to treat it ethnographically. Clifford and Marcus (1986), whose volume helped us think about the question of 'ethnographic authority', have of course inspired my attention to such a dilemma. As a result of that volume and work that stems from it, most anthropologists now consciously consider not only how they convey information in their ethnographies, but also what the particular choices made in writing suggest about the relationship between ethnographer and subject. Euro-American queer theory, which has recently taken up interest in non-western points of view, puts it this way: 'An ethical attachment to others insists that we cannot be the center of the world or act unilaterally on its behalf. It demands a world in which we must sometimes relinquish not only our epistemological but also our political certitude' (Eng with Halberstam and Muñoz 2005: 15). Much contemporary scholarship that deals with the relationship between researcher and research subject echoes this sensibility. And yet, most of the literature that has emerged about 'engaged', 'public' or 'activist' anthropology seems to assume that the meaning of 'activism' as a category of social action is both obvious and transparent.[5]

---

5. Hale (2006), a widely cited proponent of activist anthropology, indeed probes the definition of activism by criticising Marcus's (1998) discussions about how ethnography itself could be a form of activism. However, Hale's concern lies more in determining whether the anthropologist qualifies as an activist, not in assessing what qualifies as activism in the field site. His definition of activism for the researcher seems straightforward, if lacking in nuance: 'alignment with an organized group in struggle' (103). This question of alignment and how one comes to it is central to the arguments in the section 'Militant versus Objective Anthropology' in this chapter. It is also central to the understanding of activism and engagement in the collection titled *Engaged Observer: Anthropology, Advocacy, and Activism* (2006). Most of the pieces in that volume take activism to be narrowly political, however, in the sense of engaging the government or power via direct resistance, falling well on the side of the militant in the polarized debate. Warren's piece in that volume, 'Perils and Promises of Engaged Anthropology:

The story I relate here becomes additionally difficult to assess, of course, because of the complex way a non-Chinese queer ethnographer and his or her comrades from the PRC feel simultaneously connected to and dissimilar from one another. Most people involved in fieldwork with Chinese queer populations have been asked whether we are *tongzhi* upon our first visits to a community; an affirmative response allows certain doors to be opened. Despite this, sometimes non-Chinese queer researchers are seen as very different, for reasons that vary from interlocutors' presumptions that especially Euro-American researchers come from comparatively liberal queer paradises, to the idea that westerners' pronounced individualism leads us more easily to make choices favouring queer lifestyles, to the simple reality that non-native speakers could not possibly understand all the subtleties conveyed to us in Chinese. (I easily concede the last of these.) In navigating the dilemmas of similitude and difference, however, it is not only the relationship between ethnographer and subject that complicates this question of activism. We must also consider that the

---

Historical Transitions and Ethnographic Dilemmas' (2006), is one of the few that resists taking activism for granted, saying, 'We have much to learn from refusing to idealize twenty-first-century engaged anthropology even as we celebrate its rich possibilities' (214). Low and Merry (2010) present an excellent overview of the history of 'engaged anthropology' and discuss activist approaches among many others, describing the benefits and challenges of taking the many stances toward fieldwork they recount. Yet at no point is the definition of 'activism' itself explored. In the article 'Activism and Anthropology', Merry suggests, 'Academics can contribute to activism by working to refine fundamental analytical categories such as culture, tradition, gender, and rights' (2005: 255), but nowhere is 'activism' interrogated, even when referring to China – instead, one must infer from context that activism means working in an NGO. The only work I have come across that questions common premises behind scholars' approaches to activism itself is Osterweil's (2013), although his refinement of the commonplace understanding of activism is not entirely explicit. The article is concerned more with expanding our ideas of the political and of what constitutes 'movements', but it points toward a re-evaluation of the concept of activism as well. The question remains whether scholars will be willing to accept that playful enterprises like the ones I mention in this chapter can be counted as 'efficacious political action' (Osterweil 2013: 600), although they easily 'offer alternatives to what people consider reality and possibility to be' (606). Certainly, Osterweil echoes the points I make here when he says that 'there are times when anthropological knowledge cannot simply be at the service of, or determined by, the desires of activists' (615), referring to the kinds of organizers many of us easily take for granted as being the primary agents of social change.

relationship between activists (or those we might call 'activists') and their constituencies could hold its own tensions – the goals of activism may not always be the goals of the wider group.[6] For all these reasons, we must be careful about what we suppose about the epistemology of activism, and we must also have an eye for the politics of writing, which may require us to make a choice between developing ethnographies about activism and promoting activist ethnographies that, explicitly or not, advocate a narrow understanding of politics and social change.

Militant versus Objective Anthropology

Anthropologists have always debated how to do what we do, but the competing motivations that emerged from polarized debates in the 1990s concerning moral-militant versus objective-scientific approaches to research continue to influence a discourse of academic worth in anthropology (see D'Andrade 1995 and Scheper-Hughes 1995). These oppositional approaches valorize very different things. The moral approach argues that ethnography must be concerned with bringing to light and solving the problems of disadvantaged people wherever research is carried out. The objective approach encourages a more de-scriptive, holistic and relativistic tack that seeks to contribute to the science of cultural interpretation. Both approaches make excellent points. Moralists tell us that our pretensions to objectivity and our refusal to engage in the politics of the field site lead to a mystification of culture, and that this mystification can implicitly promote the toleration of some forms of evil under the guise of a dispassionate relativism. Objectivists tell us that in imagining we could make a transparent moral-ethical judgment about a field site, we actually impose an ethnocentric value system on our research subjects and cast ourselves as hero figures. Most of the commentators on the debate in which these positions were so clearly articulated point out that the opposition between the moral-militant and the objective-scientific approaches are not as dichotomous as their associated polemics suggest. For example, Marvin Harris points out to the objectivists that '[what] we choose to study or not study in the name of anthropology is a politico-moral decision' (1995: 423). And Laura

---

6.   See Engebretsen (2008) for a very good contextualization of this perspective in the queer Chinese case, where she focuses on *lala* resistance to 'activism'.

Nader suggests to the militants that even moral anthropology prizes 'integrative thinking' and 'empiricism' (1995: 427).

It is this last point about empiricism that I wish to emphasize. I take to heart the warning that 'activism *before* research is a chancy business' (Kuper 1995: 425) and consider that the benefit of not deciding in advance what is ethical and moral is a 'protection against demagogy' (O'Meara 1995: 428). Indeed Scheper-Hughes, proponent of the militant approach, asks anthropologists to 'do the best we can with the limited resources we have at hand: our ability to listen and to observe carefully and with empathy and compassion' (1995: 418). Listening continues to be emphasized as one of the key features of ethical engagement in cross-cultural 'activist' scenarios (see Boellstorff 2012).[7] Behind more militant calls, and behind the objectivist ones, an ethic of empiricism seems to drive most studies of cultural variation.

The question remains for researchers to decide when they are introducing a militancy that is not there. More specifically, in the case of queer China, researchers must decide how to characterize the relatively small but growing presence of dedicated *tongzhi* organizers and how to imagine their apparent but hesitant affinity with the kinds of activism Euro-Americans might recognize as familiar. This problem is a subtle but important one in light of critiques not only of militant or activist anthropology, but also of the general scholarly preoccupation with questions of resistance and power. Michael Brown warns that 'the indiscriminate use of resistance and related concepts undermines their analytical utility, at the same time strongly skewing the project of cultural anthropology in the direction inspired by the work of Foucault: culture as prison, culture as insane asylum, culture as 'hegemonic domination of the [insert Other of choice]'' (1996: 730).

Whether this reading of Foucault is accurate or not (and I feel that it is exaggerated), the admonition has relevance for my own work with queer groups in China that were organized and community-based but that saw their activities as having only secondarily to do with the *tongzhi*

---

7. Although Boellstorff (2012) suggests that activism is not the only path toward productive ethnography, he does not address the definition of activism itself. One of the goals of this essay is to ask readers to reconsider what counts as activism and to reflect on why researchers might choose one form of organizing over another in designing a research project, or indeed, as I will be asking myself in future research, why we might be trying to follow 'organized' groups at all.

'cause'. Therefore, to read too much into the relevance of 'hegemonic domination' to the possibly resistant but also fun activities of queer recreational groups could have the outcome of dismantling the primary logic of the ludic that I believe is so important in the creation of *tongzhi* community.[8] In addition, in the major vignette presented in this essay, resistance itself is diffuse and includes community-internal resistance to activism, too.

Sherry Ortner, who has considered the complexity of resistance and domination, addresses ethnographers who would write about this concept, asserting:

> If we are to recognize that resistors are doing more than simply opposing domination, more than simply producing a virtually mechanical *re*-action, then we must go the whole way. They have their *own* politics – not just between chiefs and commoners or landlords and peasants but within all the local categories of friction and tension: men and women, parents and children, seniors and juniors; inheritance conflicts among brothers; struggles of succession and wars of conquest between chiefs; struggles for primacy between religious sects; and on and on. (1995: 176–177, emphasis in the original)[9]

Ortner decries the ethnographer's sometimes 'bizarre refusal to know and speak and write of the lived worlds inhabited by those who resist (or do not, as the case may be)' (187–188) and seeks to re-establish the fraught paradigm of 'authenticity', recognizing that ethnographic objectivity will forever elude us – indeed is impossible – but that our writing practice should seek to collect 'the pieces of reality' that have been 'woven together through the logic of a group's own locally and historically evolved bricolage' (176).[10] Ortner and others point out that resistance studies perhaps too easily lead to ethnographic thinness because they do not allow for nuanced stories of internal micropolitics,

---

8. I build here on similar insights about play that were touched on in Engebretsen (2008).

9. Here, Ortner is referencing a host of polarizing social issues related to hierarchy and power that have long interested anthropologists who work in a variety of cultures.

10. Clifford refers to a similar type of ethnographic attention as 'textured, realistic (which is not to say objective or uncontested) understandings of contemporary cultural processes' (2000: 102).

of the ways various social stratifications are traversed in everyday life, and of the exigencies of individual preoccupations and intentions. I find that insisting on resistance as the motivation for research, as activist approaches to anthropology easily could, in fact downplays the role of 同情 (*tongqing*) – that feeling of empathy with the frustrated, sometimes defeatist, sometimes apathetic, but other times hopeful, attitudes of our interlocutors. Therefore, although I would not identify as an objectivist, I am partial to a statement made on their platform: 'It comes down to a choice: whatever one wants in the way of political change, will the first priority be to understand how things work?' (D'Andrade 1995: 408).

Ethnographic Research in *Tongzhi* Beijing

In trying to determine how things work, I have long thought that the category of 'activism' itself needs to be expanded to give us a fuller picture of the political in queer China. Thus I admit here that the question I floated in that 2012 workshop was loaded. Most of my concerted fieldwork as a sociocultural anthropologist has involved participant observation of organized queer recreational groups in Beijing, none of which was particularly political in the traditional sense but all of which were highly organized and future-oriented in a way that seemed to me to express a certain 'activism', broadly defined.[11] These groups had a large following and, from what I observed, constituted some of the major opportunities for public queer socializing in urban China. I have participated in a variety of these organizations' activities – attending meetings, doing yoga, going roller skating, simply chatting – and have come to realize the great devotion to their clubs and organizations, made by and for *tongzhi*, that my informants had. Members of these groups usually spent much of their weekends with comrades doing the things that the groups were organized to do. Their leaders worked very hard to put activities

---

11. I conducted the bulk of this fieldwork from 2005 to 2006 and did a follow-up project in 2010. From my current perspective, having returned to China most years since, although I recognize a very slow proliferation of organized community work with *tongzhi* liberation as a specific goal, I think the insights I describe here about the hesitations of many *tongzhi* to agitate for social change continue to be relevant. To be sure, the police have been cracking down lately especially hard on community organizers, hauling them in for questioning with some frequency.

together, rent venues, and keep members informed of upcoming and ongoing activities.[12]

Therefore, I imagined at first in a fairly straightforward way – the way that a naïve researcher might imagine – that my informants from these organizations would have a well-formed sense of the contribution they were making to the *tongzhi* cause. But when I asked organizers and members alike, most of the time they admitted only reluctantly that organizing for 'the movement' was a reason for keeping the clubs and groups going. That is, if I pressed them and pointed out that, in my estimation and possibly that of onlookers, what they were doing could seem like a concerted effort to benefit the wider *tongzhi* community – that their activities could be an example to be followed and could then lead to social change – they might agree that I made a good point. But really, they said, it was just about creating good feelings, making friends. Indeed, the most common response I received when I asked why participants did the things they did was that they joined these groups 'to have fun'.[13] I do realize that their reluctance on this account of activism, a feeling they possibly shared with the participants in the workshop I discussed at the beginning of this essay, could have to do with the general

---

12. As I have noted in other work, it is difficult to categorize a typical participant in these groups. Each organization had its own atmosphere, which attracted people for a variety of reasons. For example, the roller-skating group I participated in attracted for the most part 18–25 year-old men, because of the activity's reputation as something silly but also possibly injurious that younger people were better suited to doing. The yoga club events I attended attracted men from 18–50 because of the popular understanding of yoga as an all-ages self-improvement activity. The *lala* discussion salon I sometimes went to hosted a wide range of ages because it emphasized sharing between age cohorts. Most of these groups' activities required participants to pay a nominal charge to go towards renting the space in which events were held, and these charges were usually less than 20 *yuan* (about $3) and often between 5 and 10 *yuan* (about $0.75 – $1.50). Most organizers kept an eye on charges so that more people could participate. The fees were usually accessible enough to allow participants from a range of employment situations to attend, and even unemployed young people living at home were usually able to ask their families for the fees, which they would say were going towards the recreational event, not mentioning any *tongzhi* affiliation. However, workers in precarious situations, such as migrants, people with disabilities, and others, would not have had access to the groups for reasons of ability, funding, and access to the internet, on which activities were most often advertised.

13. 为了开心 *weile kaixin.*

hesitation among *tongzhi* to admit to seeking immediate social change; doing so puts people at risk of being targeted by authorities in the PRC as disruptors of stability. But separate from the political dangers generally associated with focused and organized activism, I perceived a real sense of annoyance with my attempt to introduce the seriousness of politics or the drudgery of social change campaigns into what my informants understood as an escape from the mundane. Indeed, it seems instructive here that the organizer of one of these groups once said that he hoped a member would participate 'actively' not in community-organizing but in yoga, using the very word for 'active' (积极) that the organizers I mention at the beginning of the essay refused.[14] I must admit that sometimes I felt disappointed to know that subversion was not their purpose, even if their activities could be labelled as subversive by those who might disapprove. What I finally understood, however – after much critical reflection on my own reasons for doing this research and on my prejudices about what constitutes a righteous queer political sensibility – was that I first had to address the general question of purpose, mine and my informants', and reconsider the meaning of my own research in the context of a very different set of outlooks and practices than I was used to.

The *tongzhi* recreational activities I touch on here but describe more fully in other work (Schroeder 2012a) were productive of a future and oriented towards a time to come, but without five-year plans as such or activist goals in the form of platforms and political agendas; thus, they encourage us to think about the fuzziness of the boundary between motive and purpose, two concepts that are central to the study of activism. I have found that many people may be motivated by an abstract goal but not see that goal as their purpose, even if the activities that help them achieve such a goal could in retrospect make what they did look rather purposive. In his discussion of games and play, Pierre Bourdieu (1998) also ponders this dilemma in a critique of scholarly tendencies to over-rationalize human action: '[Agents] may conduct themselves in such a way that, starting with a rational evaluation of their chances for success, it seems that they were right in doing what they did, without one being justified in saying that a rational calculation of chances was at the origin of the choices they made' (1998: 76). So it is often only

---

14. '希望你积极参加瑜伽活动!' (*xiwang ni jiji canjia yujia huodong!*)

in retrospect that researchers evaluate an activity as geared toward a particular end – that is, the sequence of events leading up to it could be identified as a causal chain. Similarly, at the time of the activity in question, the people we observe may have had stakes in it but may not have engaged in the obsessive calculation of pay-off outside of that situation that strategizing or tactical action as we usually understand these concepts require.[15] Thus one could assume the *tongzhi* play described here had broader social effects only if those could be measured at some point in the future. At that future moment, observers might indeed conclude that early 21st-century organizing had something to do with convincing hearts and minds, or creating a critical mass, or getting the *tongzhi* plight noticed. But because that calculation was not part of the planning as I witnessed it – and most especially because definitive social change benefitting *tongzhi* in China has at the time of this writing not occurred – I cannot claim that social change from community organizing was my informants' goal or that their activities were examples of purposive action meant to lead toward such things.

Yet this is the reason, I believe, that play itself is so attractive for *tongzhi*: it provides a time and place where one does not constantly have to think about the consequences of what one is doing; one can focus simply on having fun.[16] Spontaneous play especially proceeds without or despite planning as such, but it contains an element of illusion or fantasy that all play partakes of because it seems not to function by the rules of everyday life – players are momentarily detached from the banality of everything and everybody else. Bourdieu adds, speaking in particular of competitive games (which heighten the intensity of the play scenario),

15. The distinction that I will elaborate between having a purpose and being purposive might at first resemble the distinction de Certeau (1984) famously makes between 'tactic' and 'strategy'. Yet de Certeau describes even a tactic as 'a calculated action' and a 'guileful ruse' (37–38), expressing a certain explicit awareness among tacticians of overall goals, which does not seem to form the core part of *tongzhi* organizing as described in this chapter. Thus, whereas de Certeau wishes to recuperate a sense of subversion with his analyses, I would like to focus on the affective experience of doing what it is one is doing, decentering subversion, as my informants' comments suggested I do.

16. Theorists identify escapism as a primary element in play, but they also insist that play occurs under its own set of rules (for the classic account, see Huizinga 1971). Nevertheless, it is the feeling players have that play is free and removed that makes it what it is.

that such a detachment indeed involves a specific kind of removal, a fantastical rather than an indifferent one:

> *Illusio* [the quality of fantasy in play] is ... the opposite of ataraxia [serene detachment]; it is the fact of being interested, of investing in the stakes existing in a certain game, through the effect of competition, and which only exist for people who, being caught up in that game and possessing the dispositions to recognize the stakes at play, are ready to die for the stakes which, conversely, are devoid of interest for those who are not tied to that game and which leave them indifferent' (1998: 77–78).

Whereas the life-and-death stakes Bourdieu mentions here may seem exaggerated in the discussion of *tongzhi* roller-skating clubs, for example, this model of ludic commitment helps us understand what is going on in queer play and what may be motivating many other kinds of *tongzhi* activity as well.

My informants certainly were not indifferent to their recreation – and it is not as if they did not care about *tongzhi* community – but they did not usually identify broader social change as their primary goal. They recognized, however, that if their recreational activities were somehow forbidden or were to be taken as illicit by authorities, they would lose perhaps their most important link to *tongzhi* life and be that much further from being able to imagine what a future of happiness might feel like. *Tongzhi* informants' families and employers could have no idea of the social and affective importance of these recreational clubs, because the queer aspects of these activities were kept secret from them. Families and employers were therefore unaware of and, in Bourdieu's words, indifferent to, *tongzhi* recreation. This unawareness helped to preserve the escapist ethos that was so important in recreational clubs. At the same time, as we know, families and employers are not indifferent at all about the time they require of *tongzhi* family members or employees during the week, and this too explains why weekend leisure activity itself became such an important part of *tongzhi* community – its limited timeframe made it all the more precious. Though *tongzhi* leisure may not seem so precious as to warrant describing it in life-and-death terms, we might still imagine that by continuing to participate in recreational clubs, *tongzhi* avert a kind of social death.[17] Outlets of *tongzhi* recreation at least provide the psychological comfort that participants are not alone and have some prospect of a satisfying existence.[18]

Thus, even if *tongzhi* involved in recreational activities had motives that seemed frivolous from the perspective of political organizing, and even if their playful organizing did not have concrete goals other than to engage in the activity at hand, we cannot deny that their activities had purpose, although we could de-emphasize the purposiveness, as participants did, of those very same acts. Indeed, in the actual practice of recreation – going roller skating, for example – participants expressed a distinctive 'whateverness' about *tongzhi* community, that quality that Giorgio Agamben (1993) finds so remarkable in contemporary organizing practice because of its inclusivity. 'Whateverness' here describes a kind of relaxed attitude toward the attainment of *tongzhi* goals, without the obsessive quality of agitation in activism, that allows for the inclusion

17. Allen Sack (1977) reminds us that games and play can be quite different, in that games often exhibit much more of a professional character than play, which means that audiences and non-participants may also perceive a stake in the outcome (especially if they have paid to see it). This perhaps influences the perception that games are staked on life-and-death grounds because of the pressure for winning and the loss of face on losing. But this life-and-death metaphor for understanding playful activities is not unfamiliar to the members of *tongzhi* groups I studied. In other work, I have related some of the very moving reasons given by *tongzhi* participants for being active in their groups. While reflecting on the social and psycho-emotional importance of participation, a member of a *tongzhi* yoga club said: 'Some people push their cart ahead; some people are pulled by it. Those who push are alive; those who are pulled are dead'. (有些人推着车走，有些人被车拉着走。推着车走的是活人，被车拉着走的是死人。 *youxie ren tuizhe che zou, youxie ren bei che lazhe zou. tuizhe che zou de shi huoren, bei che lazhe zou de shi siren.*) In other words, being active in *tongzhi* recreational organizations means choosing to create a life for oneself. See Schroeder 2012a for a more in-depth discussion.

18. In some important contexts, the point about death actually takes on a literal tone. Having spoken with other researchers of queer China, I now realize that I should be less circumspect about the relationship between playful escape and death. Engebretsen (personal communication), recalls the vivid scars from self-harm that some of her *lala* informants showed her, the frequent discussion of suicide attempts before discovering recreational social outlets that *tongzhi* informants have recounted, and the violent pressure of hetero-marriage that causes some *lalas* to describe their engagements as the point when they died (我死了 *wosile*). These connections deserve more attention in future research.

of players who maintain a greater variety of orientations toward *tongzhi* political goals than otherwise would be possible. *Tongzhi* play does not require the exclusion of those who refuse to toe or even acknowledge a particular political or strategic line.[19] Indeed, this inclusiveness was something that the 2012 workshop participants mentioned as important to them as well.[20] Whateverness for my informants from Beijing indicates a focus on recreational activities instead of on strategizing. They thought that if their playing could be said to have led to greater social acceptance, recognition of rights, and wider tolerance at some point in the far-off future, then so be it, but in the meantime, the feeling of belonging created in community, the joy of practising and mastering a particular sport, or the perseverance required to see activities into the next weekend satisfied their desires for self-determination. These activities could be described as multipurpose, then, rather than purposive in the narrow sense that activist paradigms are normally understood.

Being Political

Most *tongzhi* are anyway extremely wary of making political agitation or activist strategizing their purpose. The *tongzhi* recreational groups I worked with functioned largely outside the purview of the government, neither seeking official sanction nor hiding their presence altogether, but remaining comfortably non-political should anyone of authority ever investigate – in other words, they were just having fun.[21] Groups were fairly content to orient themselves socially among each other rather than become overtly political (in the sense of directly confronting the domination of those who silenced and oppressed them) and instead developed an extensive network with other queer recreational groups

---

19. This inclusiveness is not limitless, however, as those who displayed a distinct politicism were unwelcome in the recreational clubs because of a fear that these people would attract too much attention and cause the clubs to be shut down.

20. Recent controversies in the *tongzhi* community involving politicized attempts to define same-sex desire in a particular way are just one example of how even those apparent 'activists' I was turning to reject the kind of activism we associate with political platforming.

21. These groups were not secretive but aimed not to be controversial. For example, most groups had public websites that openly discussed their activities in a specifically non-political fashion.

in Beijing and around China. Neither did these groups usually encourage members to involve themselves in any expressly political form or to understand being *tongzhi* in any particular way. In fact, most groups did not much talk about being *tongzhi* as such. Nevertheless, this kind of very popular *tongzhi* organizing harboured an energy that I would identify as political. This energy derives from the ability of people in community to take advantage of current opportunities (gathering for recreation, for example) and to use them to pursue short-term goals, with the idea that pursuing longer-term ones, such as general *tongzhi* liberation, should be but secondary. In many ways, the refusal of direct political action and planning in the service of attaining long-term goals was practical. As I have suggested, few Chinese people are willing to risk the kind of retribution that could result from making clear political and social demands that challenge authority or even appear to be doing so.[22]

This scepticism most *tongzhi* harbour toward organized political and social strategizing emerged starkly when a health-awareness organization in Beijing hosted an all-day meeting one Sunday during my first stint of fieldwork. The organization invited about twenty gay men, several of them culled from recreational organizations' rosters, to attend a day's seminar on *tongzhi* rights, providing lunch and offering each participant a stipend of twenty *yuan* for taking part. This may not seem like much, but it makes clear that the organization was aware that convincing comrades of the importance of rights-based activism was going to take a special effort. Most of the presentations during the morning concerned legal questions that might arise in the men's lives, such as what to do in cases of blackmail surrounding the threat of outing, or whether divorce on grounds of a husband's being gay debars him from rights to the couple's common property.[23] But the afternoon portion

---

22. People perceived to be activists are frequently detained by police or other authorities without charge or due legal process, harassed by uniformed and plainclothes officials, have their bank accounts frozen and private lives meddled with, and suffer the psychological burdens of the daily surveillance of their communications. Witness the recent detentions of feminist activists, several of whom also were tongzhi organizers, or the harassment in recent years of pride-parade organizers and other workers in any number of NGOs.

23. Although these kinds of problems have occurred, some *tongzhi* intimate that they proliferate more in people's paranoia than in reality. One participant that day criticized *tongzhi*, saying, 'Chinese people drive themselves to exhaustion' ('中国人活得很累'

of the seminar introduced a decidedly political strategy for furthering the *tongzhi* cause. The presenter, a native mainland lawyer and expert in Chinese governance and law, provided his brand of political advice for the future, propelled by the generally accepted assumption that even in the absence of concerted political action, because of China's rapid economic and social development, Chinese society would gradually support *tongzhi* rights and lifestyles. His intention, then, was to speed up the progression. However, the presenter's strategy went further than the participants were ready to accept.

He suggested placing *tongzhi* or supportive allies in positions of power through local elections, beginning at the district level, to 'represent our interests/rights'.[24] To allay participants' fears that even voting for a queer candidate or a pro-*tongzhi*-rights representative would out them, the presenter spent a great deal of time trying to convince the audience that they would not be watched while casting ballots (as might once have been the case), that their identities could not possibly be traced through ballots (ballots do not require one to provide one's name or any other identifying information – one registers, votes anonymously, and then puts one's vote with all the others into a box), and that polling-station design also would prevent the tracking of identity and voting record (the ballot box stands away from other voters and monitors). One continually sceptical participant from another province reminded everyone that this might be the case only in Beijing. But almost unanimously, participants doubted that this strategy of getting allies elected to minor posts was even worthwhile, 'considering China's past record.'

Thus, beyond scepticism about the value of getting someone elected, people doubted the process itself. Few believed that direct votes and elections were even taken seriously by the authorities and expressed their suspicions about whether, if indeed a candidate fairly won and were elected to a post, the government would duly consider his or her position on issues or even allow the person to take office if he or she

---

zhongguo ren huode hen lei), by which he meant, *tongzhi* tire themselves needlessly worrying about all the subtleties of legal protection when, if they would just come out of the closet, these kinds of problems would no longer threaten them. This participant was by far the voice of the minority at the meeting, but his attitude may ironically represent the ethos of those *tongzhi* who refuse political action in favour of recreation. Political action is also likely to tire one out.

24. 代表我们的权利 *daibiao women de quanli*

were deemed undesirable. Some participants favoured alternative strategies, which they viewed as more approachable, such as getting *tongzhi* voices heard through the media.[25] Some said the media also offered the possibility of disseminating a common voice and presenting the *tongzhi* cause as unified,[26] a quality they saw here as a benefit.[27] One wise member of the crowd, however, after a good deal of audible grumbling from the audience, pointed out that the presenter was talking about ideal strategies for the future, whereas the dissenters were pointing out practical hindrances belonging to the moment. But it seems to me that this overwhelming practicality drives most *tongzhi* approaches to social action and community-building. Indeed many of the more practical oppositions were guided by the general idea that it was too early in China for direct political strategies, with some people noting that mainland *tongzhi* would just have to wait until the PRC became a democracy like the United States or Taiwan.[28]

Despite their inability to rectify the idealism of political activism with the practicality of belonging in play, participants seemed to have a very solid concept of themselves as a group that, in the abstract, deserved particular rights and protections. They consistently referred to those in 'the circle',[29] a common way of designating people who participate in *tongzhi* life, implying the existence of a distinguishable community. Although people debated how this community should be characterized, and specifically wondered whether the often applied label 'disadvantaged

---

25. This is one strategy used by the producers of the long-running web documentary and news outlet queercomrades.com, also known as 同志亦凡人 (*tongzhi yi fanren*, 'tongzhi are like everyone else', alluding to the famous British and American TV series *Queer as Folk*). They expound on their activities in chapter 2 of this volume.

26. as a 整体 *zhengti*.

27. This may seem to work against the ethos of the *tongzhi* recreational groups I have mentioned previously, but the kind of unity discussed here is less a dogmatic than an affective one. See note 34.

28. I cannot delve into the rationale behind this form of apparently neoliberal progressivism here, but I can say that it holds sway in many Chinese people's attitudes toward the future. See Rofel (2007) for a discussion of neoliberalism in China.

29. 圈儿里 *quanr li*.

group',[30] used by well-meaning scholars and activists to categorize them, was appropriate, they nevertheless perceived that they shared something in common. Most in attendance specifically took offense to the first character in the term 'disadvantaged group', which they said implied they were 'weak'. Moreover, they felt the term was imprecise, because it makes no distinction about the kind of weakness involved – mental, physical, moral, economic – and seems to allow those outside the circle to decide who belongs to such a category.[31] I would contend that one of the reasons the participants that day bristled as they did was that they disagreed that a practical stance in the face of authority – this refusal to engage in politics – represented a weak position, especially considering the efforts they put into creating a strong sense of togetherness through such organizations as the recreational clubs to which several of them belonged.

Participants spoke instead of the importance of developing a systematized 'network of connections'[32] to gain a foothold in society. They also debated how best to create a 'chain reaction'[33] in developing the acceptance of *tongzhi* across the country, which they said first would require

---

30. 弱势群体 *ruoshi qunti*. Other groups who are sometimes also considered disadvantaged include children, the disabled and ethnic minorities. For example, in Li Yinhe's proposal to the National People's Congress to legalize same-sex marriage, she states: '我国有保护少数族群和弱势群体利益方面的成功经验，如在保护少数民族利益、保护妇女儿童利益方面都属于世界领先地位。' *woguo you baohu shaoshu qunti he ruoshi qunti liyi fangmian de chenggong jingyan, ru zai baohu shaoshu minzu liyi, baohu funü ertong liyi fangmian dou shuyu shijie lingxian diwei.* 'China has had success protecting the welfare of minority ethnic and disadvantaged groups. For example, in the area of protecting the welfare of minority nationalities and women and children, China occupies a leading position in the world'. She goes on to say that according gays and lesbians protection under the law by allowing them to marry would benefit China's standing in the world and prevent gays and lesbians from becoming a threat to stability if they engage in protests and direct political opposition, as occurs in the west.

31. Perhaps 'disadvantaged group' is another example of a 'passive noun' (see note 3) – a label bestowed rather than a category claimed. I would argue that self-determinative action of the kind expressed in organizing yoga groups, gathering for skating, and convening meetings, among many other activities, is a key to understanding what might count as activism.

32. 联络系统 *lianluo xitong*.

33. 连锁反映 *liansuo fanying*.

creating a 'progressive culture'.[34] Yet participants frequently prefaced their questions and statements with the phrase 'as an individual citizen',[35] suggesting that they saw themselves ideally as rights-holding beings regardless of their connection to any particular group or community. Similarly, an individualized sense that each person in the room had the right to 'maintain a personal opinion'[36] and not be swayed by communal rhetoric, or the rhetoric of any one leader, reigned. The tension between maintaining comfort in an autonomous individuality and the sacrificing of one's own will in order to achieve collective goals made it difficult for those present to envision coming together under any specific political platform or based on any set of clear rules for engagement, even if they shared some essential designation as *tongzhi*.

Thus, direct political action to influence the current regime remained an idealistic dream, one that no one besides the speaker on that subject found practicable. The audience was largely dismissive, and the speaker had difficulty maintaining order at times, seeming tentative about even his own views. Organizing the direct manipulation of political outcomes through a concerted campaign seemed like a radical alternative to the rather more practical advancement of *tongzhi* livelihood in the present, and this attitude may hold the key for understanding *tongzhi* activism in contemporary China.

The Politics of Having Fun

This focus on the relative short-term that many *tongzhi* shared and through which many of them created their vibrant recreational networks led me to reconsider the assumptions I had long been conditioned to make about the effectiveness of political organizing. Whereas the general avoidance of strategic and agitative resistance efforts might lead outsiders to assume *tongzhi* proceed in apathy, I think it would be more productive for researchers to recalibrate the tools with which we measure 'activism' and 'the political' so that we can better describe what is going on. Members of *tongzhi* groups continued meeting on Saturdays during my fieldwork and planned to continue to meet on

---

34. 先进文化 *xianjin wenhua*.

35. 作为一个公民的个体 *zuowei yige gongmin de geti*.

36. 保留个人意见 *baoliu geren yijian*.

Saturdays as long as they could to do their activities, socialize together, or simply chat about life. This was no dispassionate enterprise. It was a productive yet indirect approach to securing a *tongzhi* future – both the future in the great distance of generations and the future in the plans one makes for next Saturday. For *tongzhi*, whereas the grander kind of future often seems uncertain and out of reach in the context of a present in which rights and opportunities are denied and in which their voices are frequently silenced, weekends nevertheless remained accessible and liveable. My informants spoke of the relevance of their planning to the *tongzhi* community's shared long-term future only in terms of its being a by-product of their gatherings and only when pressed on the matter. Similarly, those *tongzhi* who do make it their work explicitly to provide information to or create community for *tongzhi* all over China, who do stage public awareness events, and who do run NGOs and other such organizations that could more easily be labelled 'activist', themselves by and large reject such a designation in favour of a simple description of their endeavours: providing a space for discussion, making the everyday more passable, disseminating information, and the like.

In this context, I would like to encourage a discussion of contemporary *tongzhi* politics that not only questions the staid notion that queer resistance anywhere must be overt, antagonistic and purposive, but also challenges perspectives that view resistance as the only effort worthy of documentation.[37] Regarding the political, I would argue that the planning of a Saturday skate outing with a group of one's peers constitutes a political act: in the very forecasting of oneself and those like oneself into a time to come, one implicitly engages with powers that would otherwise obstruct such an outcome. In *tongzhi* China, this politics of the everyday is frequently characterized by an emphasis on fun and does not seek to effect immediate structural change. Rather, it opens up an affective space in which change is potentiated or felt.[38] In light of this, the groups I discuss here must be regarded as political in their assumption

---

37. One might think of Scott's (1990) 'infrapolitics' here (resistance that continues on without being detected, as infrared light to the human eye), but even in the cases elaborated in Scott's volume, which has so inspired my thinking, purposiveness still underpins much infrapolitical action.

38. Space limitations prevent me from going into detail about how affect 'effects' social change, but see Schroeder 2012b for an expanded discussion.

that it is beneficial to plan a future, if only into the coming days, and in their hope that such planning coincidentally might lay the foundation for a farther-off recognition and legitimization of their desires.

Ethnography must be prepared to engage with and present this subtly political – by some definitions apolitical – attitude in order to be 'authentic' in the sense put forth by Ortner. Concerning *tongzhi* activism, the choice between activist ethnography and the ethnography of activism may not be as stark as we imagine, as long as we provide the appropriate contextualization derived from empiricism, which would allow us to see that activism is itself deeply nuanced in the PRC and that there are multiple approaches to the issue of how best to realize social change. Zhang Zhen (张真), a scholar of Chinese independent film, explains very well how we ought to view activism and the people involved in it: '[The] meaning of "activist" is not at all equivalent to someone who defends legal rights and has a meticulously planned program for social action or behaves in an organized way. Rather, it refers much more to someone who acts from a self-motivated position – interactively, with a spirit of empathy, and from an understanding of the facts – to mobilize the power of affect in order to trigger desires for social change' (2011).[39] This definition covers a range of activities that do not necessarily call for concerted resistance and allows for a more subtle and ultimately empirical ethnographic work. This empiricism prevents us from propagating an 'indifference to the question of methodology' (Harris 1995: 424) that I think is at the heart of the dilemma, and it opens up the possibility of recognizing that activism as we know it may not be the only locus of *tongzhi* culture (indeed activism as *tongzhi* understand it may not be the only locus, either). The empathy required in such an endeavour allows us to present culture in all its variation and complexity, avoiding the kind of utilitarianism that underpins both the so-called 'objective' and the so-called 'activist' or 'militant' approaches to anthropology. Such utilitarianism in the objective approach would hold that research must be undertaken at a certain remove from the situation in order to provide replicability (how it is useful to science). Utilitarianism in the moral approach would hold that the quickest means of solving the problem of

---

39. '这里 '行动主义者'（activist）并不全然等于'维权'，即有周密计划的社会方案或者组织化的行为，而更多指向出于同情心的互动关系和主动采取行动的立场，通过了解事实感动力来触发改变社会的愿望。'

domination is to resist it (and that the usefulness of the researcher is in starting or proliferating such resistance). But too strict a utilitarianism prevents us from understanding the importance of activities that are not purposive in the way we expect, requiring us to cut out a whole swathe of the vibrant and organized *tongzhi* community, not to mention the disorganized part of it, from the work we present – work that itself is obviously and inherently political and that should proceed according to an ethics not of an abstract justice but of a culturally rooted justifiability.

References

Agamben, Giorgio (1993) *The Coming Community*. Michael Hardt, trans. Minneapolis: University of Minnesota Press.

Boellstorff, Tom (2012) 'The Politics of Similitude: global sexuality activism, ethnography, and the western subject'. *Trans-Scripts: an interdisciplinary online journal in the humanities and social sciences at UC Irvine* 2: accessed 23 January 2015 at http://sites.uci.edu/transscripts/files/2014/10/2012_02_03.pdf.

Bourdieu, Pierre (1998) *Practical Reason: On the theory of action*. Palo Alto: Stanford University Press.

Brown, Michael F. (1996) 'On Resisting Resistance'. *American Anthropologist* vol. 98, no. 4, pp. 729–735.

Clifford, James (2000) 'Taking Identity Politics Seriously: The contradictory, stony ground...' In Paul Gilroy, Lawrence Grossberg, and Angela McRobbie (eds), *Without Guarantees: In honour of Stuart Hall*. London: Verso, pp. 94–112.

Clifford, James, and George E. Marcus (eds) (1986) *Writing culture: the poetics and politics of ethnography*. Berkeley: University of California Press.

D'Andrade, Roy (1995) 'Moral Models in Anthropology'. *Current Anthropology* vol. 36, no. 3, pp. 399–408.

de Certeau, Michel (1984) *The Practice of Everyday Life*. Berkeley: University of California Press.

Eng, David L., with Judith Halberstam and José Esteban Muñoz (2005) 'Introduction: What's queer about queer studies now?' *Social Text* vol. 23, nos 3–4, pp. 1–17.

Engebretsen, Elisabeth Lund (2008) 'Queer Ethnography in Theory and Practice: Reflections on studying sexual globalization and women's queer activism in Beijing'. *Graduate Journal of Social Science* vol. 5, no. 2, pp. 88–116.

Harris, Marvin (1995) 'Comments', *Current Anthropology* vol. 36, no. 3, pp. 423–424.

Huizinga, Johan (1971) *Homo Ludens: A study of the play element in culture*. Boston: The Beacon Press.

Kuper, Adam (1995) 'Comments', *Current Anthropology* vol. 36, no. 3, pp. 424–426.

Low, Setha M., and Sally Engle Merry (2010) 'Engaged Anthropology: diversity and dilemmas, an introduction to Supplement 2', *Current Anthropology* vol. 51, no. S2, pp. S203–S226.

Merry, Sally Engle (2005) 'Anthropology and Activism: Researching human rights across porous boundaries', *PoLAR: Political and Legal Anthropology Review* vol. 28, no. 2, pp. 240–257.

Nader, Laura (1995) 'Comments', *Current Anthropology* vol. 36, no. 3, pp. 426–427.

O'Meara, J. Tim (1995) 'Comments', *Current Anthropology* vol. 36, no. 3, pp. 427–428.

Ortner, Sherry B. (1995) 'Resistance and the Problem of Ethnographic Refusal', *Comparative Studies in Society and History* vol. 37, no. 1, pp. 173–193.

Osterweil, Michal (2013) 'Rethinking Public Anthropology through Epistemic Politics and Theoretical Practice', *Cultural Anthropology* vol. 28, no. 4, pp. 598–620.

Rofel, Lisa (2007) *Desiring China: Experiments in neoliberalism, sexuality, and public culture*. Durham, NC: Duke University Press.

Sack, Allen L. (1977) 'Sport: Play or work?' In Phillips Stevens, Jr. (ed.), *Studies in the Anthropology of Play: Papers in memory of B. Allan Tindall*. New York: Leisure Press, pp. 186–195.

Sanford, Victoria, and Asale Angel-Ajani (2006) *Engaged Observer: Anthropology, Advocacy, and Activism*. New Brunswick, NJ: Rutgers University Press.

Scheper-Hughes, Nancy (1995) 'The Primacy of the Ethical: Propositions for a militant anthropology', *Current Anthropology* vol. 36, no. 3, pp. 409–420.

Schroeder, William F. (2012a) 'Beyond Resistance: *Gay* and *lala* recreation in Beijing'. In Peter Aggleton, Paul Boyce, Henrietta L. Moore, and Richard Parker (eds), *Understanding Global Sexualities: New frontiers*. London: Routledge, pp. 108–123.

———— (2012b) 'On Cowboys and Aliens: Affective history and queer becoming in contemporary China', *GLQ: A Journal of Lesbian and Gay Studies*, vol. 18, no. 4, pp. 425–452.

Scott, James (1990) *Domination and the Arts of Resistance.* New Haven: Yale University Press.

Wan Yanhai (2001) 'Becoming a Gay Activist in Contemporary China' *Journal of Homosexuality* vol. 40, nos 3–4, pp. 47–64.

Warren, Kay B. (2006) 'Perils and Promises of Engaged Anthropology: Historical transitions and ethnographic dilemmas' In Victoria Sanford and Asale Angel-Ajani (eds) *Engaged Observer: Anthropology, advocacy, and activism.* New Brunswick, NJ: Rutgers University Press.

Zhang Zhen (2011) 'Art, Affect, and Activist Documentaries' ('艺术，感动力，行动主义纪录片'). *Chinese Independent Film* (《中国独立影像》), Li Xianting Film Foundation (栗宪庭电影基金), no page numbers.

CHAPTER 5

Challenging Authorities and Building Community Culture

Independent queer film making in China and the China queer film festival tour, 2008–2012

Popo Fan

The first Beijing Queer Film Festival was scheduled to take place at Peking University in 2001, but the police forced the festival to close and organizers and audience members were subjected to harassment. While this biannual festival (annual since 2010) has become an important part of the country's LGBT movement, reasonable fears of potential organizers, film-makers and audience members have limited its impact. Contrary to practices in other countries, the Chinese government labels film festivals "sensitive activities" (*mingan huodong*), which is generally interpreted as "potentially anti-government." The making, distribution, and screening of independent film (that is, a film that has not been formally approved by the government) challenges official power and, implicitly or explicitly, protests the government's tight control over information.

In regions beyond Beijing, there have been few opportunities for queer cultural events (*ku'er huati de huodong*) at all. In February of 2008, some filmmakers and activists got together for a discussion. We asked ourselves: How could more people, both in Beijing and across China, get access to queer films in a relatively safe environment? Our answer was the China Queer Film Festival Tour (CQFFT). Between 2008 and 2011, this tour visited over two dozen cities and hosted over 90 screenings before a combined audience of more than 7,000 people. This series continues to play an important role in promoting queer culture in China and helping the general public to gain a better understanding of LGBT issues.

Why are films the chosen medium for the tour?

As a popular mass medium, film is normally considered a good tool for public education. Films in the West, especially documentaries, play a pivotal role in LGBT community development. The situation in China is somewhat different. LGBT-themed films rarely gain the approvals required for showing in official cinemas. This lack of expressive platform has made gay and lesbian filmmakers turn to small-scale screenings followed by a group discussion on issues related to LGBT lives and rights. Filmmakers, LGBT rights activists and journalists are invited to participate and, although they attract less attention, these screenings are still viewed as a symbolic challenge to the status quo and censorship.

Risk and Opportunity

Participation and appreciation by the audience are often the benchmark for measuring the effectiveness and the worth of a film festival. However, in the presence of severe censorship, an open festival in one location entails inevitable risk. As mentioned, the gay film festival in Beijing encountered severe pressure and interference from the authorities. In addition, the first Beijing Gay and Lesbian Culture Festival, originally scheduled to take place in 2005, was shut down. Further, organizers and participants risked police detention and questioning.

Amid the unreasonably restrictive laws and regulations in China, one can in fact find loopholes. For example, LGBT-themed films cannot be openly screened in official cinemas, but they may be shown in coffee shops, university auditoriums, bars and independent film salons. After some careful deliberation, the organizing committee decided to spread the screenings across a period of time rather than concentrating on one location within a short span of time. Also, a screening tour in cities across different regions would encourage cooperation with various local groups. The months around the Beijing Olympics in 2008 were a politically sensitive time in China, but many independent film salons remained active. These served as a base for the screening tour.

This strategy indeed reduced risk. At the beginning, the tour was announced through mailing lists and mobile messages, but it gradually received publicity via online bulletin boards[1] and other social media.

---

1. Bulletin board system, and early form of Internet-based social communication.

By 2011, tour information could be viewed openly on such well-known LGBT websites as Aibai: www.aibai.com, Danlan: www.danlan.org, Les Sky: www.lessky.com and Feizan: www.feizan.com. Journalists from various media were occasionally invited to join events and the authorities did not interfere directly with those who chose to participate.

Reaching Out

Although the majority of filmmakers and organizers live and work in Beijing, partners and volunteers come from all over China. At first, the tour screened films already in the Beijing Queer Film Festival's collection. The Beijing LGBT Center[2] arranged for screening venues as well as human resources support. As the political and cultural centre of China, Beijing has gathered numerous talents and rights activists, but it also remains a politically sensitive spot in the nation. While talents abound in Beijing, we understood that we needed to share resources with other regions.

Fortunately, when we started out, the CQFFT received a lot of assistance from other networks. Lesbian groups such as Les+ and Common Language (*Tongyu*) had already accumulated valuable resources from throughout the country.[3] We were fortunate that local lesbian groups, all of them in a burgeoning stage, showed tremendous interest and enthusiasm for the festival tour. In 2009, other LGBT groups, including Gay Spot and Queer Comrades, also joined.[4] In addition, the Chinese Lala Alliance[5] provided important network support.

Preliminary arrangements included specifying hosts, budgeting (travel and lodging expenses for guests, screening venues, and so on), and seeking financial support. Having settled these issues, we went on to dis-

---

2. 北京同志中心. Founded in 2008, the Beijing LGBT Center serves the Beijing LGBT community. http://www.bjlgbtcenter.org.

3. 同语 or Tongyu, is one of China's longest-running LBT groups (lesbian bisexual and transgender) www.tongyulala.org. Les+ 杂志, is a famous lesbian magazine in mainland China, http://weibo.com/lesplus.

4. 点杂志, or Dian Magazine, is a famous gay men's magazine in mainland China. http://weibo.com/gayspot. 同志亦凡人, or Tongzhi Yifan Ren, is the longest-running LGBT webcast in mainland China. www.queercomrades.com. Both are based in Beijing, with a national network.

5. 华人拉拉联盟, is a network for Chinese speaking LBT (lesbian, bisexual, trans) groups.

cuss the programme for each screening. Once we reached an agreement with the local organizer, we would mail the films and publicity materials (including post cards of films, flyers of events, and so on.) to the hosts. The local hosts were in charge of selling tickets, arranging for equipment, and entertaining guests and the audience. The event would also be documented and feedback collected. Some ticket sale proceeds were sent back to the CQFFT in Beijing to cover a portion of the expenses associated with organizing the tour. In addition to keeping the project financially viable, this cooperative arrangement was a concrete manifestation of the idea that China's LGBT community spanned the country.

We learned quickly that a touring festival had to consider regional discrepancies in economic and cultural development. Some local organizers assumed that a projector would be sufficient for a screening. They were not aware that some films require a laptop or DVD player, as well as audio equipment. In addition to technical challenges, the content of the films we sent sometimes came as a surprise. Some audience members complained that some films were "too arty" for their taste; they tended to relate more to documentary films that depicted the lives of Chinese LGBT people. Feedback of this sort generated immediate adjustments back in Beijing, including revising which films would be recommended and revising descriptions of the films so that future local organizers would have a clearer idea about what to expect.

In 2011, we organized a screening of *Courage Unfolds,*[6] a short documentary about the LGBT movement in Asia produced by the International Gay and Lesbian Human Rights Commission. We hosted screenings in eight cities followed by panel discussions. It was a breakthrough success. As a result, regional audiences gained a deeper understanding of the situation for LGBTs in our neighbouring Asian countries.

Over time, the tour has grown to fill four roles in the broader development of LGBT communities in China. First, its screenings promote discussions and experience sharing that highlight rights-related issues. Second, the events enable filmmakers to interact with their audiences and produce new material, which is expected to help their work in the future; video clips made during the cross-country journey are good source materials for future documentaries. Third, the CQFFT uses the

---

6. A short documentary about the LGBT movement in Asia: http://vimeo.com/22813403

tour to carry out an "oral history" project, which records and archives the stories that participants choose to share. Finally, the evenings occasionally attract journalists, which both offers the possibility of the media presenting the community in a more accurate way and, on a personal level, generates enjoyment among LGBT community members as they see themselves in print.

We all love films

It continues to be quite a daunting task to have the tour festival cover so many lesbian and gay groups across various regions. We try our best to select films and filmmakers who represent the diversity of the LGBT community and to use the tour as a cultural stage that brings members of otherwise disparate communities together.

The tour's stop in Zhengzhou in August 2008 was the first to consciously encourage gay groups and lesbian groups to collaborate. This proved to be a good practice. Through the sharing of resources, the two groups broke barriers and built good relations. Similarly, the evening in Nanning, Guangxi Province marked the first time that this city's lesbian and gay groups worked together. This successful event started a tradition of common activities between the two groups.

Likewise, more than forty people, half gay and half lesbian, gathered to view a screening in Ji'ning in Shandong Province. One gay filmmaker and one lesbian filmmaker appeared as guests. People exchanged their thoughts on society and family, and expressed views on the LGBT rights situation in China. The organizer was a member of Shandong Rainbow, which works in the field of HIV/AIDS prevention, but he also sought to build the lesbian community. He emphasized that the event's success would have been impossible without a variety of groups cooperating to build a broader *tongzhi* community.

Obstacles to intergroup collaboration remain. Beginning in 2003, international foundations and the Center for Disease Control of China began to engage the gay community about HIV/AIDS prevention. These interventions have helped the growth of gay community, but competition for funding also causes strains in relationships among gay groups. Further, perceptions of funding restrictions have inhibited gay–lesbian collaboration. Some gay groups claimed that government funding could not be spent on female guests or that the event could only be held in venues frequented mainly by gay men. We also observed that some gay groups have to put so much energy and efforts into HIV/AIDS prevention that they have neglected broader community-building activities, including the festival tour. In contrast, many lesbian groups were much younger and had less organizational experience, especially regarding fundraising. They welcomed our logistical support and tended to make our events a top priority.

Tongzhi + Comrade

Apart from the LGBT community, we have also welcomed non-LGBT people to join our events. However, announcing a screening to a broader audience carries a risk that government authorities also will learn of intentions to screen censorable images. This increases the risk that the screening will be shut down, individuals will be harassed and inter-group cooperation will be reduced as a result of a bad experience.

To minimize these risks, we focus on collaboration with independent salons: public–private spaces where sympathetic members of the general public tend to hang out. We discovered some salons ourselves; others were referred to us by local groups. We sought first to establish a general relationship and encouraged LGBT filmmakers to build their own personal relationships with these salons by participating in non-film events hosted by the salon. Next, we engaged in a dialogue with salon owners, explaining that the LGBT rights movement is part of a broader campaign for social progress in the country. That is, we all shared the same goals. Some salon owners were not convinced. Salons dedicated to creating a safe space for conservative Christians refused to collaborate, despite their "common" position on the edges of Chinese society. Salon owners who were otherwise sympathetic hesitated when they discovered that, due to severe financial challenges, many LGBT films have relatively low production quality.

Despite these setbacks, we have established good connections with many salons. One Way Street, a famous bookstore in Beijing frequented by young writers and artists on the weekends, hosted the tour's first salon screening. Among several others, Film Fans Kindergarten in Tianjin has been tremendously supportive.

Colleges and universities are another point of entry to a broader public. College students are expected to explore and challenge difficult ideas and rules and norms about what kind of images may be screened are more relaxed. The tour worked with student groups and LGBT NGOs to show films on campus. For example, Associated Gay/ Lesbian Campus in Guangzhou has sponsored screenings on at least five campuses.

After opening the tour to more general audiences, discussion topics became more diverse. People were interested in learning more about the LGBT experience and members of our core audience were excited to share. For example, after a screening in Nanning, one member in the audience asked how *tongzhi*, which means "comrades" in the Communist ideology, became a term referring to LGBT. This gave us a good opportunity to explain the origin of this usage. After Edward Lim[7] used *tongzhi* for the first Hong Kong Lesbian and Gay Film festival in 1989, *tongzhi* became a popular term to describe homosexuals. But at the same time, it covers wider meaning than just gay and lesbian. We pointed out that *tongzhi* could also be used to refer to anyone who agreed with our agenda, regardless of their sexual orientation.

Tour Festival Plus

The organizing committee hopes to use the tour as a springboard to other activities. Even at its early stage, our sister organization, China Queer Independent Films (CQIF) discussed the options of producing and promoting LGBT-themed films and the tour has encouraged more people to join this endeavour. A T-shirt with the slogan "We Want to Watch Gay and Lesbian Films" printed in the front was worn at every event. With the event attracting more and more publicity, CQIF sought and received financial support from Astraea Lesbian Foundation for Justice and Arts Network Asia and was able to reach more cities.[8] Apart from the tour, CQIF also worked together with other groups on workshops such as "China Queer Digital Storytelling Workshop"[9] and "Queer Photographer Workshop". These projects intend to help members of the

---

7. 林奕华, Hong Kong theater director, script writer and TV host. Founder of Hong Kong Lesbian and Gay Film Festival.

8. Astraea Lesbian Foundation For Justice is based in New York and supports LGBT groups globally. http://www.astraeafoundation.org. Arts Network Asia http://www.artsnetworkasia.org supports a wide range of cultural projects.

9. 发现自我之旅 was started in 2010. It trains grassroots LGBT in making videos. http://blog.sina.com.cn/lalastories

LGBT community to learn the techniques needed for making videos and documentaries. Further, the tour attracted international interest in our films. Apart from domestic screenings, some of our films have been screened at international festivals, including in Torino, Tokyo, Copenhagen and Hong Kong.

Official censorship remains our biggest challenge. There is a still a long way to go before LGBT-themed films can be watched by the majority of the public in China, but we are making progress little by little. One day in the future, we will see the flowers of the rainbow blossom across the nation.

Appendix

Selected films screened by the film festival tour:

Mainland China:
Tang Tang 唐唐 (2005)
Douban: http://movie.douban.com/subject/2139315/

Love Mime 小树的夏天 Xiao Shu De Xia Tian (2008)
Douban: http://movie.douban.com/subject/4176575/

Mama Rainbow 彩虹伴我心 Cai Hong Ban Wo Xin (2012)
IMDB: http://www.imdb.com/title/tt2332754/
Douban: http://movie.douban.com/subject/11601812/

Hong Kong:
Soundless Wind Chime 无声风铃 (2009)
IMDB: http://www.imdb.com/title/tt1360832/
Douban: http://movie.douban.com/subject/3439354/

Taiwan:
The Corner 私角落 Si Jiao Luo (2002)
IMDB: http://www.imdb.com/title/tt0398889/
Douban: http://movie.douban.com/subject/1938315/

Other Countries:
Cowboy Forever 永远的牛仔 (2008)
IMDB: http://www.imdb.com/title/tt1073162/

Bye Bye Antonia 再见，安东尼娅 (2009)
Douban: http://movie.douban.com/subject/4207616/

CHAPTER 6

Of Pride and Visibility

The Contingent Politics of Queer Grassroots Activism in China

Elisabeth L. Engebretsen

If we organized a pride event that is not out in the press, and not known to anyone else in the world but the local gay community, that would not be pride …

Jake, organizer, Shanghai Pride, 2009[1]

A queer film festival is not an event only open to 'marginal people' who come to escape the darkness of mainstream society. A queer film festival is a platform void of prejudice, a place where people can freely express, show, explore themselves and where they can enter into meaningful exchanges … The revolution hasn't succeeded yet. Queers, keep up the good work![2]

Yang Yang, chairwoman, 6th Beijing Queer Film Festival, 2011[3]

Introduction

This chapter reflects on queer grassroots activism in contemporary mainland China, in the context of globally travelling queer and gender

---

1. Personal communication with Jake (pseudonym; email 26 October 2010).

2. This is a play on the famous words by Sun Yat Sen (Sun Zhongshan), revolutionary leader and first president of the Republic of China: The revolution is not yet completed, all my comrades must struggle on' (*geming shangwei chenggong,* **tongzhi** *rengxu nuli,* 革命尚未成功 同志仍须努力). Here, the BJQFF queerly subverts the original *tongzhi* or 'comrade' reference that alluded to fellow revolutionaries, by inserting 'queer' (酷儿) in its stead: *geming shangwei chenggong,* **ku'er** *rengxu nuli,* 革命尚未成功，酷儿仍需努力 (my emphasis).

3. Cited from BJQFF press release 2011.

theory, politics and culture.[4] Whereas queer movements around the world share the broad aim to achieve social acceptance, justice and liberation for sexual and gender minorities, locally specific strategies and priorities often differ substantially in ways that limit the usefulness of making all-encompassing generalizations. A growing body of research and activist practices have documented rich and variegated local differences – and convergences – in ways that help debunk the notion of a universal and monolithic sexual or gendered identity and ideologies that claim a single correct articulation of queer life. At the same time, there is no denial that there exists a transnational, hegemonic ideology on queerness that is centred on specific articulations of sexual rights and liberation rhetoric. This ideology promotes a particular form of identity politics based on individualism and coming-out narratives, and features public rituals such as Pride celebrations in urban space. This model has taken hold of local queer imaginations and sexual politics worldwide in a process Peter Jackson describes as 'global queering' (2009: 357). However, global queering is not a simple process of emulating Western values and 'losing' local cultural identity (see footnote 7). Jackson emphasizes the critical importance of neoliberal capitalism and market-based cultural appropriations of global flows of 'finance, goods, people, images, and ideas', but warns that these transformations are complex and always partial, with local differences and modalities. In this way, global queering involves some measure of 'Westernizing homogenization', but simultaneously 'produces hybridization in which local agency is as important as subordination to foreign influences' (Jackson 2009: 386, 387). As Ara Wilson observes in her discussion of 'Queering Asia', it is true that 'visible queer life in the region is read through the lens of Stonewall' (Wilson 2006, paragraph 3).[5] Still, expanding transnational circuits of queer liberation movements and cultures have generated considerable scholarly writing, much of which is critical of the 'globalization of the gay move-

4. In this text, I apply 'queer' as an umbrella category that incorporates a variety of subjectivities, identities, practices, and collectivities related to gender and sexual non-normativity.

5. The Stonewall riots were protests that took place in and outside the Stonewall Bar in central New York City in June 1969. This incident sparked a series of riots and is commonly considered to be one, if not the most, significant catalyst for the formation of the modern gay liberation movement. For a useful account of Stonewall and the politics that evolved in its wake, see Martin Duberman's *Stonewall* (1993).

ment' (Manalansan 1995: 427) and the underlying, often unexamined, hegemonic western paradigm that continues to frame much Anglophone scholarly literature and activist politics in this regard.[6]

Critical interdisciplinary scholarship on transnational sexualities and gender diversity, in its increasing focus on processes of globalization, power inequalities, nation and citizenship, does important work in pointing out the limited ability of western models to accurately describe and analyse realities beyond the cultural contexts in which they were produced.[7] They point out that these models reproduce a Eurocentric and monolithic version of sexuality and gender, and are therefore unable to convey the nuances and divergences of localized practices and priorities that are inconsistent with this framework. Queer anthropology in particular has offered ethnography-based critiques of how, in much of this scholarship, the quest for queer equality and liberation is folded back into a familiar narrative of identity politics and understood within an underlying framework of Western sexual modernity.[8] This perspective interprets sexuality according to a process of individual self-discovery and a journey toward self-acceptance and personal identity such as gay, lesbian or queer. This model is in turn fuelled by a powerful rhetoric of identity-based pride and public visibility (being 'out and proud'), and firmly territorialized within metropolitan urban space. Its moral opposite is shame, being in denial, closeted and silent, and defined by (residues of) tradition. But more than simply being critical and identifying shortcomings of dominant paradigms, these critical perspectives, from which I appropriate central ideas in the following pages, offer conceptual alternatives to think about difference and political possibilities in the world. Peter Jackson, in discussing the correlation between capitalism, market processes and the proliferation of 'global queering', argues that 'local forms of cultural difference exist alongside international commonalities and emphasize[s] that local forms of queer

---

6. See Arnaldo Cruz-Malavé and Martin Manalansan's *Queer Globalizations* (2002) and Gloria Wekker's *The Politics of Passion* (2008) for excellent critiques in this regard.

7. By using the term 'Western' I mean to refer to the dominant body of English-language discourse and scholarship originating in the Western European and North America academy.

8. See Boellstorff (2007) for a recent overview of this literature.

modernity have emerged from the agency of the members of each society' (Jackson 2009: 359).

China has so far figured little in this emergent critical scholarship, especially in terms of empirical research. This relative absence fuels continued perceptions of a 'stunted' queer movement and community in the country.[9] Yet all the chapters in this volume demonstrate that contemporary China offers a pertinent case study of global queerness in its local appropriations. They introduce us to an exciting new range of answers to the puzzle of how a variety of practices and ideologies related to sexual and gender non-normativity co-exist – sometimes seamlessly, sometimes with tension. Furthermore, much of the global queering literature does not adequately address the underlying assumption of a democratic civil society structure, where 'difference' is legally protected, and dissent encouraged, at least in principle. These analyses offer little guidance about how to understand queer politics in the single-party, authoritarian Chinese nation–state.

Following these insights, this chapter discusses important features of queer grassroots activism in contemporary China, as queer activists navigate an unpredictable political and social environment. I pay particular attention to locally specific strategies to circumvent official censorship and the ways in which the globally travelling ideology of 'Pride', which focuses on public visibility for sexual and gender minorities, are appropriated in a diversity of ways. To illustrate, I draw on three instances of activist events in public space that took place in three decades (the years 1996, 2009 and 2013) and in three cities: Beijing, Shanghai and Changsha. These events are exceptional and not representative of broader shifts or trends in any straightforward way. Still, these extraordinary moments and their unfolding legacies – contested and celebrated, but never ignored – illustrate the complex and shifting articulations of local agencies, the role of transnational connections, and the structural boundaries of government as they play out in Chinese society. Analytically, I situate queer grassroots activism and discourse within broader critical theorizing on transnational sexuality, gender diversity and social movements that expands the terrain for knowledge production and meaningful political possibilities, all the while recogniz-

---

9.   I discuss existing and emergent ethnographic literature and the question of why so little research is being conducted on 'Queer China' overall in Engebretsen (2013).

ing the enabling yet constraining influence of global circuits of queer politics, culture and symbolism often interpreted as 'Western'.

My inquiry here takes two main directions. First, I examine activist practices and discourses by situating activist events and movements within China's highly specific socio-political context. In an authoritarian country with neither formal recognition nor criminalization of homosexuality as such, contemporary rights activism and justice movements are in a difficult position when negotiating social visibility, outreach strategies and media profiling. Public parades and other mass events in urban centres are, not surprisingly, nearly impossible and are often met with censorship and demands of closure from authorities. Finding alternative strategies that manipulate conventional modes of organizing and interpreting the meaning – and meaningfulness – of public spatial presence and the aims of activism *tout court*, and which simultaneously minimize the likelihood of government censorship and closure, are imperative in such an environment. This context must inform our understanding of localized and multifaceted definitions of what constitutes desirable and productive celebrations, visibility and discourse – and the overall purpose of engaging in such work.

In order to situate emergent queer visibility in regional and global contexts, it is necessary to rethink the orthodox view of the inherent link between visibility, empowerment and recognition. Hegemonic models tend to emphasize values such as spectacle, confrontation and occupation of urban central space, and do so in ways that direct themselves not just at the general public or passersby, but specifically at political and moral authorities such as the government, the state leader or Church officials. As Francesca Stella has noted in the Russian context (2013), and Jason Richie in Israel-Palestine (2010), these articulations may be well received internationally but are likely to be problematic locally, in some countries drawing hostility from traditional power-holders such as the Church and conservative political factions, even provoking outright anti-queer violence, including torture and killing. Global activist discourse and academic research have especially considered homophobic currents in Africa and Eastern Europe, linking the anti-queer violence there to broader governmental anxieties regarding uneasy power shifts in the ongoing post-colonial or post-socialist transitions. In the Chinese context, such discourse and violence have hardly been present, and yet there is no denial that Chinese queers experience profound discrimination and serious forms of violence and rights deprivation. In the pages that follow, I examine how notions of Pride and visibility are often skilfully re-appropriated in more ambiguous forms of activism, with an emphasis on coop-eration, communication, similarity and shared humanity rather than a rigid politics of difference.

Second, I use the three case studies of queer grassroots activism to point to the prevailing hegemony of a particular version of transnational queer liberatory politics – especially the hyper-commercialized Pride festivals and parades – and the circuitous travel of dominant concepts including celebration, liberation, Pride and solidarity. In so doing, I seek not only to bring attention to the different ways of doing and imagining Pride worldwide, but also to challenge the underlying logics of much rights and pride discourse that unwittingly reproduce an authority in articulating 'proper' forms of activism and define what constitutes 'respectable' queer life. Attending to local and regional specificities, and placing those specificities into their broader historical, political and cultural contexts, is important in order to reorient and refigure a politics of liberation and justice.

Three Scenes of Activist Practices and Discourses

As the chapters in this volume testify to, it is the interplay among com-plex social and political institutions in China – not an essential China/ West cultural difference – that most profoundly shapes strategic activist practices.[10] As a tactical choice, Chinese queer grassroots activists have developed coping and movement strategies aptly described by some as 'guerrilla' style, due to their ad-hoc, non-territorialized use of (parts of) public space. This concept also describes activists' communicative and outreach practices, which seek to minimize the likelihood of official censorship or closure rather than maximize confrontation and general public attention (Yang 2011). Anthropologist Lisa Rofel, in a recent es-say on sexual politics and grassroots activism in China, discusses the spatial politics of movement, for example describing activists as 'nomadic

---

10. See the discussion in the Introduction chapter regarding Petrus Liu (2010) and Hans Huang's (2011) critique of Chou Wah-shan's (2000) Sinocentric analysis of Chinese *tongzhi* exceptionalism.

subjects' due to their ad-hoc event organizing at shifting locations (Rofel 2012). Argues Rofel, China's nomadic queer activists are savvy in 'reading' government authorities; they 'experiment' with shifting strategies to avoid obstacles, and they 'maneuver within and around the various powers that shape subjectivities, socialities, political beliefs and economic inequality in China' (2012: 158). In other words, activists are politically highly literate and creative agents, at once accommodating their strategies to hegemonic power structures and articulating alternative ones, some of which are successful and others that might be less so. I would argue that this is a strategic queer politics of contingency. On one level, this political strategy appropriates tacit articulations of Pride politics and rights discourses. However, it also focuses on communication and outreach to the general public, allies as well as queers, instead of giving primacy to overt political confrontation directed at the government. In turn, this strategy prioritizes ad-hoc stunts, as opposed to lingering occupation, in urban public space on symbolically significant dates, such as the last weekend of June (Stonewall), 14 February (Valentine's Day), and 17 May (International Day against Homo/Bi/TransPhobia, IDAHOBIT). In the following, I narrate three public Pride events to illustrate these strategic priorities; one that happened in 1996 in Beijing, then one in 2009 in Shanghai, and the third in May 2013, in Changsha city, Hunan province.

Celebrating Stonewall in Beijing, 1996

One of the earliest public queer events in China took place in Beijing in June 1996. Specifically, it was a party designed to celebrate the anniversary of the Stonewall movement – or, the 'birthday of all of us' as one participant movingly put it. In a sense, this early event was closely connected to international circuits of 'gay rights' activism, through its invocation of a symbolic global community rooted in the Stonewall movement.[11] At the same time, however, it was borne out of very spe-

---

11. See Wan Yanhai (2001) for an account of even earlier community activism in Beijing and its connections to the international circuits of gay rights activism already by the early years of the 1990s. Wan chronicles how gay (male) activists in Beijing began proceedings to set up a group called 'The Great Stonewall Society' in 1993. As Wan argues, 'The very reference to the New York riots of 1968 in the name of the group indicates clear knowledge of Western ideas and achievements. Indeed, it was with the help of Western human rights activists that Li contacted international lesbian and gay organizations, members of the Chinese democracy

cific local contexts and connections, some with regional, others with transnational reach. One of the leading queer activists in China since the mid-1990s and a co-organizer of this party, Xiaopei He,[12] has written about this milestone event in detail. He's narrative conveys the nuances of this key moment in queer public organizing:

> The first time we organized a politically related activity was in a small bar, to commemorate the American Stonewall homosexual movement anniversary. In 1996 in Beijing, there was still no *tongzhi* bar. This time, we learnt from past experience, and told all the people we knew to go to a very quiet bar in a small lane, to take part in a 'birthday party'. We bought a birthday cake and little presents. Sixty people came, among them eight women. This was the first time this many women took part in a get-together. Wu Chunsheng [another central community activist at the time] quietly told me that there were plainclothes police in the bar. We thought of a way to get around that.
>
> First we sang 'Happy Birthday' and cut the cake. Then I said to everyone, 'Can you guess whose birthday it is today? Come and whisper it in my ear, and if you get it right, you will get a present (which were condoms and sweets wrapped up). Everyone started to ask each other whose birthday it was. People who knew about Stonewall told those who did not, who then came and whispered to me. Everyone one by one came to me and said 'Today is the American homosexual movement commemoration day'. One boy when he heard the story ran over to me and said 'I know! I know! Today is the birthday of all of us!' When I heard his words, I was very moved, and my heart skipped a beat. I whispered what he said ... to other *tongzhi*. I thought, that's probably what the *tongzhi* movement means. We unite together, we have a common birthday.
>
> From that day, this bar became the first homosexual bar in Beijing. This backstreet bar was always empty, so we decided to make it our hangout. The owners were never fully welcoming, but needed the clientele. It became almost 100 per cent *tongzhi* every night (He 2001: 51).

The Stonewall party in Beijing in the summer of 1996 was a milestone event for several reasons. First, it brought local queers together in a decid-

---

movements overseas, and international human rights organization' (Wan 2001: 48).

12. Xiaopei He remains a key figure in China's world of sexual politics, now directing the Pink Space Sexuality Research Centre in Beijing, available at www.pinkspace.com.cn.

edly public – if not overtly visible – backstreet bar, which in itself marked a significant achievement and sense of collective empowerment (see Fu's chapter for an account of gay men's place-making in Shenyang). Second, the party hosted several women (eight) in addition to sixty men. This was the first time that so many lesbians took part in collective community activism. Due to the prevailing patriarchal social order at the time, women often lacked the degree of autonomy and resources required to participate as independent individuals; their access to urban space was often limited to family-oriented activities. It was mainly for this reason that lesbian women and their concerns had remained largely invisible in the fragmented informal queer community up until this point. Third, the many published accounts of the birthday party have been vital to generating a collective cultural memory and archive of queer existence and grassroots activism. Archived memories, such as He's description of the Stonewall anniversary party in 1996, function as starting points and sources of inspiration for activist achievement and community building in the present. A fourth reason for the Stonewall Party's importance has to do with the broader context in which the party took place: small nondescript bars in central Beijing were already sites for regular, low-key get-togethers, mostly attended only by men (He 2009). This growing informal public presence had helped generate sufficient trust to enable the Stonewall celebration to attract a critical mass of participants and ensure its success. Think, for example, of the community spirit exhibited by the whispering contest of whose birthday it was, combined with the correct answer ('all of us'). Demographically, the participants included a diverse combination of foreigners living and working in Beijing, local men and women engaged in *tongzhi* activism, and their friends.

The Beijing birthday party in 1996 was an early instance of local queer community activism in a public space. The simultaneous presence of international references (Stonewall) and foreign participants, alongside savvy locals who knew how to best manipulate the authorities, aptly demonstrates a specifically Chinese form of queer activism that cannot meaningfully be understood simply as emulating the West. By this point, economic reforms had enabled a growing market for commodity- and consumer-based leisure practices, such as bars. Beijing queers utilized this newly emergent capitalist sensibility to gain access to mainstream leisure spaces, by using the bar owners' need to generate revenue. As He put it, managers were not so much supporting queers as they 'needed the clientele' (2001: 51). Similarly, during my own fieldwork in Beijing eight years later, where I studied emergent *lala* (lesbian) social communities and activism, I found that weekly women-only bar events benefited from mainstream venues' desire to make a profit regardless of who the patrons were. *Lala* organizers were therefore able to host 'special interest' events in downtown venues (Engebretsen 2013).

In the years since the Stonewall Anniversary party, and especially after the turn of the millennium, alternative articulations of visibility and grassroots activist strategies have emerged with some urgency. Mediated by generalized and inexpensive access to social media, including the Internet, cell and smart phone communication technology, variegated voices within the broad category of the queer community have emerged. Some of these voices are orienting toward transnational practices of Pride and public protests for inspiration and, sometimes, emulation. To illustrate some key issues of these transformations and emergent tensions and conflicts of interest, I discuss two important instances of very public Pride events in the following sections, beginning with China's 'first ever Pride festival'.

Shanghai Pride, 2009: China's First Pride Festival?

The first Shanghai Pride Festival (*Shanghai Jiao'ao Zhou*) took place during the second week of June, 2009. The organizers – a mix of foreigners and Chinese – labelled the extensive bilingual (Chinese and English) promotional material that appeared both online and offline with the catchphrase 'China's first ever Pride festival.'[13] Shanghai Pride – which has become an annual event since – generated considerable global media exposure, and a string of high-profile English language media reported on it, including the *New York Times*, *Newsweek*, the BBC and the *Huffington Post* (Jacobs 2009; Rauhala 2009). The dominant media narrative presented a sparkling picture of glitzy cosmopolitan liberation and celebration whereby the country's queer population, finally, came out proudly in public. Exemplifying the general focus from Western media outlets, a *Newsweek* article – aptly titled 'Pride without a Parade,' given that public mass parades of any kind are nearly impossible to carry out – argued as

---

13. See the Shanghai PRIDE 2009 website: http://www.shpride.com/pride2009/.

follows: 'Gay pride in China? This week's coming-out party in Shanghai for the country's lesbian and gay community was touted as a first' (Liu and Hewitt, 2009). News of the festival also made it to the state-run English-language newspaper *China Daily*, which hailed the festival as a sign of China's successful social reforms (Jacobs 2009). Notably, however, news of the festival did not appear in its Chinese-language edition, *Zhongguo Ribao*. When authorities closed down some of the festival's scheduled events – including a film screening and a play – the overseas media resorted to the familiar story of governmental repression and lack of civil rights progress in China.

The selective emphasis on Shanghai Pride as 'a first' in China carried certain side effects that have political consequences for activist concerns. Most importantly, this discourse effectively erased knowledge regarding previous local initiatives that played with alternative, roundabout definitions of 'Pride' and 'the public'. Earlier years of Pride month activities such as flying rainbow-patterned kites (*fang fengzheng de huodong*) on the Great Wall and in public squares in numerous provincial cities, despite vigorous online and social media publicity and archiving of images and narratives, were invisible. In short, the violence of the discursive claim to a 'first' is to eliminate pre-existing practices from the emergent archive. It reproduces a familiar binary understanding of queerness and/in China: being out and proud can only happen in the cosmopolitan public, by utilizing globally travelling Pride symbolism and LGBT rights discourse, and by being organized and supported by foreigners.

At the time of Shanghai Pride I was in Beijing for a research project, and I could not help feeling intrigued by the festival organizers' promotion of it as 'China's first' such festival, given the vibrant recent history of similar festivals, festive events and other annually held community markers of 'Pride Month' (*jiao'ao yue*) within LGBT communities. I wondered what definitions of Pride they had developed for their festival and how they considered Shanghai Pride's relationship with the broader queer grassroots activist initiatives in China. How different and new was Shanghai Pride, really, when set against the *longue duré* of low-key queer activism prior to its inception? Many earlier events, some of them held ritually every June with explicit references to 'Pride' and Stonewall – such as the kite flying – used Rainbow and Pink Triangle symbols, such as flags, kites, wristbands and buttons. Contrary to what the overseas media reports seemed to suggest, I knew that Chinese queers were already deeply immersed in queer pop culture and rights politics, organizing festivals and similar activist events on a regular basis, and they had been for years.

In light of this, I contacted the festival organizers to find out more about Shanghai Pride and the organizers' thinking around this discourse. Eventually, I got in touch with Jake, a Shanghai resident originally from another country in the region and one of the organizers of 2009 Pride. When I asked him about their use of the 'China's first Pride' catchphrase, Jake was quick to correct me. More than a slogan, he explained, this wording was simply a description of a known fact. To illustrate what he meant, he went on to define the Pride concept:

> [It] should be multi-dimensional, multi-day, it should cut across various spheres: celebration, education, arts/cultural, sports, etc, and most of all, it should be an opportunity for a *collective coming out* for the LGBT community as a whole. This *coming out* element is a key crucial element: if I and my friends waved rainbow flags in the privacy of our own homes, that would not be pride. If we organised a one-off hush-hush event at some back alley local bar preaching to the converted (as has been done many times before), that would not be pride. If we organized a pride event that is not out in the press, and not known to anyone else in the world but the local gay community, that would not be pride, too.[14]

Our conversations allowed me to gain a deeper understanding of the politics of Shanghai Pride at that time and what distinguished it from previous events. Their intention was to organize a public event over several days, spanning both fun and politics, both satisfying a seasoned existing queer community and 'showing off' to the rest of society. With almost limitless enthusiasm, overseas connections and experience, and considerable local support, they succeeded in many ways with their 'first' Pride festival, despite suffering a few setbacks caused by the local police.[15] Shanghai Pride has since become an annual event, continuing to draw considerable overseas media attention.

---

14. Personal communication with Jake (email 26 October 2010).

15. Police appeared at many festival locations and demanded closure of events. They could frequently be pacified, but not always. The setbacks included having to cancel one film screening and halt the performance of a play based on 'The Laramie

What we might call the event of the 2009 Shanghai Pride illustrates broader tensions regarding the role and purpose of grassroots activism in light of competing ambitions and the transnational and regional travelling of people, resources, and media cultures. The stakes involved are particularly high in locations such as China, where social and activist movements are illegal or at the very least politically problematic, where personal risk is considerable if you get involved, and where formal protective legislation is absent or minimal. To illustrate, let me highlight three interrelated concerns regarding the 2009 Shanghai Pride event: spatial location, public visibility and the limits of identity politics. First, the public urban spatiality necessary for Pride reaches beyond 'the privacy of our own homes' and communities, into the hyper-visible general public. It thus transcends the discrete visibility of the private, personal sphere – to which backstreet bars belong – to enter public space marked by qualities such as being mainstream, hypermodern and cosmopolitan. This kind of ideal definition, however, equates Pride with a very particular narrative of urban citizenship and queer belonging: one that excludes certain groups of people and experiential domains. This erasure is perhaps most poignantly related to socio-economic class: poorer people not only have less money but also less free time, they face greater risk and greater consequences of exposure (because they have less social capital that might influence authorities), and they have less access to transnational cultural capital, including English language proficiency. Participating in big events like Shanghai Pride is thus more risky and less fun for some members of the queer community. Nonetheless, this hegemonic politics – by preferring to highlight commonalities and assimilate into a dominant Pride politics – forecloses the possibility of a co-existent discursive space to articulate needs and make visible a broader array of queer lives, voices and desires.

The second issue concerns media visibility that extends beyond 'the local gay community' into mainstream society and creates a media event of global reach. This implies that public Pride festivals connect to global circuits of queer activism and justice-seeking movements. According to the Shanghai Pride narrative, being out and coming out is a categorical

---

Project', which chronicles the life and murder of Matthew Shepard, a gay college student in the U.S.

– and implicitly identity-based – collective event that connects individuals to local and transnational communities of like-minded people. This Pride definition aspires to represent the 'LGBT community as a whole', inside and outside of China's national borders. Simultaneously, however, this discourse goes a significant way toward reproducing certain structural power inequalities, whereby 'local' events that do not readily translate into established transnational gay and lesbian rights and identity discourse are invisible, implicitly dismissed, for instance for being too secretive, small-scale, and internal – located in 'back alley bars' and being 'hush hush' one-off events.

The Pride narrative that emerges here could be considered a hegemonic Pride politics, in that it instructs on the desirable ways to celebrate queer life in the cosmopolitan city of Shanghai. This aligns in important ways with dominant discourses of 'global queering' as noted by Jackson (2009). An effect of this discourse – however unintentional this effect might be – is that alternative articulations of Pride and different kinds of visibility strategies are at best side-lined and at worst erased or discredited. By taking a closer look at the specific event and narrative of Shanghai Pride and situating it within a broader historical context and alongside the multiple versions of Pride that pre-dated it, the picture that emerges is one of multiple strands of generative activist events and narratives. Some of them actively re-appropriate the globally circulating Pride concept; others do not. I would suggest that what we could usefully take away from these interpretive tensions is less the observation that different community groups articulate Pride politics in different ways, than the recognition of an expansive coexistence of diverse forms of queer activism, some of which align more closely with global flows of queer activist ideology and discourse than others. Hence, they also display broader, emerging power inequalities and their local manifestations as they relate, however unevenly, to global capitalist market flows and cultural globalization.

The expansions in the vision for political possibilities for queer activism not surprisingly include ever more creative strategies of merging globally circulating ideologies and practices with locally specific conditions and desires for Pride and overcoming the perils of (in)visibility and (il)legibility. My final case study considers a Pride Parade in Changsha, the provincial capital of Hunan, set alongside other public events that took place at the same time across the country, and which were reported in a wide variety of media platforms.

From Hunan with Love: A Public Pride Parade, 2013

On 17 May 2013, more than one hundred queers and allies gathered in Changsha for a public parade near a scenic university campus, in order to demand equal rights and protest against discrimination. Participants carried rainbow flags, large banners and signs demanding rights and equality. The organizers titled it the 'Mainland China (Changsha) Anti-Discrimination Summer Event' (2013 年夏季大陆长沙同志 反歧视活动).[16] Many commentators within the queer community in China have labelled this an unequivocally successful event, as it happened peacefully and without incident and because it was the first public parade in the country. Both the location and timing of the parade are notable. Changsha is Mao Zedong's birthplace and thus the city is deeply invested with political symbolism. Moreover, alongside the dates associated with Pride and Stonewall, May 17 is gaining global activist significance as the International Day against Homophobia, Biphobia, and Transphobia (IDAHOBIT), celebrated annually in a large number of countries around the world and in China since 2008. While the event itself did not trigger any official interference, police took away four people for questioning later that day. All but one were released after just a few hours, but the main organizer of the Parade, an activist with the Changsha LGBT group 'Hunan with Love', was held for twelve days before the police finally let him go without filing charges.

Interestingly, Changsha Pride took place just as public queer activist events in support of IDAHOBIT happened in several other Chinese cities on the very same day. In Chengdu, capital of southwestern Sichuan province, members of local queer groups LES Chengdu and Tongle Chengdu organized a flash mob dance stunt to American pop singer Kelly Clarkson's song 'Stronger' outside a Starbucks coffee shop in a downtown shopping mall. In the southern city of Guangzhou, local activists

---

16. The Changsha event was a feature of a Queer Comrades webisode in June 2013 titled 'Changsha LGBT Pride Takes Place, Organizer Detained'. I draw mainly on information presented here in my discussion. The webcast is available from http://www.queercomrades.com/en/news/china/长沙同志反歧视活动/ (last accessed 10 June 2014).

handed out homemade IDAHOBIT fliers to passers-by outside a busy shopping mall. Police approached them, took some of the activists away for questioning, and released them later that day. According to published reports, the police's main concern was the act of distributing fliers without a proper permit, not the fliers' contents as such. And in the capital city Beijing, renowned queer film maker and activist Popo Fan, wearing a t-shirt saying 'We want to see gay movies', demanded that the State Press and Publication Administration of Radio, Film, and Television overturn the ban on queer topics (alongside 'pornographic and vulgar' topics) and called for transparency in their review processes. Finally, this remarkable day began with an unusal post on *Weibo*, a popular micro-blogging service similar to Twitter, advocating the worldwide celebration of IDAHOBIT and promoting respect for sexual minorities (Li 2013). In fact, this post was made by the China Central Television (*Yangshi Xinwen*), which is the Communist Party's official mouthpiece. It is the first example of support for sexual minorities to appear on an official government website. It is not clear who posted the announcement and it was deleted quickly, but not before attentive activists saved a screenshot and shared it in online social media. Some hours after the deletion, CCTV published a new post but with heavily modified content, saying simply 'homosexuality is not a mental disease' (Li 2013). This second post, which was undoubtedly official, was also a cause for celebration.

The public Pride events that took place across Chinese cities on this symbolically significant date demonstrate the growing confidence of local and regional queer activists to articulate their needs and show their existence in general public space. In particular, Changsha Pride Parade turned a corner in activist appropriation of public space. Yet by holding the Parade on the scenic riverside streets in Changsha's university area, the organizers demonstrated a sensitivity to their appropriation of 'public space' that probably allowed the event to take place without being shut down. Had they attempted a Parade at the public square downtown, the outcome would likely be different and less positive. The main organizer in Changsha later said that their Pride Parade that day was worth the twelve days in detainment and he would risk it again. Taken together, the diversity of this day's events in their appropriations of urban public space – including the use of compelling global LGBT rights symbolism, all the while demonstrating their keen awareness of local political constraints, and playing queerly with the grey area of holding unauthorized events and public visibility – show the contingent politics and practices of queer activism across China today.

The Contingencies of China's Queer Grassroots Activism

The three snapshots of grassroots organizing that I have discussed in this chapter make clear that the modes of organizing and ideologies of activism are becoming increasingly diverse, inspired as they are by regionally and globally circulating discourses and practices regarding sexual rights and diversity cultures. Moreover, it is important to note that this form of activism – mobile, transformative, multilingual and based on a multi-media platform – feeds off the almost unlimited speed and reach of new media technologies. This sense of 'time-space compression', to use David Harvey's famous notion, engenders possibilities of connection, identification and inspiration for those traditionally disenfranchised by hegemonic national structures, especially in non-democratic locations like China (Harvey 2009). At the same time, the discussion also shows that the structural constraints that shape and, ultimately, limit activist visibility remain dominant, and local and regional activists show tremendous creativity and strength in continuously adapting to, and (usually) staying a step ahead of censorship and closure. Therefore, experimenting with alternative and shifting notions such as the 'public', 'Pride', and alternative forms of 'activism' is critical to China's queer movement and its future.

Queer community events in China, then – whether they are categorically out in public or they take place in semi-private space such as community centres or online micro-blogs – do important work of intervening and interrupting dominant cultural and political representations of sexual and gender minorities as morally deviant, mentally ill and infected (as carriers of HIV). On a local level, these events help to push queer voices up from the underground and into the social consciousness of those taking part in queer communities, in other activisms directed at other kinds of minority life in the country, and sometimes into mainstream society.

Accounts of such activist strategies – as they, too, travel transnationally in the mainstream media as well as via digital media channels such as Queer Comrades webcasts (see Chapter 2) – challenge dominant versions of gender and sexuality theory and queer politics more broadly.

Several chapters in the volume document this well, such as those by Popo Fan, Stijn Deklerck and Jiangang Wei, Ana Huang, and certainly the interview with Cui Zi'en. Queer theorist Petrus Liu has insightfully shown how Anglo-American queer theory typically sees China as a relevant concern 'only as the producer of differences from Western queer theory' (Liu 2010: 297; see also this volume's Introduction). The referent of Chinese specificity, Liu suggests, often has the effect of establishing China as existing in the past and lagging behind in progressive queer development. Alternatively, he offers, China is placed as exceptional and unique, and therefore categorically outside of (and hence irrelevant to) queer theory proper. A 'Queer China' focus, Liu proposes, adds local knowledge to the existing body of transnational queer studies and academic-activist politics; not only that, but as the chapters of this volume testify, a 'queer China' perspective' complicates simplistic theories and politics of queer pride and liberation more generally. In turn, the emergent catalogue of queer activist world-making – the fractions, instances, ad hoc organizing alongside digital archiving and storytelling of transnational reach – are likely to be better situated to organize meaningfully for justice and equality in lasting ways.

It remains true that, due to the political situation in China, queer public participation remains dependent on assimilationist strategies, at least on a (sur)face level. Despite the general absence of confrontational political rhetoric, queer modalities of public visibility and participation are decidedly political. As we have seen here, as well as in other chapters in this book, activists use nuanced modes of articulation and develop meaningful ways to further their political agendas while minimizing the risk of censorship and violence. These communicative strategies convey messages of difference and sameness, or of transgression and compliance, depending on the perspectives of the audiences. In this way, they contribute toward creating powerful, and complex, and yet paradoxical discourses of what it means to be Chinese *and* queer, in a comparative, geopolitical perspective.

The examples discussed in this chapter highlight complex intersections in the practice and imagination of queer grassroots activism in China today. Here, I have set out to show how local nuances and variations in the appropriation of Pride rhetoric and visibility strategies as well as creative uses of urban space speak to the importance of what we might call situated visibilities. I would thus argue that such seemingly inconsequential occurrences as semi-public/semi-private, intra-community and 'preaching to the converted' events are in fact the foundation for creating a lasting community; they also foster aspirations for future collective events in public that blur the public/private distinctions more directly, for example a festival like Shanghai Pride. In China, the fact remains that social stigma, violence and exclusion are the norm for sexual and gender minorities: no formal legal protection exists, heterofamilial norms dominate, public awareness remains at a minimum and independent primary research and literature on this topic remains largely absent. In light of this, and as I have argued elsewhere, the hard work of basic consciousness-raising within the queer population and the mainstream public is ongoing and essential (Engebretsen 2013).

As the snapshots of Stonewall Birthday, Shanghai Pride and Changsha Parade exemplify, it is quite possible to engage in celebration and communication, openly and publicly, without provoking the kinds of confrontation that sometimes accompany direct speech acts and parades in city space. As Rofel writes: 'Government officials' close monitoring of these activities derives from their anxiety about any social movement that might create social instability as well as from their own felt need to uphold the dominant moral order. Since the government has no legal grounds for outlawing gay life, they often cleverly use commercial laws or procedural regulations to harass gay activists' (Rofel 2012: 158). It is in light of this unpredictable reality, and the risks involved for those who seek change, that queer grassroots activists have developed a perceptive repertoire of strategies to best manipulate the terrain of organizational possibilities. However, these 'nomadic' and 'guerrilla' strategies are not simply to be read as necessary responses to local political circumstances, or even as acts of complicity or assimilation that indicate shortcomings of agency, initiative and power. What contemporary queer grassroots activisms in all their diverse manifestations demonstrate, rather, is the nuanced ways in which they challenge rigid models that prescribe how queer justice movements should act in order to incite systemic change toward inclusion, equality, and freedom. Through the conceptual lens of Pride and public visibility, and by discussing three specific events as illustrations, I have sought to highlight these diverse ways of thinking about activist struggles and their sensibilities – they shift our attention to ad hoc commonalities, strategic alliances, and expose the continued challenges posed by hegemonic structures and inequalities at the heart of activist movements.

Author's Note

Earlier versions of this paper were presented at the 4th Sino-Nordic Gender and Women's Studies Conference, Travelling Theories within the Context of Globalisation, Aalborg University (25–27 October 2011); the Queer Theory and/in China workshop at the Nordic Institute of Asian Studies, University of Copenhagen (28 October 2011); the 5th Christina Conference on Gender Studies, Feminist Thought – Politics of Concepts, University of Helsinki (23–25 May 2013). I thank the conference and workshop organizers for their support, especially Cecilia Milwertz, and the session participants and audiences for their feedback. I am grateful to the two anonymous reviewers for helpful feedback, Alanna Cant and Fran Martin for generous comments on earlier drafts, and NIAS Press editors Gerald Jackson and David Stuligross for meticulous copyediting and helpful feedback that significantly improved the argument. Special thanks to Hongwei Bao and Will Schroeder for our enduring collaborative comradeship.

References

Beijing Queer Film Festival Organization Committee (2011) 5th Beijing Queer Film Festival Press Release. First published online 19 June. Accessed at: http://www.bjqff.com/?p=446.

Boellstorff, Tom (2007) 'Queer Studies in the House of Anthropology'. *Annual Review of Anthropology* vol. 36, pp. 17–35.

Cruz-Malavé, Arnaldo and Martin Manalansan IV, eds. (2002) *Queer Globalizations: Citizenship and the afterlife of colonialism.* New York: New York University Press.

Duberman, Martin (1993) *Stonewall.* Boston: Dutton.

Engebretsen, Elisabeth L. (2013) *Queer Women in Urban China: An ethnography.* New York: Routledge.

Harvey, David (1990) *The Condition of Postmodernity: An enquiry into the origins of cultural change.* London: Blackwell.

He Xiaopei (2009) Creating the First Dyke/Gay Bar in Beijing. (First published online 1 December 2009; last accessed 20 May 2013) http://www.pinkspace.com.cn/Art/Show.asp?id=28.

——— (2001) 'Chinese Queer (Tongzhi) Women Organizing in the 1990s', in Ping-chin Hsiung, Maria Jaschok and Cecilia Milwertz (with Red Chan) (eds), *Chinese Women Organizing: Cadres, feminists, Muslims, queers.* pp. 41–59. Oxford: Berg.

Jackson, Peter A. (2009) 'Capitalism and Global Queering: National markets, parallels among sexual cultures, and multiple queer modernities'. *GLQ,* vol. 15, no. 3, pp. 357–395.

Jacobs, Andrew (2009) 'Gay Festival in China Pushes Official Boundaries'. *New York Times,* 14 June. http://www.nytimes.com/2009/06/15/world/asia/15shanghai.html?pagewanted=1&ref=world&_r=0 (accessed online 30 July 2009).

Li, Amy (2013) 'LGBT Activists Detained during Celebrations of International Day against Homophobia'. *South China Morning Post,* 18 May. http://www.scmp.com/news/china/article/1240512/lgbt-activists-detained-during-celebrations-international-day-against (accessed online 21 May 2013).

Liu, Melinda and Duncan Hewitt (2009) 'Pride without a Parade'. *Newsweek.* 12 June. http://www.thedailybeast.com/newsweek/2009/06/12/pride-without-a-parade.html (accessed online 20 June 2009).

Liu, Petrus (2010) 'Why does Queer Theory need China?' *positions: east asia cultures critique.* vol. 18, no. 2, pp. 291–320.

Manalansan, Martin F. (1995) 'In the Shadow of Stonewall: Examining Gay Transnational Politics and the Diasporic Dilemma'. *GLQ,* vol. 2, no. 4, pp. 425–438.

Queer Comrades (Tongzhi yi Fanren 同志亦凡人) (2013) *Changsha LGBT Pride Takes Place, Organizer Detained* [Changsha 5.17 Huodong Chenggong Juxing Zuzhizhe bei Ju 长沙 5。17 活动成功举行，组织者 被拘]. Webcast published 4 June 2013. http://www.queercomrades.com/en/news/china/长沙同志反歧视活动/

Rauhala, Emily (2009) 'Shanghai Pride: China gay pride festival its first ever' *The Huffington Post* (first published by *Global Post*). First published 16 July, 2009. Accessed 20 July 2009. Available at: http://www.huffington-post.com/2009/06/15/shanghai-pride-china-gay_n_215785.html.

Richie, Jason (2010) 'How do You Say 'Come Out of the Closet' in Arabic? Queer activism and the politics of visibility in Israel-Palestine'. *GLQ,* vol. 16, no. 4, pp. 557–575.

Rofel, Lisa (2012) 'Grassroots Activism: Non-normative sexual politics in post-socialist China', in Wanning Sun and Yingjie Guo (eds.), *Unequal China: The political economy and cultural politics of inequality in China*, pp. 154–167. New York: Routledge.

Stella, Francesca (2013) 'Queer Space, Pride, and Shame in Moscow'. *Slavic Review* vol. 72, no. 3, pp. 458–479.

Wan Yanhai (2001) 'Becoming a Gay Activist in Contemporary China', in Gerard Sullivan and Peter A. Jackson (eds.), *Gay and Lesbian Asia: Culture,identity, community*, pp. 47–64. New York: Harrington Park Press.

Wekker, Gloria (2006) *The Politics of Passion: Women's sexual culture in the Afro-Surinamese diaspora*. New York: Columbia University Press.

Wilson, Ara (2006) 'Queering Asia'. *Intersections: Gender, History and Culture in the Asian Context*. Issue 14 (Nov.) http://intersections.anu.edu.au/issue14/wilson.html.

CHAPTER 7

On the Surface
'T' and Transgender Identity in Chinese Lesbian Culture

Ana Huang

The Inconsistent Self-Narrative

Growing up, I have always looked the way I do right now [like a *T*]. The first day I reported for work, the director of the hospital called me to her office. She told me to grow my hair longer. She said I was too individualist, why was my hat crooked? I said, director, this is how berets are supposed to be worn. She wanted me to perm my hair. She said, if I really can't change, that's okay, but she still recommend that I try. So I got a perm, and even wore a cheongsam to work. The director and my coworkers all gave me compliments! It was great.

I've been wearing high heels at work, and I'm getting used to it. But it's not like the director changed me into something new. Most of my life I was like a *T*, but there were a few short years when I had shoulder-length hair too. Her talk embarrassed me, so I recalled those few years, and found that feeling again…

I'm still a pure *T*, that can't change. I can't be touched that way [during sex]. It feels very uncomfortable. I simply can't do it…

Kai, quoted from a group discussion at Beijing Lala Salon.[1]

This rich narrative of a *T* exemplifies the complexity of gender and sexuality in contemporary Chinese *lala* culture.[2] *Lala* (拉拉) is a recently coined Chinese term for queer women. Short for 'tomboy,' *T* represents the more masculine partner in a female same-sex couple, while *P*, short

---

1. Only a selection of the conversation is translated into English here.
2. *Lala* (拉拉) is defined as lesbian, bisexual, and women-loving transgender people by the Chinese *Lala* Alliance. Its inclusivity contracts and expands in popular usage.

for the Chinese term wife (*laopo, 老婆*), indicates the more feminine counterpart. A proliferation of finer distinctions such as versatile *T*, sissy *T*, pure *T*, and iron *T* reveals a diversity of gender practices within each category.[3] *Lala* collective desires, relationships and conversations congeal around *T/P* roles, making up a vibrant queer subculture that demands analysis.

Kai tells her story at a *lala* group discussion on *T/P* matters in Beijing, yet the untouchability Kai insists upon could very well be heard at transgender group discussions anywhere. Indeed, an exploration of *T/P* categories in China must give central attention to the issue of overlap between transgender and lesbian identity. Through an in-depth ethnographic analysis of female masculinity in *lala* culture, this chapter moves to incorporate an analysis of transgender[4] as a part of *lala* subjectivity.

Kai is not the only *T* who refuses to involve her own sexual body parts in sexual activity. Many *T*s hold fast to this practice and some refuse to expose their naked bodies at all. They only take the active role of the penetrator during sex and may wear chest bindings on a daily basis. Mainstream narratives of transgender identity in the United States would recognize these bodily practices as denials of female identity and affirmations of female-to-male (FTM) identity. Pure *T*s who carry out these practices consistently over the long term, along with articulated masculine identification, could qualify as full-fledged transsexuals who can receive gender reassignment surgery under the standards of the medical establishment and transition fully into living as men. It might be tempting at first to suggest that China is full of transgender men who have not yet discovered themselves, but would embrace the transgender identity if it were a more widely available and realistic option. But such a hypothesis is based upon faulty assumptions. It betrays a dependence on the developmental narrative that positions Western identity politics as the goal of advanced civilization; it also assumes the existence of a universal, individual subject buried underneath social entanglements, across cultures.

---

3. In Chinese, versatile is *bufen* (不分), sissy *T* is *niang T* (娘T), pure *T* is *chun T* (纯T), and iron *T* is *tie T* (铁T). *Bufen* is an important role that, for some *lalas*, defies the dominant *T* and *P* binary, but it also resides comfortably among other *T* and *P* categories for many.

4. In popular American use, transgender is an umbrella term used by people whose gender identity differs from the sex they were assigned at birth.

Indeed, some *T*s may embrace the transgender identity if given the choice. But we can also safely predict that many will not. Kai's willingness to present as 'feminine' at work, and later outside of work, is inconsistent with the dominant transsexual narrative. She does not resent the changes as oppressive or involuntary, but attributes her comfort with them to a part of herself, rooted in a different period of her life. Kai's nuanced understanding of her gendered possibilities separates her experience from the widely accepted belief that the FTM is 'a man born into the wrong body'. She does not articulate a consistent transsexual narrative.

Kai's ability to change and 'get used to it' appears to be an illustration of Butler's theory of performativity, which argues that gender is constructed in the body through repetitive, ongoing performances of femininity or masculinity that produce natural feelings, as if the performed gender came from deep within. Butler (1997: 24) rejects the idea that gender is the expression of 'a psychic reality that precedes it.' However, Kai's insistent claim that her refusal to be touched is a permanent feature does not lie comfortably with theories of gender fluidity. To credit her self-narrative as more than false consciousness would imply some core of unchangeable gender that counters much of the deconstructive work that queer and feminist theory tries to do. The flexibility and fluidity of queer theory, as well as the definitive narrative of transsexual identity, does not adequately address the multiple components of Kai's self-narrative. Both modes of understanding involve a tension between her insistence on untouchability and her comfort with high heels. I explore this presumed tension and search for an alternative model of understanding that reflects the coherence of Kai's lived experience.

Expanding the Transgender Imaginary

Gayle Rubin offers the idea of 'partial masculine identification'. She notes, 'Within the group of women labeled butch, there are many individuals who are gender dysphoric to varying degrees. Many butches have partially male gender identities. Others border on being, and some are, female-to-male transsexuals ...' (1992: 468). Rubin recognizes a continuum of masculinities among lesbians and the possibility of transgender identification that resides within rather than exclusive of butch identities. Kai's ability to adopt certain feminine practices but not others could be understood as a position on this continuum.

Rubin's work precedes the more recent work by David Valentine, who calls into question the distinction of gender and sexuality as separate categories in themselves. In *Imagining Transgender: An Ethnography of a Category*, Valentine argues that '"gender" and "sexuality" are not simply universal experiences or categories that are shaped in different ways by different "cultures" but, rather, *that they are themselves transformed as categories* in different contexts.'(2007: 165; emphasis in the original) Tracing the emergence of the transgender category in New York City in the 1990s, he finds that many working-class people of colour whose experiences match perfectly the institutional definition of transgender saw themselves as gay, instead of transgender, or used both terms interchangeably to describe themselves.

Valentine's argument is immensely useful in an analysis of Chinese *lala* culture. It opens up the possibilities of imagining *T* as outside of a transgender/lesbian binary, and imagining *T/P* roles as a melding of both gender and sexuality into one categorization system. Though the category of *lala* is based on a common female biology, it encompasses gender variance in addition to female relationships, a point I will demonstrate with ethnographic data.

Valentine points out the erasure of human experiences that result from the institutionalization of identity. At the end, he calls for activists and ethnographers to 'attend to differences beyond identity categories' and to expand the imagination around transgender (*ibid*: 249–255). Here I present a culturally grounded theory of difference in China. I argue that *T* blurs the distinction between butch and transgender identities and occupies a social position that accommodates both same-sex desire and gender variance. The way in which *T*- and *P*-roles facilitate social interactions in *lala* culture rests upon the Chinese notion of face, or *mianzi* (面子). Prior to addressing face, however, I shall discuss the related concept of surface.

On the Surface

The concept of surface is distinct from the Western notion of the subject as defined by an essential, inner self. While Western theory has long wrestled with the questions of subject formation – whether the self originates from within or without – surface sidesteps the whole interiority/exteriority debate. It enables *T*s to occupy masculine, female-bodied roles in relation to others in their intimate relationships while still negotiating varying stances toward gender reassignment surgery on their bodies.

Surface is not the same as interiorized notions of individual identity, because surface is concerned first and foremost with the relational. Surface is not the antonym of depth, just as the function of face does not depend upon the truth of the flesh and bones underneath. Surface undercuts penetrating inquiries into one's authentic essence. As such, it can be liberating as well as oppressive. One can claim to be a *T* without calling upon identity narratives to buttress the claim. Nevertheless, surface is not antithetical to identity politics: some *T*s do claim that their gender is an essential identity that was evident even in childhood. But such claims operate on a selective, personal basis, and no clear line of legitimacy has been drawn between *T*s who do and do not lay claim to such essentialist narratives. In other words, *lala* culture does not require examinations of internal cavities as a prerequisite for adopting the role of *T*.

Inspired by Valentine's work on the construction of transgender as an identity category in the United States, I study Chinese *lala* subculture through an anthropological lens. I demonstrate through ethnography the incongruence between Chinese *lala* subculture as it is and the American transgender discourse that threatens to flatten the field of possibilities with its claim to universalism. My informants' own articulations suggest that the concept of surface offers a more fitting interpretation of *T* and other gender roles in Chinese *lala* culture.

The Chinese Face

Rosalind Morris's analysis on gender and sexuality in Thailand has striking theoretical parallels to China. She introduces the Thai concept of *kraeng cai*, which denotes the presentation of a social mask in order to pay respect to others. It is based on the importance of *naa*, or face, which has an equivalent in the Chinese term *mianzi* (面子). Morris (1994: 36) explains that 'this masking is not sublimation or repression in the Freudian sense … but is, instead, the proper mode of social interaction. The concept of face reflects a similar valorisation of surfaces.'

Likewise, the important Chinese concept of face demands the enactment of a certain social role in relation to other people, without inquiry into any kind of authentic inner psyche. There is no pretence that one's positive public persona should come about without making an intentional effort to present oneself favourably.

Scholars have argued that in pre-modern Chinese society before Westernization, the self did not exist except in social relations. In *Desiring China*, Lisa Rofel puts forth that China does not have a deeply rooted history of the inner psyche. Writing in a post-Foucauldian age, Rofel argues that though 'the discursive production of the psyche in China proceeded apace throughout the twentieth century... nonetheless China does not have a history of Christian pastoral care or confessional therapy' which centres on an inner self (2007: 101).

Her discussion of the notion of 'face' or *mianzi* closely binds the self to social life (*ibid.*: 101–102). Face is the medium through which one interacts with the social environment and other people contained in it. It is not concerned with the expression of inner depth, but is predominantly invested in external interactions. For *lalas*, face enables a relational understanding of gender roles that recognizes gender difference and allows for role changes, providing a sense of authenticity that does not rely on inner depth. Morris (1994: 37) describes the significance of the separation of public persona from the private self as enabling 'great mobility and fluidity of practice, preserving the rights of individuals to pursue whatever pleasures, desires, or fascinations they choose.' Reality might be less idyllic than she portrays, since the demands of social responsibility can be just as overwhelming as inner turmoils over identity. However, externalized subjectivity does enable a (non-exclusive) way of imagining *T/P* gender roles as a surface quality.[5]

The notion of *mianzi* has been widely written about by Euroamerican scholars, in regard to LGBT populations and in general as well. Casual use of the concept runs the risk of tapping into an essentialism that reduces Chinese culture to a dialectical other,[6] yet the frequency in which *mianzi* has sparked scholarly interest in regard to LGBT studies also indicates that the concept does mark a distinctiveness we must recognize in any discussion of Chinese LGBT identities, against a backdrop of globalizing gay discourse. Most work gives attention to sexual orientation as the identity

---

5. Other scholars have also discussed the notion of surface in China in regard to other topics of analysis. For examples, see Angela Zito, Zito and Barlow, and Fran Martin.

6. Martin, Fran. 2000. "Surface Tensions: Reading Productions of *Tongzhi* in Contemporary Taiwan." *GLQ* 6(1): 61-86.

that affects face. Here I employ the notion of face in regard to gender, and propose that it indicates a fusion between gender and sexuality in practice that is often elided and denied by the vocabulary available to us (i.e. lesbian and transgender), both in English and in its Chinese translations.

I employ surface as a more expansive term than *mianzi*, going beyond the highly visible and richly symbolic features of the human face to include the entire body as a contoured social canvas upon which social interactions take place. *Lalas* do not perceive intersubjective gender roles to be expressive of their inner selves, but rather as useful categories that facilitate ways of relating to others. In this light, I argue that the cultural category of *T* fulfils the social needs of gender variance as well as female partnership for many people, as it melds the ontologically separated realms of gender and sexuality, and in particular transgender and lesbian identity.

T is for Transgender

Keeping in mind Rubin's and Valentine's analyses, I read the category of *T* through a transgender lens, as a first step towards expanding the definition of *T* beyond an exclusively female identity. The category of *T* aligns a predominantly masculine subject with a biologically female body. I first demonstrate that *Ts* have a set of common experiences that closely resemble narratives of transgender identity.

My ethnographic data comes from fieldwork I conducted in Beijing and Shanghai between 2006 and 2008. In addition to interviews with strangers and friends, I engaged in participant observation in the *lala* community and worked closely with many queer Chinese activists.[7] While my own familiarity with American queer culture inevitably informs my research, I strive to refrain from comparative tendencies that might pit China against the West through evolutionary timelines or Eurocentric benchmarks. Instead, I provide thick descriptions of Chinese *lala* culture on its own terms.

In practice, most *Ts* consider themselves *lala* and/or lesbian; few would describe themselves as transgender. This must be contextualized by the fact that currently mainland China does not have a significant community of female-born, transgender-identified people. The average person is not

---

7.   Most of my informants are in their 20s or 30s, and include a range of gender roles. Some informants' names have been changed to ensure their anonymity. I conducted semi-structured interviews with consent for the purpose of writing my thesis.

familiar with the available medical procedures for transitioning, and many hold the belief that medical technology fails to construct an adequate male anatomy. People understand the available Chinese terms of *yixingpi* (异性癖) and *bianxingren* (变性人) to refer strictly to the transsexual person who pursues surgical intervention as well as hormonal therapy. The term *yixingpi*[8] carries pathological associations of perversion and comes closest to the psychiatric term of 'gender dysphoria'. *Kuaxingbie* (跨性别) is a direct translation of the English word 'transgender' that is only recently introduced by a small community of queer activists. The dearth of neutral or expansive vocabulary for transgender in China illustrates a context where medical transition is not perceived as a popular or attractive option, and queer or transgender politics is only marginally known by an elite few with heavy Western contact.

Given this setting, people do not articulate male identification, viewing their own female biology as an unchangeable fact of life. Nevertheless, many *T*s are taken to be boys by passers-by on a daily basis, and some regularly use men's bathrooms. In addition to adopting masculine or androgynous nicknames, *T*s as a whole are also called the husband (*laogong*, 老公) in a relationship, and the *P* partner of an older *T* friend would be *saozi* (嫂子), the Chinese term for an older brother's wife. *T*s express various degrees of the desire to become men, ranging from a fleeting thought about the possibility of marrying their girlfriends, to a childhood longing that has never been quite forgotten.

The most masculine end of the spectrum, where Kai falls, is named pure *T* (纯T) or iron *T* (铁T). This position is associated with chest binding and a rejection of having one's own body touched sexually. Such practices closely mirror the definitive traits of a stone butch in English usage.[9] Many in the *lala* community have watched the Hollywood adaptation of the Brandon Teena story, *Boys Don't Cry*. Despite the film's narrative presentation of the protagonist as transgender-identified,

---

8. *Yixing* literally means "of the other sex." *Pi* means perversion or obsession, with a medical connotation.

9. Interestingly, Leslie Feinberg's classic novel, *Stone Butch Blues,* has been translated into Chinese with "T" in its title (蓝调石墙T). At the same time, the preface to the Chinese edition is titled "The Song of Transgender (跨性别之歌)." Though this is presumably the decision of its translator, Taiwanese queer scholar Josephine Ho (何春蕤), it reflects a fascinating convergence between the two identity categories in the process of translation.

every *lala* who has spoken about this film with me refers to the main character as a *T*, albeit one of the most masculine types of *T*. Their interpretation of Brandon Teena's identity into a Chinese category reflects the expansive capacity of *T* to absorb all sorts of people. It is impossible to tease out the overlaps and differences between *T* and the Western understanding of transgender, as these two terms operate on different planes of subjectivity. The murky waters that we confront when one cultural term is translated into another serve as a reminder that *T* cannot be reduced to either lesbian or transgender.

Names and Business Cards

Surface is the mechanism that enables the merging of transgender and lesbian needs. The category of *T* accommodates both the need for masculine social status and the need for sexual involvement with women, needs which might be identifiers of transgender and lesbian in another place and time. The capacity of the *T* category to provide for this set of social privileges and burdens is the practical manifestation of surface in the way that *lalas* conceive of categories. The *T/P* system defines a range of roles that play different functions in how one relates to partners, friends and the social environment. They are not categories of being, but categories of social practices and ways of relating to others.

In many *lalas'* experience, people do not try to fit into given categories; categories are made to fit with people's realities. *T/P* roles are descriptions of how people already behave. For some, *T/P* categories are tools that facilitate the dynamics of an intimate relationship. My interviewee Ice explains that '*T* represents certain behaviours. If I say I'm a pure *T*, that means don't touch me please. Pure *T*s will not take off their clothes, will not wear dresses, will not be penetrated in sex. Once I've clearly labelled myself a pure *T*, you are aware that I won't do certain things.' People want to inform potential lovers of certain practices they maintain, and having a shared repertoire of *T/P* categories help some people to communicate that message. Xian, a queer Chinese activist, says laughingly, 'Looks like *T/P* is most importantly serving a goal - who do you want to fuck?'

Bebe tells me about a friend's experience, 'Her *T* [girlfriend] used to be really manly. Now the *T* has been transformed by her to be more feminine.' She attributes this change to the natural process of *mohe* (磨合), which always occurs in a new relationship. The Chinese term *mohe* means breaking-in or mutual adaptation, and suggests the polishing of rough surfaces; it literally translates into *mo* (contact involving friction) and *he* (fit or bond). In Bebe's view, the surface role of *T* serves the purpose of facilitating intimate relationships. It follows that adjustments to the role are made at times in order to form more fitting bonds. *T/P* roles reside in the realm of relationality, and the facilitation of social interactions take priority over the expressive mode of identification.

The practice of naming in *lala* culture points to a general recognition of names as functions of social settings. Almost all *lalas* use a chosen name apart from their legal given names, which are rarely mentioned at all within *lala* spaces. *T*s have either androgynous or boy's names, such as Chris and Sam. One informant has different nicknames she uses in school, in the *lala* community, at work, and online. Yet the multiplicity of these names does not produce feelings or appearances of artificiality. Names are specific to social contexts, and people in general recognize the pragmatic nature of names as markers of various social positions instead of representations of a single self. Thus, names are treated lightly as the surface of a person, and seriously as the media through which one interacts.

To explain the widespread deployment of *T/P* categories outside of romantic and erotic situations, Pan offers an illustrative analogy: 'Some people need *T/P* as a business card to give to others, to help them make friends and to draw lines around [their] social circle.' Sam offers a nuanced observation on the community's use of *T/P* categories:

> Say we have a party today, and someone you're meeting for the first time asks are you a *T* or a *P*? She [might] not mean that you have to meet traditional templates. We just want to get to know, through this, whether or not you are a bit more boyish, or if you are more in line with traditional women. To know the most *surface* and most general things about you, it doesn't represent everything about you. It's like getting to know what horoscope you are ... It's not complete, it's also not the *deepest* [emphases mine].

Sam points out that *T/P* roles function in the culture as matters of surface, allowing for the possibility of someone having a sense of deep self while not devaluing the functionality of the surface. The meaning of *T/P* is produced in social contact and takes more elaborate shapes under the active reading practice of others.

Behind widespread use of *T/P* categories lay both serious and light attitudes towards their use. These categories are acknowledged as more useful to some people than to others. Xian appreciates the flexibility of its use: 'The definition of *T/P* isn't a definition about essence or nature. It's a tool. It's a game. If you want it, you can play it... But it won't limit your essence itself. If it's just a business card, then you can change this business card as you wish. You can use different cards for different settings.' This statement concisely echoes the point that *T/P* categories are surface-oriented tools used to facilitate relationality, without laying claims to any truth (or falsehood) regarding gender identity.

Three Ways to Live

Though most Chinese people have limited familiarity with transsexuality and gender reassignment surgery, three of my interviewees did explicitly align themselves with it, each in a different way. Quentin is saving up money for surgery, rejects the *lala* label and emphasizes the distinction between himself and *T*s, whom he perceives to be still women and therefore feminine.[10] His attitude is rare in the *lala* community. I first made contact with Quentin through mutual *lala* friends, who were aware that he thought of himself as a man but introduced him as a *T* anyway. To them, living and thinking of oneself as a man are simply descriptions that can be applied to many *T*s. Though Quentin himself defined his maleness through negation of *lala* subjectivity, others saw the two as compatible.

Henry also wants surgery at some point.[11] Though he stated at the start of our formal interview that he is not actually a *T*, but a transsexual, he shares an apartment with several *lala*s and has a giant letter '*T*' painted next to his door with an arrow pointing inside, which he obviously did not mind. Henry articulates a distinction between himself and *T*s during the interviews, but does not invest as much as Quentin in that border. He socializes with other *lala*s and finds that the *T* category is a liveable one for him, though he articulates that, technically, he is not a lesbian.

10. The third-person pronoun in Chinese is conveniently gender-ambiguous in its homophonous pronunciation of ta (她/他). It is impossible to determine which gender pronouns each of my interviewees would prefer to use in English translation. Therefore, my strategy is to detach the significance of gendered pronouns from internal identification, and openly use them as external readings of someone's social gender. English pronoun usage represents my own attribution.

11. I discuss surgery rather than hormonal therapy, because both top and bottom surgery are required for legal transitions in China, and testosterone therapy is often administered post-operative. Most people imagine surgery as the definitive act of sex change.

A more typical example of *T*s, Joe fully embraces the labels of *lala* and *T*. At the same time, he thinks of himself as 'a little bit *yixingpi*.' Joe describes partial transgender feelings as a quantifiable trait, which is very much included within *T*-dom. Joe says, 'You can't choose your biological sex, but you can choose what gender you are in your heart/mind. I always thought of myself as a boy ever since I was little ... I hate being called feminine titles like "sister".'

Others treat Joe as a non-feminine person as well. Joe's girlfriend Bebe comments that 'sometimes Joe plays around and puts my bras on. It looks strange to me too, like a *renyao* (人妖, male-to-female transvestite).' When I asked who would give birth if they had kids, Bebe laughs again at the ridiculous idea of Joe pregnant. Joe's younger sister calls him *gege* (哥哥, older brother), except for when she uses *jiejie* (姐姐, older sister) in the presence of their mother.

Joe spoke of another friend who is 'the purest kind of *T* I've seen, extremely *yixingpi*. With their girlfriend, they're basically like how a guy is with a girl.' Using *yixingpi* as an adjective rather than a noun, Joe imagines that others are closer to the most masculine end of the spectrum. He sees a lesser quantity of transsexuality in himself, since the 'pure *T*' apparently behaves in thoroughly masculine way in relation to his girlfriends, while Joe cries and 'whines like a baby' in front of Bebe from time to time. Instead of discrete identities, most people, like Henry and Joe, perceive a range of masculinities, upon which transsexuality is not an all-or-nothing identity, but can be a quantity or a grammatical modifier.[12] The *T* category demonstrates the capacity to include diverse gender and sexual practices within its ambiguous borders.

Relationality and Surgery

The mainstream transsexual narrative explains bodily modification as the need to align the physical body with an unchangeable inner psychic

---

12. Continuums of identity have been critiqued for their failures to allow fluidity and flexibility. Addressing the conflicts between FTMs and butches in so-called border wars, Judith Halberstam argues against the continuum of masculinity that marks a rupture between stone butch and transgender butch and places FTM at the end, because it makes the faulty assumption that "the greater the gender dysphoria the likelier a transsexual identification.' Likewise, transsexual identification, or not, does not correlate directly to the degree of masculinity in *lala* culture.

reality. It is a self-driven project. But surgery cannot be extricated from the social reality for Chinese *lalas*. The gendered body acquires its meaning through surface interactions. Bodily desires do not exist in a vacuum; they are not a priori. Many people discuss their desire for gender reassignment surgery through highly practical evaluations of the social benefits and costs. Generally speaking, going to great lengths to maintain one's face, or *mianzi*, does not imply a sense of falsehood or repression in their experience. Likewise, *lalas* do not associate such surface-oriented considerations regarding surgery with negative connotations, but present their motivations and calculations as a matter of course.

For example, Joe embraced the *T* category and did not want to pursue surgical transition:

> Joe: Because that thing men have, [penis], is disgusting.
> Bebe: That's weird, you told me you wanted to do it before.
> Joe: That was for a period of time. Later on I thought about all the problems you'd face if you did do it, like your family won't accept it, other people….

Joe's practical analysis of the situation found that negative social consequences outweighed whatever motivations he had for pursuing a bodily transition. He does not seem to resent his present situation as being in an unfulfilled and inauthentic state of being, but lives rather comfortably in the role of *T* and actively participates in the *lala* community, contributing to a *lala* magazine. The category of *T* can accommodate his social needs without requiring him to choose between lesbian and transgender identity. It provides for both masculine gender and desire for women. Defined by function instead of self-expression, the category of *T* indicates someone with a masculine social position, which includes having relationships with relatively more feminine women. Since most strangers already read him as male, albeit a young one, surgery would have little effect on Joe's social privileges and responsibilities.

Danny has a similar experience to Joe, even though Danny does not describe himself as *yixingpi*:

> Some want surgery, but I find it scary. Hormones have a lot of negative side effects. I thought about it in elementary school, when I read about someone in a newspaper. I said, I want to do it too. Later I found out it was too expensive, surgery was 30,000 RMB. Then, I felt like, well, it

doesn't actually matter. Now I feel okay, there's no need to change that thoroughly. After you change sex, societal pressure would be hundreds of times greater than how it is now. People will think, oh, like those male transvestites they have in Thailand.[13] That's pretty scary.

Danny's reasoning is strikingly similar to Joe's, emphasizing practical obstacles to medical transition. To clarify, I asked Danny, 'What if you can transition just by saying so, with no effort at all?' He responds, 'Oh sure, I'll do it.' However, given the social reality, Danny has come to terms with his way of being in the world, feeling 'no need' for a male body, because a biological change will not 'actually matter' for the way he functions in the *lala* world. For many *Ts*, the social desire to be treated as the 'husband' in a relationship doesn't entail the bodily desire to pee standing up. In fact, biological transition might worsen Danny's situation, because he perceives much more societal prejudice against transsexuality than homosexuality. The relatively tolerant societal atmosphere towards masculinity in girls and young women in China means that the category of *T* offers the most essential accommodations at a lower premium. Thus, it is a welcoming category.

When *T/P* categories are defined according to what people *do* in social interactions rather than what people *are*, gender shifts from the individual body to the social realm. The demands of Kai's new job did not amount to a conflict with an authentic interior. The change to feminine clothing was not an external intrusion on the masculine internal self, since Kai denies that the hospital director 'changed me into something new.' The social situation asked for a particular mode of interaction from Kai, who cooperated and felt great satisfaction from the praise of her boss and co-workers in return. But the mode of interaction Kai desired in sexual situations was not affected by her feminine public appearance. Willingness to wear high heels does not disqualify someone from enacting the masculine *T* position in the intimate setting. The pure *T* role did not demand to know the topography of Kai's femininity or masculinity underneath, and we still cannot speak to this interior world definitively. With the primacy of surface, a uniform type of interiority is not necessary for anyone's inclusion in a certain category. Different sets

---

13. The original term used here, *renyao* (人妖) loosely translates into male transvestite. It is a derogatory term that conjures up impressions of male-to-female transgender performers for tourists in Thailand.

of gender practices operate like various business cards that Kai presents in corresponding settings, according to the type of social relationship that is desired in each interaction. Putting on feminine clothing, refusing to be touched during sex, using a boy's nickname and choosing surgery (or not) are all part of putting on a particular *mianzi*, or face.

Beyond the Problem of Interiority/Exteriority

The mainstream transsexual narrative of an innate, psychic gender that mismatches one's body presumes the interiority and exteriority distinction and valorises the former, calling for consistency between the two as the most desirable. Such a one-dimensional approach to gender and sexuality has been subject to much academic critique. David Valentine (2007: 246) points out that the organization of gender and sexuality is rooted in 'a longer history of the disaggregation and reintegration of the self in modernity', which is also evident in 'the growth of psychiatric diagnostic categories, the assertion of "identity" as a central paradigm in politics, and the elaboration of niche markets for consumption.' His point resounds with Foucault's work (1990) on the emergence of the homosexual in modernity, as a product of the taxonomic drive in 19th century Europe that attempted to categorize people into myriad species.

Western social theorists no longer hold onto the notion of the asocial, individualized subject, and anthropologists continue to demonstrate the social embeddedness of all subjects. Yet the terse relationship between the self and the social remains a site of ongoing debate and re-definition. Striving to move beyond this dilemma, Butler (2006: 65–80) writes that 'gender is to be found neither inside nor outside', since 'a self is precisely that perpetual problem with boundedness that is resolved, or not, in various ways and in response to an array of demands and challenges.' Not only does she reject the 'expressive fallacy'; Butler also repudiates the idea that cultural norms 'surround this bounded being and then find their way inside through various mechanisms of incorporation or internalization.'

Valentine, Butler and many others have performed the critical task of deconstruction, but much scholarship remains entrenched in efforts to point out what the self is not. Such approaches are still intimately connected to the ontological framework that presumes an interior/exterior distinction, with the self located somewhere along this mapping. Even when scholars conclude that gender and sexuality cannot be found in either location alone, the epistemological framework continues to be shaped by a philosophical heritage that places the essentialized self at centre stage. In full admission, my own initial interest in this project also reflects a fascination with the interiority/exteriority debate, but my informants' articulate insistence on the functional value of gender roles made me realize the limitations that result from this epistemological obsession with ontology, of which I am guilty.

T/P culture does not invest heavily in the matter of origins. The concept of surface enables us to ask a different set of questions, questions that emphasize desiring production in the Deleuzian sense. Instead of trying to determine whether *T*s are really transgender men or butch lesbians, we might imagine *T* as its own category. Rather than placing *T*s along a continuum of masculinity according to the truth of their gender selves, we might ask which masculine/feminine social roles are practised and desired by a subject across different social contexts. We might also set our inquisitive gaze upon the lubricating functions, as well as frictions, that are produced by *T* and *P* roles, thus moving beyond an obsessive quest for origins and definitions.

While surface might not be a universal constant, it is a more relevant ethnographic interpretation of the Chinese *lala* experience. Surface is not simply a unique Chinese cultural tradition. It is a particular mode of relationality, an enactment of meaningful roles within an understood social context. By linking *T* with queer and transgender scholarship, we shift China out of the theoretical ghetto, taking a step towards de-centring the Western dominance in queer studies. *T* isn't just an exotic oriental phenomenon that serves as the anthropological Other to a faulty model of lesbian and transgender identity politics. Attentiveness to the implications that *T* has for gender and sexuality studies might help inject new ways of imagining into transgender scholarship, in the trajectory called for by Valentine.

The Politics of Surface

In much of China scholarship, face, or *mianzi,* is examined for its heteronormative function in the instance of saving face, particularly when gay and lesbian subjects obscure their sexuality in the public presence. Here I am interested in something else, in the way that face reaches across all social interactions, facilitating gender and sexual practices within the *lala* community, where there is no need to hide. It is common to blame the notion of face as the uniquely Chinese cultural culprit responsible for heteronormative tragedies, but face is not inherently oppressive, just as the social is not inherently oppressive. Without romanticizing the Chinese notion of surface, I recognize that the homophobic or oppressive applications of face have already been treated in depth by scholars elsewhere.[14]

In the activist project against heternormativity, we should realize that the social, or the relational, is not the enemy and individualism is not the antidote to a heterosexual, patriarchal system. Though the mainstream public demands a potentially uncomfortable presentation of face from queer subjects, we might find relief and empowerment in the social faces available for our use within *lala* subculture. As a counterpublic, *lala* culture offers alternative types of relationality that may provide soothing effects for marginalized people. Specifically, *T*s might encounter the uncomfortable frictions produced in surface interactions with a mainstream public that insists upon their femininity. Their potential responses to such friction might include intensified conflict with the public, disengagement or withdrawal from the social altogether, or living at ease in the *lala* community in accordance to one's preferred masculine, female-bodied position. The self is never fully alone, always bounded up with and constituted by the social. Surfaces are omnipresent. Queer genders and sexualities require lubricated social surfaces to survive and flourish, and *lala* culture is one of the most likely sites for the production of such surfaces. *T/P* roles reside on the surface, where gender and sexuality overlap and flow into each other.

Future Developments

I write against a context of globalization and cultural imperialism, where LGBT identity politics as practiced in the United States are actively imported by and distributed in the Chinese queer community. Often well-intentioned Chinese activists, in an effort to be inclusive of diverse genders and sexualities, have set out an empty seat at the table for the 'T' in 'LGBT', waiting for transgender-identified representatives to fill the chair. In the years that I've been involved in Chinese queer activism,

---

14. See Andrew Kipnis, Jen-peng Liu and Naifei Ding.

it has been ironically difficult to find trans-identified men to step up. In the strange temporal space of cosmopolitan China, LGBT politics that might have developed in response to existing community needs is actually being played back in reverse, with the name plate circulated before the transgender subject himself is fully formed.

Just as Rofel (2007: 102) carefully avoided setting up an antinomy between surface and depth, I do not deny the validity or even the necessity of transgender identification for some people in China. Indeed, an exclusive transgender identity should be among the social positions available in China. Some people have already undergone medical transition without any publicity. Most notably, a *lala* organization in Shandong Province has witnessed several members change their identification from *T* to transgender, upon learning of the definition of transgender. One transgender-identified FtM in particular stars in the 2012 documentary film *Brothers*, though his intersex condition was later discovered during a medical examination.

However, I do question the disproportionate weight being placed on the conscious creation of the transgender category by well-intentioned Chinese *lala* activists, in accordance with international LGBT standards.[15] Recognizing the expansive surface functions of the role of *T* is also an urgent task for Chinese *lala* activism, so that we do not bury *T* alive with a restrictive notion of 'lesbian' female identity in the process of raising transgender awareness. In recent years, the rigidity of *T/P* roles has been criticized within the *lala* community and many now practice gender roles with increased creativity and flexibility. At the same time, many *lalas* in the broader community increasingly voice an insistence on the purity of their lesbianism: 'I am just a woman who loves women.' This widespread claim to superiority is often infused with negative implications for pure *T*s like Kai, whose masculine identification is seen as a misguided attempt to imitate men.

As Chinese *lala* culture becomes more structured and increasingly informed by the West, it runs the risk of misrecognizing itself. The normative Western discourse of equality-based same-sex identity threatens

---

15. My argument is limited to FtMs, since MtFs are an entirely different story to which my analysis of *T* does not apply. With less cultural tolerance for femininity in men in China, male-bodied people passing as women do not occupy as significant of a place within gay male culture as *T*s do in *lala* culture.

to erase the ongoing, local practices of gender variance within the existing *lala* community. It is impossible to predict how *T*s throughout China would interact with an emerging transgender identity, or whether border wars will occur in the process. What we can say is that the globalization of transgender identity will be filtered through the strategic presentation of queer activists and the creative adaptation of *lala* subculture.

Thus, I argue that we should not eject *T*s from the *lala* category and push them into the transgender box. To date, surface is a mechanism that allows the role of *T* to occupy an ambiguous social position between the sexuality and gender binary, but its effectiveness and social currency will only last as long as we allow it.

References

Butler, Judith (1988) 'Performative Acts and Gender Constitution: An essay in phenomenology and feminist theory'. *Theatre Journal*, vol. 40, no. 4, pp. 519–531.

——— (1997) 'Imitation and Gender Subordination.' In Linda Nicholson (ed.), *The Second Wave: A reader in feminist theory*. New York & London: Routledge.

——— (2013) 'Transgender and the Spirit of the Revolt'. In Catherine Lord and Richard Meyer (eds.), *Art & Queer Culture*. London: Phaidon Press Limited.

Foucault, Michel (1990) *The History of Sexuality, Vol. 1: An Introduction*, trans. Robert Hurley. New York: Vintage Books.

Halberstam, Judith (1998) 'Transgender Butch: Butch/FTM border wars and the masculine continuum.' *GLQ: A journal of lesbian and gay studies*, vol. 4, no. 2, pp. 287–310.

He, Chun-rui 何春蕤. (2005) 'Kua xingbie zhi ge: 'Landiao Shiqiang *T*' xu 跨性別之歌：『蓝调石墙T』序 [Song of transgender: preface to *Stone Butch Blues*].' http://www.lalabar.com/news/ReadNews. asp?NewsID=286. Retrieved October 2, 2008

Kipnis, Andrew (1995) '"Face": An Adaptable Discourse of Social Surfaces.' *Positions,* vol. 3, no. 1, pp. 119–48.

Liu, Jen-peng, and Naifei Ding (2005) 'Reticent Poetics, Queer Politics.' *Inter-Asia Cultural Studies,* vol. 6, no. 1, pp. 30–55.

Martin, Fran (2000) 'Surface Tensions: Reading productions of *tongzhi* in contemporary Taiwan.' *GLQ: A journal of lesbian and gay studies,* vol. 6, no. 1, pp. 61–86.

Morris, Rosalind (1994) 'Three Sexes and Four Sexualities: Redressing the discourses on gender and sexuality in contemporary Thailand.' *Social Positions,* vol. 2, no. 1, pp. 15–43.

Rofel, Lisa (2007) *Desiring China: Experiments in neoliberalism, sexuality, and public culture.* Durham: Duke University Press.

Rubin, Gayle (1992) 'Of Catamites and Kings: Reflections on butch, gender, and boundaries'. In Joan Nestle (ed.), *The Persistent Desire.* Boston: Alyson Publications.

Valentine, David (2007) *Imagining Transgender: An ethnography of a category.* Durham: Duke University Press.

Zito, Angela (1997) *Of Body and Brush: Grand sacrifices as text/performance in eighteenth-century China.* Chicago: Chicago University Press.

Zito, Angela and Tani Barlow (1994) *Body, Subject and Power in China.* Chicago: Chicago University Press.

CHAPTER 8

Queer Texts, Gendered Imagination, and Grassroots Feminism in Chinese Web Literature

Ling Yang and Yanrui Xu

In mainland China (hereafter China), the term 'web literature' (*wangluo wenxue* 网络文学) generally refers to original works of more or less literary merit, mainly serialized novels, that have been published, circulated and read online for commercial or non-commercial purposes since the Internet infrastructure emerged in China in 1994. Unlike electronic literature or hypertext, which has much in common with poststructuralist literary and critical theory (Landow 1994: 1), Chinese web fiction is more directly related to *zhanghui xiaoshuo* (章回小说), a traditional type of Chinese chaptered novel, written in the vernacular with each chapter headed by a couplet hinting at the gist of its content. Since Chinese web writers by and large use the Internet as a publishing medium, not as a creative medium, there is no strict boundary between web literature and print literature; most works initially published on the Internet could easily be reproduced in print. However, hypertextual features are not absent from Chinese web literature. As researchers (Feng 2009, 2013; Zhao 2011) have pointed out, the interaction between writers and readers is much stronger in web literature than in print literature as readers and writers can exchange ideas and comments on the webpages where the works are posted, and many online writings reflect the constant negotiation between readers' expectations and authorial intentions.

Statistics released by China Internet Network Information Center (2014: 36) show that readers of web literature surged to 274 million in 2013, which accounts for 44.4 per cent of Internet users in China. Bolstered by such an enormous market, web literature has evolved from what Michel Hockx's (2004: 691) described as 'only mildly innovative' into a veritable laboratory for experimentation on new genres and subject matters, a training school for amateur writers, a testing ground for the popularity of new works, and an indispensable marketplace for multi-million bestsellers in the book industry. More importantly, cyber-space has become a critical and contesting site, where competing ideas of sex, gender and sexuality can be fully fleshed out. Web literature not only creates taste cultures that highly value 'grassroots participation' and 'light entertainment', as Alexander Lugg (2011: 134) has observed, but first and foremost produces complex re-imaginations of gender relations that could simultaneously confirm and challenge traditional gender norms. For instance, the phenomenal growth of web literature has enabled website specialization, which magnifies the salience of genre preferences and gender gaps. Some literature websites such as Jinjiang Literature City (晋江文学城, 2003–), commonly called Jinjiang, and Hongxiu Tianxiang (红袖添香, 1999–) have particularly appealed to female readers and writers. The former is renowned for its homosexual 'Boys' Love' novels, while the latter attracts readers who are interested in heterosexual romance. Qidian (起点, 2002–), the largest literary website in China, is filled with male-preferred historical, military and fantasy novels, some of which have earned the nickname of 'stud fiction' (*zhongma wen* 种马文), as they tend to portray a charismatic and powerful male protagonist with numerous sexual conquests. Although Qidian established a 'girls' channel', an affiliated website for female writers and readers in 2005, Jinjiang remains the largest women's literature website in China.

Harriet Evans (2008) has asserted that, despite the pluralization of sexual culture and the increasing prominence of 'alternative' sexualities in 'postmillennial consumerist' China, public discourse of sex and sexuality consistently frames them as personal acts and choices, rarely linking them to the broader issues of gender relationships and social power. It is therefore still difficult for young Chinese women to find 'a language to articulate their changing gendered subjectivities in a discursive environment that endlessly repeats the conventional descriptors of gender difference' (p. 375).

This chapter, by contrast, offers a more optimistic view of the evolution of gender norms in contemporary China by taking a look at three genres of web literature that have been favoured by female writers and readers, namely, Boys' Love, Body Change and Superior Women. Mostly produced and consumed by a young generation of Chinese women born in the 1980s and 1990s, these genres constitute a 'spectrum of gender bending' (Feng 2009: 18) that boldly and playfully subverts gender stereotypes and the heterosexual regime. To understand the significance of this spectrum, we trace the origins and developments of the three genres, examine the textual and sexual politics of representative texts from each genre, and discuss the ensuing controversies and their implications. We argue that the low threshold of online publishing and the relative freedom of cyberspace combine to provide a unique opportunity for young Chinese women to express their desires and aspirations in a supportive community, without worrying about being censored and censured by the male-dominated official literary circle. Through online literary activities, Chinese women are collectively forging a new language and narrative that imagines more egalitarian gender relations, more fluid gender roles, more diverse sexualities and more social power for women. The grassroots feminist sentiments articulated in women's online writings, intentionally or not, pose serious challenges to the widely held ideal' of 'harmony between the two sexes' advocated by some academic feminists in China and the 'pervasive heterosexual assumption' (Butler 1999: viii) behind this ideal.

Boys' Love: Beyond Womanhood

Originating from Japan, Boys' Love, frequently abbreviated as 'BL', is a genre about male–male romance that is produced and consumed primarily by women. It was first introduced to China in early 1990s under the name *danmei* (耽美), literally meaning 'indulging in or addicted to beauty'. After more than a decade of rapid expansion, BL has turned from a secret topic discussed in small, closed, online communities into a major web genre and a massive Internet-based subculture. Although it is difficult to estimate the number of Chinese BL fans, judging from the millions of hits received by hot BL novels at Jinjiang, the fandom is obviously huge and stable. The development of BL fiction in China can be divided into two stages: early non-commercial offerings in small online fan communities and recent commercial works posted on large literature websites. Early generations of BL writers were usually fans who wrote out of interest and posted their works for free on fan-managed 'bulletin boards' or websites. While some writers did attempt to get published in Taiwan, their main purpose was to preserve their works in print, rather than to make money; it has been very difficult, if not completely impossible, for BL novels to be published or distributed legally on the mainland. Heavily influenced by Japanese BL novels and *manga* (graphic novels), early BL fiction generally highlights the transgressiveness of same-sex love and conveys a strong sense of grief and desolation. It was often deemed as a spin-off of the traditional heterosexual romance, dubbed 'BG' (Boy and Girl) by BL fans. Unlike BG, however, sex in BL is usually more direct and intense; BL characters also tend to be more active in public affairs.

Most of the early writers who joined the BL community around the year 2000 have given up writing due to job, marriage, pregnancy, loss of interest, or other pressures but many of them continue to be loyal readers. Feng Nong (风弄), currently the most influential BL writer in China, is probably the only one who remains active. She is known for her portrayal of stubborn and devoted lovers. Her very first novel, *Xueye (Bloody Night)*,[1] features the love between a domineering king and a delicate but tough spirited young boy. The king first rapes the boy and holds him in captivity because of his extraordinary beauty. Later, when the king gets to know more about the boy, he is deeply attracted by the boy's inner qualities. Sensing the true love from the king, the boy also changes his attitude from abhorrence to acceptance. The theme of forcible love and the pairing of an overbearing but passionate *seme* (attacker, top 攻) with a kind, innocent *uke* (receiver, bottom 受) recurs in Feng Nong's later works and is given more reasonable explanation as to why the *seme* has to act domineeringly. In those works, the *seme*'s overbearing manner is no longer a simple display of power, but a defiant gesture against social conventions so that he can pursue his forbidden

---

1. *Xueye* was written and serialized between 2000–2001. It was first published on a Taiwanese BL website, and later reposted at Lucifer Club (1999–), the then leading online BL fan community in China. A high recommendation from the club administrator increased its visibility.

love of the *uke*. Moved by the passion of the *seme*, the *uke* also decides to stand by him and the two men fight against societal pressures together.

With the growth of readership and the commercialization of the genre at Jinjiang since 2008, BL fiction has undergone a significant change. Since their income is based on a chapter's length and the number of hits, writers have good reason to cater to the taste of mainstream readers and stretch their works as much as possible by incorporating themes, styles and characters from other popular genres. As a result, recent BL fiction has shifted its focus from the 'feminine' themes of love and passion to the more 'masculine' themes of war, aliens, zombies, robot fighters and sports. For example, Zhang Dingding (张鼎鼎), an author with 13,000 fans at Jinjiang, specializes in the sports theme. Rather than depicting romantic love at length, her novels feature long and colourful depictions of sports training and matches. Regarded as the quintessential expression of masculinity, those themes had been assumed to belong exclusively to the men's sphere. Women were believed to be uninterested or even alienated by those subjects and would presumably lose their femininity if they attempted to poach on men's territory. At a time when heterosexual romance on the mainland Chinese Internet is still obsessed with women's rivalries in the imperial harem and feudal families, BL fiction displays a wider range of social concerns and a more vivid imagination. All subjects are 'fair game' for BL appropriation and can be harnessed to the purposes and interests of the BL readership. In this sense, BL provides not only a queer narrative framework of male–male relationship, but a revolutionary 'mental tool' that helps women imagine alternative gender relations, explore new self-identities and consider strategies for re-inventing the big wide world outside the prison-house of patriarchal gender roles (Xu and Yang 2013).

Chinese scholars offer a variety of reasons to account for the immense popularity of BL in China (see for example, Yang 2006; Ruan 2008; Zheng and Wu 2009; Du and Ren 2010; Song and Wang 2011; Wu 2011). The first reason is the egalitarian appeal of BL narratives. Although there is a distinction between the aggressive *seme* and the passive *uke* in the relationship, the two men are fundamentally equal, as the *uke* is neither secondary to nor dependent on the *seme*. For instance, in the story of *Xueye* mentioned above, the *uke* boy refuses to be the sex slave of the *seme* king and manages to run away from his captor. After years of martial arts training, he transforms himself into the powerful leader of a military uprising. It is only after the *uke* boy could rival the king in status and power that he finally makes peace with the king and accepts his love. Besides, those roles are by no means fixed; well-written BL stories would always make sure to give the *seme* and the *uke* a chance to switch their positions. In his study of Japanese BL, Mark McLelland (2006–2007) also notes that 'in Confucian Japan, women's sexuality has long been tied up with reproduction and the family system and this has made it difficult to represent women romantically involved with men as their partners and equals'. Hence, one Japanese woman who is a BL fan has asserted, 'Images of male homosexuality are the only picture we have of men loving someone as an equal, it's the kind of love we want to have' (*ibid.*).

Secondly, many female readers are tired of women being presented as passive sex objects in traditional male-dominated literature. They are drawn to BL because it is loaded with graphic descriptions of the beautiful male body and passionate sex. Since BL centres on male homosexuality, female readers, as mere onlookers, can watch the sex scenes without moral guilt or anxiety. This advantage over heterosexual romance renders BL an excellent platform for women to unleash their sexual fantasy and release sexual tension. Fan-researcher Ruan Yaona (2008) adds one more intriguing cause in her master's thesis on BL fans. She observes that many BL fans have the expressed desire to be gay men. Such a BL fan is biologically female, but male by gender and gay by sexual orientation. Ruan believes that this phenomenon is the result of BL fans' long term immersion in the BL community and their lack of real life experience with the opposite sex. This kind of sexual and gender 'confusion' is also visible among Japanese BL fans. Sakakibara Shihomi, a popular Japanese *yaoi*[2] novelist, once described herself as 'a gay man in a woman's body (a "female-to-male gay" transsexual)' (Thorn 2004: 177). Similarly, and contrary to the common presumption that BL is new, unusual or even unnatural, Uli Meyer (2011) boldly asserts that 'female interest for gay male sexuality' may have been 'a cause rather than an effect of BL', as 'female-to-gay-male eroticism can be traced back for at least 100 years' and still exists in many Western countries.

---

2.   *Yaoi* is an acronym for the Japanese expression 'yama nashi, ochi nashi, imi nashi', meaning 'no climax, no punch line and no meaning'. It is an early term of BL but still widely used among Western fans of Japanese manga and games.

The objectification of the male body, along with the marginalization of women in BL, has provoked criticism from both gay men and feminists. In Japan's 'yaoi dispute' in the early 1990s, Satō Masaki, a Japanese gay writer and drag queen, compared *yaoi* fans to the 'dirty old men' who watch lesbian pornography, and accused *yaoi* of misrepresenting all gay men as beautiful and handsome (Lunsing 2006). Despite Satō's claim that *yaoi* has damaged the human rights of gay men, the Chinese gay community in general has chosen to engage in open dialogue with China's hardcore BL fans, the so-called 'rotten girls' (腐女 *funü*), about fantasy versus reality in male homosexuality. For example, in an anonymous online post titled 'Some Words a Gay Wants to Tell Rotten Girls' (2010), the gay author first appreciates the rotten girls' contribution to the increasing tolerance of homosexuality in Chinese society. He then calmly reminds them that not all gay men are handsome in real life and real gay sex does not make a clear distinction between *seme* and *uke*. He concludes that, even though some rotten girls struggle with the idea of real-life gay men, as long as they acknowledge the existence of sexual minorities, they already show more tolerance than is typical of mainstream society.

Interestingly, the most scathing critique of BL in China comes from critics with an ostensibly feminist leaning.[3] Using a well-known BL novel that features strong *seme* x weak *uke* as an example, Wang (2010) points out that the *seme* character in BL is often depicted as the protector of the *uke*, as the former is superior to the latter in terms of age, experience, power, and social status. The feminized and helpless image of *uke* suggests that women still expect some stronger men to be their saviours and their wish for an egalitarian relationship is complicated by a dependency mentality. Drawing on psychoanalytic concepts of castration complex and penis envy, Zhang (2011) contends that BL reflects heterosexual women's desire to assume the male role so that they can enjoy more sexual freedom with men. Hence, according to Zhang, female BL lovers have no intention to subvert the patriarchal order, but merely demand men's privileges under patriarchy to treat women (men

---

3. Since it is difficult for scholars to publish research related to homosexuality in Chinese academic journals unless they cast the issue in a negative light, those critical stances could be strategic or may not reflect the genuine intentions of the authors.

in BL) as sex objects. In a strikingly similar vein, Wu (2011: 160) argues that BL reveals women's difficulty in dealing with their own sexual identity, claiming that BL's 'borrowing of the male body to express female expectation and desire' (借男性的身体来表达女性的期望和欲望) shows that 'women do not know what kind of people they want to be and therefore simply erase themselves all together' (女人不知道自己希望成为什么样的人，于是干脆将本身取消). The assessments of Chinese researchers concerning BL's benefit to women are echoed by Pagliassotti (2010: 77), who observes that 'BL manga may open a space for women's creativity and sexual pleasure, but they seem to do so at the price of devaluing or erasing women as positive presences within the narrative'.

While the above criticisms have raised some tough ethical questions concerning BL fantasies and their relations to gender inequality in the real world, they tend to overlook the multiple complexities of the genre itself and its transgender fandom. As one of the most popular genres in Chinese web literature, BL authors' styles, meanings, and subject areas are as diverse as their vast readership. The idea of *uke* has evolved to include arrogant *uke*, masochist *uke*, masculine *uke*, girly *uke*, and many others. In addition to the general coupling pattern of 'strong *seme* X weak *uke*', the pattern of 'strong *seme* X strong *uke*' has become increasingly common in recent years. Even the portrayal of a weak *uke* in BL need not be interpreted as women's dependency on men; the imaginative interaction between author and reader open the possibility of many layers of meaning, including queer layers. For instance, through a close reading of Gilbert, the main character of Takemiya Keiko's (1976-1984) foundational BL text *Song of Wind and Trees*, McHarry (2010) examines the appeal of BL to gay readers. He argues that the effeminate *uke* symbolizes the 'abjection in subject formation' of young boys who are struggling for sexual autonomy outside the state-organized 'unitary sexual identity in children' (p. 183). Moreover, empirical studies (Feng 2009; Su 2009) show that there is a significant number of gay and lesbian BL readers in China. Such 'queer' reading tastes among readers suggest that pleasure in writing and reading BL may not be fully understood within the boundary of heteronormativity. As to the charge of BL's trivialization of women, there are actually many positive women figures in Chinese BL novels. Yet unlike heterosexual romance, strong BL women are portrayed as the male protagonists' mothers and sisters, rather than lovers. In the following two sections, we examine two other genres that offer a more direct reflection on and critique of women's existence under patriarchy.

Body Change: Into Androgynism

Mostly written by women, Body Change, or *bainshen* (变身) in Chinese, is a mixed genre that combines elements of time travel, BL and traditional heterosexual romance. Its basic narrative formula is that the soul of a man or woman enters into the body of a person of the opposite sex because of disease, calamity, or some other reason, and then learns to live with the new body and new sexual identity. To achieve maximum dramatic effect, most Body Change novels are set in ancient times, where the contrast between men and women is most prominent. The Body Change genre includes two subcategories: male-to-female and female-to-male. Although both respond to their readers' strong desire to imagine a world without fixed gender roles, the two subcategories are not mirror images. In the male-to-female subgenre, the male protagonist lives as a heterosexual woman but keeps some male mentality and habits. Rather than hindering her adaptation of the new sexual/social identity, retained male traits enable her to gain love and happiness. In the female-to-male subgenre, the female protagonist is transformed into a homosexual man and takes advantage of her new male identity to change the world. Although there have been prolonged debates on Jinjiang's bulletin boards and elsewhere regarding whether the female-to-male category can be truly qualified as BL – because the protagonist's soul and consciousness remain female despite the sex change – its inner logic of appropriating male body to articulate female desire is very much in accord with BL.

A Dou's 2009 novella *Fugui Ronghua* (*Rich and Prosperous*) is an example of a male-to-female story. It portrays an ordinary white-collar man named Lin Nan, who wakes up one morning to find himself transformed into the 3-year-old daughter of a rich family in traditional China. While acquiring all the knowledge and skills to be a 'proper' lady, Lin Nan keeps her male perseverance and generosity. At the age of 17, she marries a simple-natured but somewhat self-centred scholar-gentleman. Since Lin Nan was an experienced bisexual in her past life, she is quite sexually compatible with her husband. Following the traditional norm of polygamy, her husband later takes a number of concubines. While those concubines are fixated on the doomed attempt to seek for their husband's exclusive favour, Lin Nan maintains emotional and sexual independence from her husband and harbours no envy or resentment of her competitors. She also helps her husband advance his official career and produces three sons for him. As time passes, the generous Lin Nan eventually wins loyalty and attachment from her husband.

Readers' comments on the story suggest that the character of Lin Nan offers a welcome role model for those women who want to cling to the romantic ideal of one true love, yet are fully aware that men may demand a sexual freedom unfettered by love or marriage. Lin Nan's cool-headed attitude towards her heterosexual relationship, an inheritance of her past life as a libertine, seemingly offers a solution to the problem of expectation gap between men and women in modern relationships. The change of sexual identity and the preservation of the old male interest in women endow Lin Nan with an androgynous personality, keeping her aloof from women's struggle to please men and the consequent same-sex jealousy. The convergence of two kinds of sexual consciousness in a single body means not only the doubling of sex roles – a fusion of the heterosexual female and the homosexual *uke* – but the freedom to deal with people from both male and female perspectives and to play either gender role as one likes. In this way, the male-to-female transgender character offers both an escape from and a challenge to the deeply unfair gender norms traditionally imposed on women.

Originally named 'A Bad Luck Woman Who Has Been Turned into a BL Man', Pu Tao's three-year (2005–08) serial is a typical female-to-male Body Change narrative. Topping Jinjing's ranking chart in 2005, the novel was later renamed *Qinglian Jishi* (*The Chronicles of Qinglian*) and published in two volumes, each by a different publishing house. It tells the story of a 26-year-old elite businesswoman named Qiaochu, literally meaning 'outstanding' or 'distinguished', whose soul after her death in a plane crash inhabits the body of an elegant but treacherous court official, Zhang Qinglian, in an unspecified ancient era. Zhang used to be the emperor's male favourite. After the emperor passes away, Zhang runs the government on behalf of the emperor's young son. A lecherous and cruel man, he has forced many handsome boys to become his lovers and even engineered the ruination of the family of a handsome marital arts master, Yao Jinzi, so that he could incarcerate Yao and make him into his plaything. With an IQ score of 179, a superb business acumen and the mentality of an emancipated modern woman, Qiaochu reverses the evil ways of Zhang Qinglian and starts to do many good deeds for the country. Detecting the change of 'heart and soul' in the body of Zhang Qinglian, Yao Jinzi cannot help falling in love with 'him'. After the young emperor grows up, Qiaochu gives up his supervision of the ruler and lives a carefree life with Yao Jinzi in a faraway place.

The Chronicles of Qinglian could be read as a commentary on Chinese social reality. The setting in the ancient world alludes to the dynastic aspects of contemporary Chinese society, characterized by an opaque and totalitarian political system, an overstaffed and corrupt bureaucracy, and the lack of basic human rights protections. The concept of the female-to-male body change is an implicit critique of women's political development in China; despite three decades of rapid economic growth and the expansion of higher education, Chinese women continue to be politically excluded (Min 2012). As a result, although Qiaochu has already combined femininity and masculinity for her survival in the job market, she cannot affect the world and achieve a distinguished life until she is transformed into a biological man in her second life. The *Qinglian* series illustrates Jin Feng's (2009: 23) more general characterization of women's literature on Jinjiang: female-to-male sex change 'enables women to shed the burdens of their female bodies and disadvantageous gender identity to seize power'. Moreover, *Qinglian* also reveals a women's sense of vigilance against the negative effect of power on personality and personal relationships. In the end, after the political situation has been stabilized, Qiaochu chooses to relinquish her supreme authority and adopt a simple life in the countryside with her lover.

Feng (2009: 30) claims that 'a significant number' of BL writers and readers at Jinjiang prefer the 'modern time traveler, whether originally male or female' to play the role of *seme* after they travel to the other world. Taking Liu Yue's well-known Jinjiang serial novel *Feng Ba Tianxia* (*The Phoenix That Rules the World*, 2005–2007) as an example, Feng argues that this kind of female-to-male novel 'reverses the model of male supremacy and promiscuity' in contemporary male-authored 'stud fiction' and pre-modern vernacular novels (*ibid.*). Yet the example Feng gives is actually an exceptional male-to-female-then-to-male story, rather than the more common male-to-female or female-to-male Body

Change novels. Based on our own participant observation of women's writings on Jinjiang and other online BL communities, we find that, regardless of their original sexual identity, protagonists in the majority of Body Changes novels are positioned as *uke*, rather than *seme*, after undergoing the sex change. First-person narratives in particular tend to be written from the perspective of *uke*, because women readers in general more readily identify with *uke* protagonists. It is perhaps only in the genre of Superior Woman that female characters are commonly portrayed as *seme* in sexual relationships.

Superior Women: Down with the Patriarchy

If BL examines love between equals outside the heterosexual norms and Body Change explores the advantages of androgynism for women under the patriarchy, the genre of Superior Women (*nüzun* 女尊) is bent on depicting a new configuration of love, marriage and family by imagining a matriarchal society where the Confucian maxim 'men are superior to women' (男尊女卑) is turned upside down. To be sure, it is hardly the first time that Chinese writers play with alternative gender roles. The 16th-century classic, *The Journey to the West (Xiyou Ji)*, describes a 'Women's Kingdom of Western Liang', a place populated and governed by women. Since no men live there, women reproduce by drinking the water of Child-and-Mother River. The 18th-century novel, *Flowers in the Mirror (Jinghua Yuan)*, also presents a fictional women's kingdom across the sea. While men do exist in this outlandish women's nation, they assume women's roles – staying home, wearing cosmetics and binding their feet – while women work outside and handle public duties. Contemporary Superior Women stories have incorporated elements of those pioneer works with a heightened gender consciousness or, more accurately, twist still further the traditional gendered imagination of what life under female rule would be like. Rather than focusing on men's suffering from a male standpoint, Superior Women stories are told from a female perspective, sometimes in first person narrative, and raise the provocative question: how would women feel and act if they happen to live in a society where women are superior to men in every way: physically, psychologically, socially and politically?

Superior Women stories are often set in an ancient women's kingdom, similar to the fictional world of *Flowers in the Mirror*. In that kingdom,

142

the gender hierarchy of the patriarchal feudal China is thoroughly re-versed. All social and sexual privileges 'normally' reserved for men now go to women: instead of an emperor and a male ruling class, there is an empress and female officials and aristocrats. Instead of polygamy, there is polyandry. Since women are usually taller and stronger than men in the world of Superior Women, they are the 'natural' *seme* in sex. The scene of a group of high-ranking women revelling in a brothel packed with beautiful male prostitutes has become a narrative convention in Superior Women stories. On the other hand, men are usually the *uke* and are forced to be chaste, delicate and submissive. They not only have to obey their wife-master (*qizhu* 妻主) but also carry, bear, and rear children. Like *The Journey to the West* and *Flowers in the Mirror*, the contrast between conventional and alternative gender systems in con-temporary Superior Women stories is dramatized via spatial and time travel. While male characters in those two classical novels unexpect-edly encounter women's kingdoms in their travels to foreign countries, Superior Women protagonists are often modern women accidentally traveling back to ancient China in their afterlives. Contrary to male char-acters' lasting anxiety and fear in their sojourn to women's kingdoms, female protagonists living in Superior Women societies undergo only temporary bewilderment and then perfectly adjust to their elevated social positions.

Among the dozens of Superior Women stories frequently recom-mended by readers, *Sishi Huakai Zhi Huanhun Nüerguo* (*Four Seasons of Blossom: Soul Returning to the Women's Kingdom*) by Gongteng Shenxiu (2006–2007) is probably the most influential.[4] Its reputation as the 'Bible of Superior Women' may not be an exaggeration, as it has set up a canonic relationship model of one woman versus multiple male partners. The novel follows the adventure of a plain, loveless and spiteful contemporary young girl whose soul travels to an ancient women's kingdom called the 'Habitat of Phoenix' and enters the body of Ruizhu, the Empress's sister. With the help of King Yan, the lord of

---

4. In her 2013 book *Romancing the Internet*, Jin Feng devotes a whole chapter to the genre of Superior Women, including an analysis of Gongteng Shenxiu's novel *Four Seasons of Blossom*. Feng translates the name of the genre into 'matriarchal fiction' and the title of the novel into 'Flowers of Four Seasons'. We came across Feng's book at the stage of final edits and were delighted to find that some of our viewpoints coincide with hers.

death in Chinese mythology, the ugly duckling turns into a privileged young woman and starts a brand new life. The first half of the novel details Ruizhu's relationship with a number of men (one husband and several male concubines) in her household, especially how she builds trust and understanding with those men. The second half shifts the scene from the domestic environment to the royal court and military battlefield. Although Ruizhu is not politically ambitious, she inevitably gets involved in a precarious power struggle within the royal family and between neighbouring kingdoms. With intelligence and secret archery talents, Ruizhu bravely defeats the rebel army and wins the trust of the Empress. Later, she lives a peaceful life with her men – seven of them by the end of the novel – and all of the children they have borne her.

At first glance, the novel might seem to be a reversed version of Su Tong's 苏童 well-known novella *Qiqie Chengqun* (*Wives and Concubines,* 2002 [1989]), which was adapted into an award-winning film *Raise the Red Lantern* in 1991. Like *Wives and Concubines,* which depicts the subtle emotional conflicts between the four wives of Master Chen, *Four Seasons* offers a credible account of men's fear, insecurity and jealousy towards one other when they are put in an utterly powerless situation and have to compete for the favour of their wife-master. Yet unlike the cruel and indifferent Master Chen in Su Tong's novella, Ruizhu genuinely tries to care for and protect her men. The misery in her previous life has made her highly sensitive to other people's anguish. Her kindness and sincerity are warmly embraced by her husband and male concubines; in the end, they tacitly agree to share her love in a harmonious way. Ruizhu's sexual prowess has also played an important role in her relationship with men, as Ruizhu often uses her outstanding sex skills to pacify and satisfy her men. In contrast, the fifty-year-old Master Chen suffers from sagging sex drive, subsequently driving one of his concubines into adultery and another one into madness. *Four Seasons* dwells at length on the rich emotional and sexual tension of the 'bed scenes', including a playful threesome, as if to prove the possibility of love and fun between female *seme* and male *uke.* When women are on top of men, literally and figuratively, it is the men, rather than women, who have to use their physical look to seduce the more powerful sex and are associated with the ominous image of 'femme fatale'.

Compared to the wide readership of BL and Body Change, Superior Women has so far enjoyed less popularity. One common objection to the genre is that it has excessively altered the biological and psychological features of the two sexes, so that men have lost their masculinity and women their femininity. Some readers claim that they could no more accept a chauvinistic male pig than a sissy boy; they detest lasciviousness in either sex. Another argument is that the genre's simple role reversals have done nothing to change the power imbalance in gender relations. It is still a form of patriarchal thinking, albeit in the guise of feminism. The fanciful description of men's pregnancy and child delivery in many Superior Women stories has also led to displeasure or even disgust among female readers who consider women's reproductive capacity as a 'sacred' duty, rather than a punishment borne by the inferior sex. Significantly, those who criticize the genre often end up being the defenders of conventional gender roles. For example, in a serialized treatise on young people's writings on the Internet, a web writer/reader who describes herself as a female in her late 20s passionately denounces Superior Women as 'the most perverse' (最为变态) genre of web literature (Boboxixi 2011). The author argues that Chinese women have already achieved equal status to men in education, employment, and family. It is therefore absurd for Superior Women stories to demand more rights for women. Besides, it is quite 'fair' (公平) that men are superior to women not only because it is the 'natural law' (自然规律) but because men are more hardworking, independent and socially responsible than women.

Despite such criticism, Superior Women has attracted its own followers. In 2006, a discussion forum of the genre named 'Superior Women Inferior Men' (女尊男卑) was set up at Baidu Post Bar (*tieba* 贴吧), the largest Chinese-language online community in the world. Supporters contend that the genre is neither extravagant nor horrible, because women have held higher status than men in some societies during certain historical periods. An 18-year-old girl (DHROCK 2011) once posted an open letter to anti-fans of the genre in the Bar. She claimed that fans of Superior Women are girls who believe in self-reliance and self-determination, and Superior Women promotes the status of women with no contempt for men. It merely gives men a new choice when they want to be a *uke* or to be taken care of. In a reply to this post, another fan (Canyue Sixin 2011) asserted that the genre could help women build up a strong mentality and realize that they are not the weaker sex:

It is actually the men who are weak. They dare not make us strong, for they are afraid that once we become strong, we'll surpass them. It's not surprising that some women dislike the genre, because they are more or less trapped by tradition and dare not challenge it.

Apparently, for some Chinese women born in the 1980s and 1990s, the label of 'strong woman' (*nü qiangren* 女强人) is no longer a stigmatization to be avoided but an identity to be proud of. While their feminist foremothers born in the 1950s and 1960s have been searching vainly for the 'female essence' in an attempt to reclaim a sexualized identity 'from the asexual "iron-girl" ethos of the Maoist era' (Schaffer and Song 2007: 28), the young generation of Chinese women has taken up the task of dismantling the rigid boundary between femininity and masculinity and fiercely upholding gender and sexual equality. Meanwhile, in a sharp contrast to the 1980s' national craving for what Zhong (2000) describes as 'the real man' (*nanzihan* 男子汉), contemporary young Chinese women seem to prefer men who possess both handsome appearance and a certain degree of feminine features. Both BL and Superior Women stories are populated with androgynous male figures that are more beautiful than women. While obviously influenced by a 'pan East-Asian soft masculinity' that has come into vogue in South Korea, Japan, Taiwan and China since late 1990s (Jung 2009), this changing ideal of masculinity reveals substantial change in Chinese women's perception of gender norms. When women have more confidence in their own ability to survive in the patriarchal system, they tend to care less about the traditional gender stereotypes and to be more tolerant, or even appreciative, of effeminate men. Following this line of reasoning, it seems to be easier for the general public to accept feminized homosexual men, like those depicted in BL and Body Change, than powerful heterosexual women in Superior Women.

Conclusion

Currently, the slogan of 'harmony between the two sexes' (*liangxing hexie* 两性和谐) has gained wide currency in Chinese academic feminist discourse. Recalling Huang Lin's 'smiling feminism', which was proposed in the 1990s and seeks to ease the tension between dominant male scholars and militant feminists, scholars (e.g. Wang and Wu 2008: 24) now claim that feminism should 'transcend the one-sided stance of women' (超越女性一己的立场) and take the quest for harmony and partnership between the two sexes as its ultimate goal. An offshoot of 'the broader concept of a "harmonious society" (*hexie shehui*) that has been promoted by the Chinese government since 2004' (Spakowski 2011: 41), the ambiguous slogan on one hand promotes the equality of men and women in social, economic and political realms and views this equality as the basis of a harmonious society, while on the other it revives the spectre of biological determinism that has been used to justify gender inequality, as the distinction between the 'two sexes', male and female, rests solely on biological differences. Many 'harmonious society' advocates specifically evoke the binary of *yin-yang* to illustrate the complementary and harmonious heterosexual relations, oblivious to the fact that the binary has been used by Confucian scholars to establish and perpetuate a gender hierarchy that privileges *yang*/men over *yin*/women since the second century BCE (Yun 2012).

The gender-bending genres discussed in this chapter not only raise serious questions about the validity of the heterosexual assumption underpinning the thesis of 'harmony between the two sexes', but also interrogate the presumptively natural and fixed categories of sex, gender, and sexuality, putting deep-rooted binaries of male/female, masculine/feminine, and heterosexual/homosexual all on trial. BL breaks up the neat alignment of gender and sexuality via a deft detour to male homosexuality and tactically replaces the binary of male/female with a more fluid dyad of *seme/uke*. Instead of depicting women's femininity as traditional literature generally does, BL portrays feminized beautiful boys and reveals that the category of male is by no means unified or monolithic. Body Change uses the dual tropes of sex change and time travel to explore the necessity of androgynism for women to survive in a patriarchal society. The contrast between the achievements of the androgynous protagonist and the suffering of traditional female characters indicates that women's adherence to gender stereotypes will only bring them an unhappy and unfulfilled life. Superior Women confronts women's assumed passivity and sexual reliance on men head-on by imagining 'masculine' and sexually assertive women. It shows that, when women are sufficiently empowered in society and when their sexual energy is normalized rather than pathologized, they would be able to thrive while filling a far greater variety of social and sexual roles. To borrow Andrea Wood's (2006: 397) comment about BL manga, literary genres of BL,

Body Change and Superior Women are not simply queer because they tell stories of homosexuals, transgenders and masculine women, 'but rather because they ultimately reject any monolithic understanding of gendered or sexual identity'. Sooner or later, this new type of grassroots feminism and creative energy will reshape the vision of Chinese feminism and deepen the academic understanding of the category of gender.

Author's Note

This research was supported by a grant for Japan-related research projects from the Sumitomo Foundation (Reg. No.: 128017). We would like to thank Alexander Lugg and Elaine Jing Zhao for their careful readings and valuable suggestions on an earlier draft of this chapter.

References

A Dou(pseudonym) (2009) 'Fugui Ronghua' [Rich and prosperous]. http://www.jjwxc.net/onebook.php?novelid=587337, accessed 6 June 2012.

Anonymous (2010) 'Yige tongzhi dui funümen shuo de hua' [Some words a gay wants to tell the rotten girls], http://www.danlan.org/disparticle_28451_4_1.htm, accessed 17 July 2013.

Boboxixi (pseudonym) (2011) 'Nüzun wen, nüren de beiai' [Superior women fiction, women's pity], http://www.17k.com/chapter/113125/3335820.html, accessed 17 July 2013.

Butler, Judith (1999) *Gender Trouble: Feminism and the subversion of identity*. 2nd edition. New York: Routledge.

Canyue Sixin (2011) 'Ruode shi naxie nanzi' [It is actually the men who are weak] [Online forum comment], 15 September, http://tieba.baidu.com/p/1131024304?pn=2, accessed 3 April 2015.

China Internet Network Information Center (2014) 'Di sanshisan ci zhongguo hulian wangluo fazhan zhuangkuang tongji baogao' [The 33rd Statistical Report of the Situation of Development of Chinese Internet Network], http://www.cnnic.net.cn/hlwfzyj/hlwxzbg/hlwtjbg/201403/P020140305346585959798.pdf, accessed 10 July 2014.

DHROCK (pseudonym) (2011) 'Gei naxie fan nüzun de renmen' [To those who are against superior women], 5 July, http://tieba.baidu.com/p/1131024304, accessed 17 July 2013.

Du, Rui, and Min Ren (2010) 'Jiedu 'tongrennü' wenxue chuangzuo qunti jiqi shehui wenhua genyuan' [Interpreting the literary writing community of

'*Dōjinonna*' and its sociocultural roots]. *Shengyang Nongye Daxue Xuebao* [Journal of Shenyang Agricultural University], vol. 12, no. 2, pp. 247–249.

Feng, Jin (2013) *Romancing the Internet: Producing and consuming Chinese web romance*. London: Brill.

———— (2009) 'Addicted to Beauty: Consuming and producing web-based Chinese *Danmei* fiction at Jinjiang'. *Modern Chinese Literature and Culture* vol. 21, pp. 1–41.

Feng Nong (pseudonym) (2000–2001) *Xue Ye* [Bloody night], http://tieba. baidu.com/p/152416301?pn=1, accessed 6 June 2012.

Evans, Harriet. (2008) 'Sexed Bodies, Sexualized Identities, and the Limits of Gender'. *China Information* vol. 22, pp. 361–386.

Gongteng Shenxiu (2006–2007) *Sishi Huakai Zhi Huanhun Nüerguo* [Four seasons of blossom: soul returning to the women's kingdom], http:// ishare.iask.sina.com.cn/f/5103185.html, accessed 6 June 2012.

Hockx, Michel (2005) 'Virtual Chinese Literature: A comparative case study of online poetry communities'. *The China Quarterly* vol. 183, pp. 670–691.

Jung, Sun (2009) 'The Shared Imagination of *Bishōnen*, Pan-East Asian Soft Masculinity: Reading DBSK, *Youtube.com* and transcultural new media consumption'. *Intersections: Gender and Sexuality in Asia and the Pacific*, vol. 20, http://intersections.anu.edu.au/issue20/jung.htm, accessed 6 June 2012.

Liu Yue (pseudonym) (2005–2007) Feng Ba Tianxia [The phoenix that rules the world], http://www.jjwxc.net/onebook.php?novelid=59052, accessed 6 June 2012.

Landow, George P. (1994) 'What's a Critic to Do?: Critical theory in the age of hypertext'. In George P. Landow (ed.) *Hyper/Text/Theory*. Baltimore: Johns Hopkins University Press, pp. 1–48.

Lugg, Alexander (2011) 'Chinese Online Fiction: Taste publics, entertainment, and "Candle in the Tomb"'. *Chinese Journal of Communication* vol. 4, pp. 121–136.

Lunsing, Wim (2006) '*Yaoi Ronsō*: Discussing depictions of male homosexuality in Japanese girls' comics, gay comics and gay pornography'. *Intersections: Gender, History and Culture in the Asian Context*, vol 12, http://intersections.anu.edu.au/issue12/lunsing.html, accessed 6 June 2012.

McHarry, Mark (2010) 'Boys in Love in Boys' Love: Discourses West/East and the abject in subject formation'. In Antonia Levi, Mark McHarry and Dru Pagliassotti (eds), *Boys' Love Manga: Essays on the Sexual Ambiguity and Cross-Cultural Fandom of the Genre.* Jefferson, NC: McFarland pp. 177–189.

McLelland, Mark (2006 - 2007). 'Why Are Japanese Girls' Comics Full of Boys Bonking?' *Refractory: A Journal of Entertainment Media* vol. 10. http://refractory.unimelb.edu.au/2006/12/04/why-are-japanese-girls%E2%80%99-comics-full-of-boys-bonking1-mark-mclelland/, accessed 6 June 2012.

Meyer, Uli (2011) 'Hidden in Straight Sight, the Sequel: Trans*gressing gender and sexuality via BL'. Paper presented at the 'Global Polemics of 'BL' (Boys Love): Production, Circulation, and Censorship' workshop, Oita University, Japan, January 22–23.

Min, Jie (2012) 'Zhongguo funü canzheng bujin zetui shi shang jin chansheng guo siwei nü shengzhang' [Chinese women's political participation either advances or retreats: Only four female provincial governors in history]. *Zhongguo Xinwen Zhoukan* [China Newsweek], April 20, http://www.chinanews.com/gn/2012/04-20/3834668.shtml, accessed 6 June 2012.

Pagliassotti, Dru (2010) 'Better than Romance? Japanese BL manga and the subgenre of male/male romantic fiction'. In Antonia Levi, Mark McHarry and Dru Pagliassotti (eds), *Boys' Love Manga: Essays on the sexual ambiguity and cross-cultural fandom of the genre.* Jefferson, NC: McFarland, pp. 59–83.

Pu Tao (2005–2008) *Qinglian Jishi* [The Chronicles of Qinglian], http://www.jjwxc.net/onebook.php?novelid=57114, accessed 6 June 2012.

Ruan, Yaona (2008) 'Tongrennü' qunti de lunli kunjing yanjiu' [A study of the ethical dilemma of the fan girl community]. MA thesis, Zhejiang University. CNKI.

Schaffer, Kay, and Xianlin Song (2007) 'Unruly Spaces: Gender, women's writing and indigenous feminism in China'. *Journal of Gender Studies* vol. 16, pp. 17–30.

Song, Jia and Mingyang Wang (2011) 'Wangluo shang danmei yawenhua shengxing de xinlixue sikao' [A psychological reflection on the boom of BL subculture on the internet]. *Heihe Xuekan* [Heihe Journal], no.8, pp. 22–24.

Spakowski, Nicola (2011) '"Gender" Trouble: Feminism in China under the impact of western theory and the spatialization of identity'. *Positions* vol. 19, pp. 31–54.

Su, Tong (2002 [1989]) *Qiqie Chengqun* [Wives and concubines]. Kunming: Yunnan renmin chubanshe.

Su, Wei (2009) 'Danmei wenhua zai woguo dalu liuxing de yuanyin jiqi wangluo chuanbo yanjiu' [A Study of the Causes of popularity of BL and Its Online Dissemination in Mainland China]. MA thesis, Shanghai Foreign Studies University. CNKI.

Takemiya, Keiko (1995) *Kaze to ki no uta* [Song of wind and trees]. Tokyo: Hakusensha. Ten Volumes. First published in 1976 by Shōgakukan.

Thorn, Matthew (2004) 'Girls and Women Getting Out of Hand: The Pleasure and Politics of Japan's Amateur Comics Community'. In *Fanning the Flames: Fans and Consumer Culture in Contemporary Japan*, edited by William W. Kelly, 169–187. Albany: State University of New York Press.

Wang, Chunrong and Yujie Wu (2008) 'Fansi,tiaozheng yu chaoyue: ershiyi shiji chu de nüxing wenxue piping' [Reflection, Adjustment and Transcendence: Women's literary criticism at the beginning of the 21st century]. *Wenxue Pinglun* [Literature review], no. 6, pp. 23–27.

Wang, Jing (2010) 'Yawenhua xiade danmei xiaoshuo – xiao nüren men tianbu qinggan kongque de wanju' [BL fiction in the perspective of subculture: a toy for small women to fill their emotional gap]. *Wenxue Jie* [Literary circle], no. 9, pp. 33–34.

Wood, Andrea (2006) ''Straight' Women, Queer Texts: boy-love manga and the rise of a global counterpublic'. *Women's Studies Quarterly*, vol. 34, pp. 394–414.

Wu, Di (2011) 'Yi ru danmei shen si hai – wo de geren "danmei·tongren" shi' [Once enters BL it's as deep as the sea – my personal reading history of BL and *dōjin*]. In Guangdong Writers' Association and Guangdong Web Literature Institute (eds) *Wangluo wenxue pinglun diyi ji* [Web literature review, Vol. 1], Guangzhou: Huacheng chubanshe, pp. 150–167.

Xu, Yanrui and Ling Yang (2013) 'Forbidden Love: Incest, generational conflict, and the erotics of power in Chinese BL fiction'. *Journal of Graphic Novels and Comics* vol. 4, pp. 30–43.

Yang, Ya (2006) 'Tongrennü qunti: danmei xianxiang beihou' [The fan girl community: behind the BL phenomenon]. *Zhongguo Qingnian Yanjiu* [China youth studies], no. 7, pp. 63–66.

Yun, Sung Hyun (2012) 'An Analysis of Confucianism's *Yin-Yang* Harmony with Nature and the Traditional Oppression of Women: Implications for social work practice'. *Journal of Social Work*, doi: 10.1177/1468017312436445, accessed July 17, 2013.

Zhang, Bo (2011) 'Fuquan de touhuan – lun danmei xiaoshuo de nüxing yange qingjie' [The secret displacement of patriarchal power – on the female castration complex in BL fiction]. *Wenxue Jie* [Literary Circle], no.9, pp. 11–12.

Zhao, Elaine Jing (2011) 'Social Network Market: Storytelling on a web 2.0 original literature site'. *Convergence: The International Journal of Research into New Media Technologies* vol. 17, pp. 85–99.

Zheng, Dandan, and Di Wu (2009) 'Danmei xianxiang beihou de nüxing su-qiu – dui danmei zuoping ji tongrenü de kaocha' [Female appeals behind BL phenomenon: an investigation of BL works and *Dōjinonna*]. *Zhejiang Xuekan* [Zhejiang Academic Journal], no. 6, pp. 214–219.

Zhong, Xueping (2000) *Masculinity Besieged? Issues of Modernity and Male Subjectivity in Chinese Literature of Late Twentieth Century*. Durham: Duke University Press.

CHAPTER 9

Queerness, Entertainment, and Politics

Queer performance and performativity in Chinese pop

Qian Wang

This chapter applies the concepts of performance and performativity from Butler (1993) to an examination of when and why the image of queerness in Chinese pop transcends performance and becomes queer performativity. I understand performance as the presentation of a static identity or visual image that might suggest queerness but that ultimately does not have the ability to influence society and culture in a profound way. Performativity, by contrast, integrates image with a self-conscious political commitment to a productive process of identity making at the societal level.

In consideration of China's transformation in the past three decades and the reserved political and social system of power, queer is undoubtedly a highly sensitive issue in terms of politics, morality, and tradition. Queer is an umbrella term not only indicating the sexual acts and identities for the sexual and gender minorities who do not fit into the fixed conventional heterosexual category, but also indicating the abnormality, deviance, and alternativeness of ideologies, activities, and lifestyles for some marginal communities who challenge the social structure and formation controlled by the governing body and the dominating groups. The queer, therefore, encompasses the sexual and non-sexual minorities who are viewed as the trouble-makers and noise-makers in China's otherwise harmonious society. Queerness, as the expression of queer ideologies and identities, is often delivered through various forms of popular culture, but this connection also gives creative industries the opportunity to explore and capitalize on queerness for profit, including fabricating queerness for the sake of publicity and marketing.

Queer messages, found in lyrics, sound and visual images, and which allow fans to structure vital social contexts, can be delivered through all forms of popular culture and arts. Yet, it is fair to say that, since the middle of the 20th century, popular music has played a leading role in articulating the queerness of lifestyles and social relations. Glam rock, punk rock and disco, for example, interacted with social movements in the 1970s, such as the gay rights movement, the second-wave feminist movement and the African American civil rights movement. The queer message in those music genres was political and reflected the tension between the dominant and the submissive, the mainstream and the marginal, the global and the local. But why popular music?

The simplest definition of popular music is based on the criteria of mass production, mass dissemination and mass consumption. Popular music is an industrial, multi-functional product. Between art and commerce, enlightenment and entertainment, factors including cultural capital, willingness, and autonomy all affect the endpoint of a process that begins with artistic creativity. Popular music as a genre is value-neutral; it can be (and has been) a politicised cultural force that challenges governing bodies, yet can just as easily be used by governing bodies and powerful social actors to deceive the masses (Waldman 2003). Similarly, Chinese rock music was regarded as an ideological weapon against the government in the 1980s and 1990s until it was incorporated by the music industry in the late 1990s (Jones 1992; Baranovitch 2003). Popular music is definitely more than merely a form of entertainment.

Queer issues in western popular music were first examined as part of the new gay and lesbian musicology (Brett, Thomas and Woods 1994). Whiteley and Rycenga (2006:xiii) explain the relation between popular music and the queer in this way:

> Popular music is not a neatly squared-off discourse; rather, it can be considered as a social force that constructs heteronormativity *and* resistant queer sexualities, whether gay, lesbian, bisexual, transsexual, or transgender, and can thus claim to have played a significant, if often ambiguous role, in the shaping of queer identity and queer self-consciousness. In doing so, it has merged queer social relations with queer musical ones, thus demonstrating the transforming significance of musical discourse and the ways in which these are situated in historical time.

In Chinese cultural studies, the queer has been examined in film and literature (Martin 2003a; Ruan and Tsai 1987; Song 2007), and a few scholars (such as de Kloet 2001; Baranovitch 2003; and Martin 2003b) have discussed gender issues in Chinese popular music. The presentation of queerness in Chinese pop is an experiment in glocalisation,[1] but compared to the western experience, tight governmental control is likely to limit the extent of popular music's contribution to queer communities in China.

Worries about marketability and political confrontation have shaped the Chinese music industry's approaches to presenting the queer. Nonetheless, queer images and themes have successfully attracted younger consumers of both music and fashion. Chinese popular music is an Inter-Asian phenomenon, covering the territories of China, Hong Kong, Taiwan, Singapore, Malaysia, and other countries and regions with diasporic Chinese populations since the formation of the Greater China market in the late 1990s.[2] In Hong Kong and Taiwan, LGBTQ movements have developed in parallel with popular media presentations of the queer. However, Chinese government policies and actions have raised the cost of linking queer images with queer sexuality. Further, China's market power has forced record companies in Greater China to make compromises in order to sell their products – both music and stars – in China. Although the list of suspected LGBT pop artists since the 1980s is long, including Leslie Cheung, Anthony Wong, Lin Yifeng, He Yunshi and Lin Xi in Hong Kong; Fei Yuqing, Lin Liangyue, Pan Meichen and Wu Qingfeng in Taiwan; and Mao Ning, Gao Feng, Dai Jun and Han Hong in China, no one was willing to address queer issues in public until 2009. In that

1. Glocalisation is the combination of global and local elements within human activities in order to make 'outside' ideas more attractive to 'insiders.' Through explicit or implicit dialogue and compromise, global ideologies are revised and repackaged in ways that make sense to local audiences while not provoking the governing body or the dominating organization for the sake of politics, morality and economy.

2. Popular culture from Hong Kong and Taiwan dominated the mainland market in the 1980s and 1990s. Power stemming from internal economic development enabled China to negotiate with Hong Kong and Taiwan for the reform of the market in the late 1990s. After China joined the WTO, the Big Five (Universal, EMI, BMG, Warner, and Sony) formally entered into China's market from Hong Kong and Taiwan. This symbolized the formal formation of the Greater China market.

year, Taiwanese pop superstar Zhang Huimei (*A'mei*) surprised the music industry and audiences with her new album *A Mi Te* (阿密特, Zhang's original ethnic name). The surprise lay in her open show of support for gay people through the song *Caihong* (彩虹, Rainbow)[3]

> ...The closet is not very big
> It hides your heaven
> You still welcome me to share it with you
> Our love is similar
> We all get hurt because of men
> And continuously clash with them
> When the sky is dark
> When the temperature is unusual
> You can always resist with your great strength
> For the unfriendly glance
> For the unpleasant voice
> You pack them gently with the romance of the rainbow...

The lyrics can have multiple meanings, but Zhang left no room for confusion when, onstage before performing the song, she said:

> There are many kinds of love around me, and I treasure all very much... we have different love between siblings, relatives, friends, classmates, and lovers. No matter whether it is love between men or women, all are worthy of treasuring... no matter if you are at this concert or somewhere else, I dedicate this song 'Rainbow' to my all colleagues and all my dearest gay friends.[4]

During her performance, the giant screen at the back of the stage displayed a massive LGBT pride flag. The message was clear: this song is dedicated to queer people as its clarified social context. Zhang was already the 'rainbow ambassador' for the 2007 gay parade in Taipei, but in the history of Chinese popular music, it was the first time that a superstar dared

3. This song was originally called 'My Gay Friends' (我的同志男友). In order to avoid unnecessary trouble—for example, censorship in the mainland—the less explicit and more metaphoric name 'Rainbow' was used in the end. The music video can be watched on Youku website (accessed 18 September 2014): http://v.youku.com/v_show/id_XMTExNzkzOTUy.html?tpa=dW5pb25faWQ9MjAwMDA4XzEwMDAwM18wMV8wMQ

4. Zhang Huimei made this speech at the 33rd minute during her concert. This concert video is from the Internet (accessed 10 August 2010): http://v.youku.com/v_show/id_XMTg3OTc0ODAw.html

making a queer anthem publicly. It was like a domino effect, other pop artists soon released more *Tongzhi Ticai* (同志题材 gay-themed) pop songs and music videos, such as Zuo Guangping's '1/0' (Top or Bottom), 2moro 'Shaole' (少了 Less), Yinguo Brothers *'Ni Zhende Ai Wo Ma'* (你真的爱我吗？ Do You Really Love Me?), Fan Siwei *'Xiabeizi Zai Ai Ni'* (下辈子再爱你 Love You Again in the Next Life), Ma Qiguang *'Wangzi Zaijian'* (王子，再见 Goodbye Prince), Dongpinxicou *'Zhuanjiao Xiatian'* (转角夏天 Summer at the Corner), Qiaoqiao *'Ai Bufen'* (爱不分 Regardless of Love), and Yu Siyuan *'Xinli You Ge Ta'* (心里有个他 He is in My Heart).[5] Meanwhile, openly gay pop stars are increasingly visible in the Chinese popular music scene, as if queerness has become a popularity strategy. Most importantly, even though there is no evidence to prove what political, social and cultural impact Zhang might have generated in Greater Chinese societies after her brave musical statement, a number of pop stars (including Anthony Wong, Lin Yifeng, and He Yunshi) came out of the closet and became involved with various LGBT activities, such as the Pink Dot HK Carnival on 15 June 2014.

Whiteley and Rycenga (2006: xiv) are correct that 'popular music can be seen as a catalyst for the different truths, for different interpretations that have worked to free the queer imaginary.' Unlike other forms of popular culture, popular music can easily and frequently be played, performed, parodied and discussed by fans in their daily lives for the demonstration of cultural taste and social identity in a way that is similar to what Bourdieu (1984) discovered in his research on cultural consumption in France. Popular music simply creates one of the most convenient and widespread media through which to demonstrate differences of 'capital' in Bourdieu's sense.

The Cult of Queerness

With the continuous innovation of new technologies and products, the visual text of popular music becomes increasingly important for the creation of theatricality and the generation of social context. Television allowed Elvis Presley simultaneously to win millions of teenage fans and anger parents with his provocative imagery and performance in 1950s America. He sparked teenagers' sexual passions with the way he rotated

---

5.   Those music videos can be watched on www.youku.com, www.tudou.com, www.ku6.com and many other websites in China.

his pelvis when dancing, but he was rewarded with the unpleasant nickname 'Elvis the Pelvis'. Jimi Hendrix's setting fire to his guitar and Jim Morrison's showing his genitals on stage are just two classical moments of 1960s American pop resistance. When David Bowie appeared on the stage as the fictional androgynous alien character Ziggy Stardust in 1972, his performance empowered what could be called queer performativity. Like Elvis and Hendrix, Bowie's performance challenged mainstream morality of the time. Bowie created a holistic, theatrical, socially queer experience that included not only music and costumes by also an array of new technical possibilities, all harnessed to a story. Bowie's story suggested a queerness that audiences could interpret in a number of ways, but it also developed the vital social context of popular music that exists between musicians and their audiences.

Lady Gaga and her 'little monsters' harness similar techniques as they construct a 21st-century context for socially queer performativity. The release of 'Bad Romance' in November 2009 symbolises the beginning of Lady Gaga's reign as the new global pop queen. The attention paid to her from the Chinese audiences, though great, was not initially focused on her music, but rather on the queerness of her image and performance. Indeed, surprisingly, lesbian audiences in China did not fully understand her music video 'Telephone' and gay audiences did not get the message from 'Born This Way'.[6] Although image and performance as visual text are extremely important parts of her ideological expression, and her music, image and performance seem inseparable in ways reminiscent of earlier artists such as Andy Warhol, David Bowie and Freddie Mercury, most of her Chinese fans understood her image as something cool, avant-garde, and weird in a funny way, but devoid of the LGBT component that is linked to queer identity. What is seen by many in the West as her sophisticated queerness came to be defined in internet jargon as *Leiren* (雷人, weirdo), and she has been called *Leiren Jiaomu* (雷人教母, the Godmother of weirdoes).

This simplification cuts off the etymological relation between queer and queerness in Chinese language, but is perfect for the logic of com-

---

6. Like the middle-school students I researched (described later), I noted that a large number of Chinese adults with decent language capabilities also could not really understand what Lady Gaga expresses in her music and music videos. A paucity of queer cultural capital could be a reason.

mercialisation. The understanding of 'queerness as weirdness' in China allows some people to wear provocative make-up and costumes in public without linking that visual image to a socially conscious queer agenda (at the same time sidestepping the political confrontation that might would accompany such an agenda), as when Lady Gaga speaks for those who are discriminated against, mistreated, or bullied in the USA. Many local pop stars have sought to use queer images, but not a queer social or political agenda, to market themselves. Shang Wenjie (*Laure Shang*) and Jiang Yingrong presented these images when they were rising stars; Sun Yue, among others, hoped that a queer image would boost her popularity near the end of a long career. The queerness as weirdness image has such a powerful appeal that Furong Jiejie (芙蓉姐姐) and Feng Jie (凤姐) achieved pop and internet stardom despite an apparent absence of artistic talent.[7]

The content of popular music can be roughly divided into four parts: lyrics, music, visual text, and social context. Chinese pop stars have separated an apparently queer visual text from their lyrics, music and social context. Hence it is no surprise that they have not had the social impact of punk artists or modern-day avant-garde musicians like Lady Gaga Thoughtful musicians express their ideologies using all four parts and extend their creativity into new forms; punk artists in the 1970s developed their music into a diversified subculture that included punk fashion, literature, film, visual art, and ideology. Under pressure to compromise on ideology and autonomy, a genuine musician would negotiate, balancing the logics of avant-gardism and commercialisation. But a pop star could be expected to concede and follow the instruction of the record company, because sales rather than musical purity or social message may be the ultimate goal.

Lady Gaga's queer ideology is clearly based on her personal life experience and her understanding of being part of a marginalised social group – for example, her own experience of being bullied by fellow

---

7. Furong Jiejie and Feng Jie are individualistic, opportunistic, commodified, and controversial Internet celebrities in China. Both are famous for their misplaced confidence in their looks, writing, singing and dancing ability. After they gained their popularity, the government used censorship to control their influence. To a certain extent, they represent the conflict between the government and common people, official culture and grassroots culture.

students at school.[8] Calls for help from her fans inspired her to write her 2011 song 'Born this way', and she founded her Born This Way Foundation to empower people considered by mainstream society to be abnormal. 'Born This Way' clearly addresses the idea that no matter whether one is gay, straight or bi, black, white or beige, people cannot change who they are and should be accepted by others. Such a demand for equality and human rights for sexual minorities is at the heart of the queer agenda. But the queerness as weirdness visual text used by many Chinese pop stars is generally a fabrication of the music industry for publicity's sake. Comparing Lady Gaga with Laure Shang – known as the *Chaoliu Nüwang* (潮流女王, Fashion Queen) and *Gexing Tianhou* (个性天后, Queen of Individuality) – Shang uses lyrics that touch on politics, religion, sexuality and feminism, yet her music is lacking a clearly defined ideology that would authenticate her performance and expression through either its musicality or its visual imagery. Shang released a song titled 'Jinguzhou' (紧箍咒 The Band-tightening Spell) in August 2011 that addressed similar themes to Lady Gaga's 'Born This Way'. Through Hong Kong lyricist Lin Ruoning's words, Shang publicly expressed her support for non-mainstream race, age, gender, class and religious groups. The difference between Lady Gaga and Shang here lies in the level of authentic social context, which determines who becomes a cultural icon for queer performativity in societies and who becomes a pop star for queer performance on the stage.

Although no pop star can truly escape industrial manipulation, Lady Gaga's life experiences and her interactions with queer people suggest that her creativity and expression come from somewhere not imaginary. This is a key factor of judging authenticity in popular music studies. Comparatively, there is no context or evidence to prove why Laura Shang wants to make such expression in her music. It may not be that Laure Shang herself lacks ideology, but rather that her music cannot be said to express one. Popular music is produced through a 'filter-flow' model where musicians cannot have total autonomy to produce their music and are under the control of industrial production. Interpreting Shang's motives is more difficult because she faces a challenge that Lady Gaga need not worry about: the risk of governmental intervention. As

---

8.   For a Chinese-subtitled interview with Lady Gaga, see http://v.youku.com/v_
     show/id_XMzk1MjQxNTI4.html (accessed 6 June 2012).

a mainland musician, her expression is under the pressure of censorship and self-censorship, which is probably the reason that she designs and presents queer content in her music and videos without clarification. Nevertheless, the consequence of this lack of context is that during my fieldwork, many queer people who like Shang still often question what she means and whether she really understands them, whether she is a supporter, or if she is simply an opportunist.

In the process of transforming queerness to weirdness, the LGBT origin of the queer has been well disguised in Chinese pop. This transformation draws the borderline between politics and entertainment. Queer in the context of LGBT is political and dangerous, but queerness as weirdness is viewed as politically harmless and the government employs this simple rule to control queer cultures. From the moment she was spotted by the public until the moment she was crowned 2005 *Chaoji Nü Sheng* (超级女声, Super Voice Girls), Li Yuchun was a constant topic in lesbian and queer discussions. Regardless of her real sexual orientation, those discussions remained entertaining gossip because Li never clarified her sexuality, and the government could not take any actions against her. Liu Zhu, however, paid the price for his honesty. In early May 2010, Liu appeared on *Kuaile Nan Sheng* (快乐男声, Super Boy), a men's television singing competition, and shocked judges at the audition for not only his women's dress style, hairstyle, and make-up, but also his feminine demeanour. A female judge, Annirose, rudely interrupted his performance and demanded to verify his sex three times, which angered many viewers. Being a student of Sichuan Conservatory of Music, however, Liu won votes from the other two judges and progressed in the competition, becoming an instant media sensation. During a few interviews, he admitted that he loved men, not women, which constituted a public statement that he was gay and clearly overstepped the mark for the government. On 21 May 2010, a report revealed the State Administration of Radio, Film and Television warned Hunan Satellite TV that Weiniang (伪娘 pseudo-ladies) were not suitable for mainstream culture and the influential Liu had to be eliminated from the show to control the situation.[9] The next day, as expected, Liu was eliminated.

---

9. See http://music.yule.sohu.com/20100521/n272252441.shtml (accessed 21 May 2010).

Jin Xing, one of the best modern dance artists in China, received similar treatment. Although Jin is an artist with global reputation, she is unknown to the majority of the public and, consequently, the government views her transgender identity as sensitive but acceptable. Becoming a judge of the dancing show *Wu Lin Dahui* (舞林大会, Let's Shake It) on Dragon TV in 2011, however, introduced her to millions of Chinese television viewers. Despite her sharp tongue, her attitude towards dance and arts won her many fans, which resulted in extensive reports about her atypical life journey. The public soon learned from her frank speaking that she was born and lived as a man for most of her life. Jin was a colonel in the army, a dancer in the military singing and dancing troupe, and in 1988 became the first Chinese dancer to study in New York with governmental financial support. Jin married an American woman in 1990 and divorced her in 2000. While married, Jin had three homosexual love relationships with an American cowboy, an Italian psychiatrist, and a Belgian politician. After moving back to China, Jin underwent sex reassignment surgery in 1995, and eventually transformed into the woman she had wanted to become since the age of six. Jin then adopted three children and married a German businessman, Heinz-Gerd Oidtmann.

Following her success on *Wu Lin Dahui*, Jin became a national queer icon. Fearing that she would use her newfound television popularity to spread queer ideologies to national audiences, the State Administration of Radio, Film and Television demanded TV stations remove her and she was immediately taken off her second show, *Feitongfanxiang* (非同凡响, We are the Music). Her increasing popularity and the development of the LGBTQ movement in China, however, forced the government to tolerate her; for her part, Jin has become more careful about what she says in public. Her latest talk show, 'Jin Xing Show', is airing in China in 2015.

The formation of Chinese pop's cult of queerness has been influenced by multiple forces. Firstly, Chinese popular music has been a product of cultural globalisation since its birth in the early 20th century, but localising western popular music into Chinese popular music is never easy: musicians' cultural capital, education, life experience and attitudes all influence their music. Secondly, in the second half of the 20th century, the production of popular music developed into a broader cultural industry. The sharp decline of profit from conventional products like CDs and

DVDs forced the music industry to work closely with other industries, most notably internet-based companies, in their search for new markets and products. Burnett (1996) believes popular music might be the essential component in linking various sectors of the global entertainment industry. One effect of these linkages is that musical enterprises like these singing-talent TV shows, co-produced with the media industry, have reconstructed the production process. Now, at the stage of exploring new 'raw materials', the media industry and other business forces determine the extent to which entertainment value will be stressed more than musical and cultural value. Thirdly, music companies that wish to profit from the production of queer images must be sensitive to government concerns. The Chinese government will tolerate 'academic' voices in queer politics, such as the legislative campaign for civil partnership advocated by Li Yinhe, but it will not allow such campaigns to succeed and seems to become nervous when they move beyond formal, intellectual settings. The presentation of the queer in Chinese pop music is a 'one stone, two birds' strategy for the government and the creative industries. Allowing intellectual debate gives the outside world the opportunity to conclude that the government is politically tolerant and that the social environment for queer communities has improved. At the same time, allowing a politically neutralised cult of queerness benefits China's economy without generating 'real' social change. Flamboyant pop stars entertain TV or live audiences with a cheerful and liberal picture of today's China, but the truth is that the government continuously intervenes in all social activities of queer communities, demonstrated in the way that, for example, the Beijing Queer Film Festival has been forced into conducting itself as a semi-underground event.

Entertainment and Mediation

Probably having learned from their experience of dealing with rebellious Chinese rock music in the 1990s, the government knows that the most dangerous message does not come from the music itself, but from the social context that is generated from the interaction and communication between musicians and fans or social groups. Mediation, a sophisticated process generally open for all relevant social forces, affects the interpretation of ideologies from encoding to decoding. In our discussion, mediation shapes the development of music's significance from text to social

163

context. Although no one specific mediatory force can solely determine this process, the media, as the conventional gatekeeper, plays a vital role in filtering the content and message of cultural works. Since the media is controlled by the government, music mediation often becomes a means of blocking rebellious voices and engendering public support for official ideologies. A Taiwan indie record company *Hen Liuxing* (恨流行 Hate the Popular), for example, released two queer albums, *Touch* in 1997 and *Touch Together* in 1998. Most songs were written and performed by queer people, which reflected their real lives. Culturally, the two albums should have been extremely important as the earliest Chinese queer music, but since both albums were circulated only within underground communities, the albums did not communicate to a broader public, could not develop a social context, and ultimately made no contribution to the development of queer communities in Greater China. The media industry holds the key position in this process and the government employs a censorship system to control the media industry.

In reaction to various problems in the 1980s and with the development of the second economic reform in the 1990s, the government pushed the media industry towards a market economy by cutting down governmental subsidies. In order to earn profits, the media industry produced entertainment programmes to attract audiences and advertisers. This development shifted the government's direct role from away from production and toward cultural dissemination. Hence, the government could claim that the market was responsible for whatever the media chose to broadcast (Donald, Keane and Hong 2002). However, it was no accident that market incentives led to shows that redirected people's attention toward something less or even non-political. Baranovitch (2003) believes this helps to explain why politicised Chinese rock was no longer attractive in the 1990s. Public media often chose to embed ideological education into entertainment as *Hong ge* (红歌 red songs) – revolutionary songs have been repacked as popular music (Wang 2012).

Due to governmental control over the media industry, the queer message in Chinese pop is often mediated into plain entertainment. When Leslie Cheung had his final tour in 2000, he saved his statement song *Wo* (我 I) for last. He took off his glamorous costumes, washed off his makeup and came back to the stage wearing just a white bathrobe. He spoke to the audiences: 'The theme of this tour is "me". For human beings, in addition to loving other people, the most important thing is appreciating yourself.'[10] He then started singing 'I am what I am'. This performance was a powerful example of queer performativity – the song and staging were not just about his personal life, but also about queer people throughout Greater China. As a role model, he encouraged audience members to be honest with themselves and embrace themselves. Much later, Ma Haisheng performed 'Wo' in front of millions of TV viewers at the CCTV 14th National Youth Singing Contest in May 2010. It was not clear whether the programme producer and judges really understood this song, as only Ma's vocal performance was discussed. The political and cultural significance of this song had been completely mediated.

But not all performance in the contemporary Chinese scene mediates queerness away. In the face of governmental control, Li Yugang, a Chinese opera / popular music singer and actor, rapidly reached stardom by developing a connection between queer performance and traditional arts like Beijing opera as a strategy for capitalising on the market. Putting the question of the operatic authenticity of Li's performance aside, the cross-dressing (*fanchuan*) of his Nandan (男旦 male Dan performer) character from Beijing opera offers a protective umbrella to his queer performance. Cross-dressing as the traditional art of *fanchuan* is considered politically acceptable, but the so-called 'pseudo-ladies' of popular culture are not. Li was therefore welcomed to perform in the Great Hall of the People, but pseudo-ladies can only play in night clubs. The problem seems to lie in government censors' perception that queerness has sex appeal and is lustful while they see *fanchuan* to be sex-free. For these reasons, queer performers must repeatedly claim their normality. At the end of his performances, Li would change from his female costumes back to normal male clothes and stop singing in a falsetto but use his normal male vocal to sing a pop song to prove his gender normality Other entertainers also understand the rule. Facing doubts about whether he is gay, the extremely feminine-looking entertainer Ma Lishan has sought to prove his normality by publicly insulting women and declaring that he likes to touch women's breasts and that he can give women orgasms.[11]

---

10. This video clip can be watched on Youku website (accessed 10 June 2012): http://v.youku.com/v_show/id_XMzc0NzE1MzM2.html

11. This video clip can be watched online (accessed 9 June 2012): http://v.youku.com/v_show/id_XMzYyMTc3MTYw.html

The media industry is not alone in its engagement with the queer world. The fashion and beauty industries are keen to explore the queer market. They work together to promote and sell the idea of queerness as a modern lifestyle. The presenters and so-called experts on televised fashion or lifestyle programmes repeatedly urge audiences that it is time to join the global trend of crossing conventional gender borders; pop stars serve as perfect models.[12] Musically, the contribution of Taiwan boy group F4 is arguably limited, but culturally and economically, the cult of metro-sexuality *Huayang Meinan* (花样美男 Flower-like Beautiful Men) led by them since 2001 contributes massively to China's economy and the public presentation of gay men. Men's fashion magazines are the frontrunners in extracting wealth from the queer market. *Men's Style, Men's Uno, Men's Vogue, Bazaar Men's Style* and *L'Officiel Hommes*, all advocate *Nanxing Shishang* (男性时尚 male fashion), which is tightly linked to queer culture because gay designers, Chinese and foreign, are the major forces behind this fashion. *iLook* magazine released a special volume '*Gay China*' (translated as 中国真高兴 China is really happy) in August 2009, frankly stating that men's fashion is actually gay men's fashion, with straight men following the bold homo-style of gay men under the guise of following global fashion. Under these circumstances, the queer has infused what is seen as an avant-garde standard in fashion and daily life and the metrosexual, straight or gay, can be spotted easily in many metropolitan streets. Influenced by queer fashion style, a number of young people boldly and smartly seize every opportunity to show off their fashion sense in front of the media, gaining popularity and reward, such as Ma Lishan and Kongque Gege (孔雀哥哥 Peacock Brother).[13] This phenomenon might yet be deemed a cult of queerness, despite the fact that many men who dress fashionably insist they are not gay. The perception among many people that these styles are 'queer' may on the one hand offer an opportunity for queer people to be themselves, but on the other hand those in image-conscious industries may feel compelled to a certain extent to perform a kind of queerness in order to be fashion-

---

12. The fashion industry plays an important role in pushing Chinese men to embrace femininity and homosexuality as a part of their daily lives, see Tong Ting, 'Accentuate the Feminine', *Metro Beijing*, June 9, 2010, p.11

13. Both men are at pains to demonstrate that they are not gay, despite their queer-inflected style. See their blogs: http://blog.sina.com.cn/tel15910693940

able. A local hair stylist once reported to me that his boss demanded he dress more queerly. The hair stylist did not want to, but he kept his hair long and dyed it into a bright and strange colour, wearing an earring and tight clothes that showed his body shape in order to keep his job.[14]

In discussing the relationship between the media and sexuality, scholars like Gunter (2002) have introduced the term 'media sex' to explain how sex has been controlled and regulated in the mainstream media and consequently influenced the understanding of sex in society. The media structures a 'media queerness' to meet the needs of the government and creative industries, which can be seen especially in the popular TV singing-talent programmes. Season one of *Super Girl* was successful in 2004, but season two was phenomenal partially for the androgyny of the winner Li Yuchun and the rumours of her lesbian preferences. After Li Yuchun, each season saw several androgynous women, such as Zeng Yike and Li Xiaoyun, become the figures of a national debate related to queer issues. Because what they wear and use would be adored and bought by their fans, a kind of queer niche market has emerged in China as a result of this social and cultural phenomenon. In opposition to these stars' millions of admirers, millions of detractors have called them *Chun Ge* (春哥, Brother Li Yuchun) and *Zeng Ge* (曾哥 Brother Zeng Yike) in disgust towards their gender-ambiguous images and styles. Nevertheless, other TV programmes quickly learned that queerness could sell. When Dragon TV produced *Jiayou, Hao Nan'er* (加油，好男儿 My Hero) in 2006, feminine and beautiful young men, such as Xiang Ding, Pu Bajia and Song Xiaobo, dominated the show. If *Super Girl* symbolises the emergence of lesbianism, *My Hero* symbolises the coming out of gay men. In 2010, *Super Boy* pushed the trend to new heights by presenting transgender contestants. A group of 'pseudo-ladies', including Liu Zhu, Lai Chuan and Shang Chen, were placed in the spotlight and caused great controversy among audiences about the borders between sexuality and morality, homosexuality and heterosexuality, masculinity and femininity among the younger generations in today's China. Unlike Liu, Lai

---

14. His boss firstly said to him, '打扮时尚点儿' (dress more fashionably), and he responded by changing his dress style a bit. But his boss was not happy and then told him to '妖娆点儿' (be more alluring), showing him pictures on the Internet. The images were androgynous and sexualized. For men, '妖娆点儿' suggests a rather gay or queer style. The variety of ways people are asked to adapt to social expectations is striking.

and Shang managed to dodge governmental criticism by limiting their queerness to physical presentation rather than discussing in interviews what it might or might not mean.

Queerness mediated by the fashion industry for entertainment purposes has a double effect. In a positive way, the frequent presentation of queer effects in popular music, television, film, video and other forms of popular culture across a collective of different industries and regions can be regarded as a kind of cultural activism, especially with the development of convergence culture all over the world. Jenkins rightly points out that 'convergence refers to a process, not an endpoint' (2006: 16), which includes 'a top-down corporate-driven process and a bottom-up consumer-driven process' (*ibid.* 18). Jenkins argues that the relationship between media convergence, participatory culture and collective intelligence determines how content flows across multiple media platforms, continuously producing new content in transmedial storytelling and pushing the development of cultural activism. Activism consists of efforts to promote, impede or direct political, economic and social change. As collective actions, regardless of which method has been employed by activist groups – whether street protest, consumer activism, internet activism or culture jamming – activism can generate unpredictable social power and change the way people think, act and live their daily lives. In comparison with other forms of direct conflict with governing or dominating bodies, cultural activism seems to be less political, aggressive and radical, but its wide influence can guarantee that it is an effective and efficient way of alluding to political and social problems or conflicts by using symbolic, cultural and artistic expressions to produce enlightenment, reflection and awareness. For example, one of my informants knew that she was a lesbian for years but, before the Li Yuchun phenomenon in 2005, she had considered getting married. After Li won the show, she said she observed lesbians more often in public and regained her faith in a queer lifestyle. Media reports about introduced the idea of queerness to her parents and, when she finally came out to them, they accepted it without any of the ugly episodes she had imagined and feared for years.[15]

---

15. This is one among hundreds of stories collected during fieldwork conducted at the Beijing LGBT Center, Lesbian Salon, universities, and other social occasions in Beijing from 2009 to 2012.. In total, over 100 queer and heterosexual people

On the negative side, in order to avoid government intervention, the creative industries purposely make queerness ambiguous by presenting it in an exaggerated but entertaining style, as, for example, with those rather shallow and flamboyant gay characters in *Chou Nü Wudi* (丑女无敌 the Invincible Ugly Girl, Chinese version of *Ugly Betty*). Li Yuchun won the 2005 *Super Girl* competition because of her queer image, personality and charisma, but her vocal and singing skills were no better than those of the other two finalists. Even though a seemingly queer image got Li Yuchun the prize, her 'image team' tried very hard to devalue the symbolic capital of her queerness and to remake her into a mainstream heterosexual woman. This process left her image neither queer nor normal. Li and her team succeeded in persuading Jean Paul Gaultier to provide five sets of clothes for her 'Crazy World' concert tour in 2012, but all Li could deliver was the performance of a fashion model, generating little more than entertainment news. Clearly, performers must go beyond simply showing a queer image and follow through with involvement or clear statements of support in order to create the kinds of cultural and social influence that other Gaultier-clad artists such as Madonna in the 1990s and Leslie Cheung during his 'Passion' concert tour in 2000.

My queer informants perceived the differences between performance and performativity – the difference between Li Yuchun and Leslie Cheung, for example – and were generally highly critical of the media. Because queer issues are less directly important for heterosexual people, they are perhaps less interested in finding out what the queer really is about and they often take what the media give to them. Queer people, however, are much more critical and go to greater lengths to find trustworthy resources, generally being upset about queer content reported by or presented in the media. In my study, I used a scale of one to ten to measure the influence of the media on people's ideas about queerness and found that for straight people, the significance of the media on their ideas about the queer measured 6.9, but for queer people, the significance of the media in this respect was 3.7. A 22-year-old gay student told

---

were involved with interviews, questionnaires, and open discussions. Their ages ranged from 18 to mid-40s, and all except one had graduate or post-graduate educational backgrounds. Quantitative data is based on completed questionnaires, 14 from queer people, and 10 from heterosexual people.

me, 'The modern media are demons!' A 24-year-old lesbian editor said, 'The influence of the media on me is limited because I am very vigilant, and I do not want to be controlled by the media. What influences me the most comes from books and music.' A 26-year-old lesbian accused the media: 'Reports on queer issues are always negative, and the media's influence is really bad. I think the media are really important. It is exciting to have them report about the queer, but why do they always treat it as something negative?' As long as the governmental control over the media and the creative industries remains the same, media reports and uses of the queer will be continuously mediated into a form of entertainment in order to prevent a transformation from queer-seeming performance to queer performativity.

The Twofold Logic of Queer Politics

Pop, it seems clear, cannot automatically become a queer political medium; how it functions depends on how it interacts with record companies, the media, the audiences and the government. For example, one radio station in Singapore selected the top ten pop songs welcomed by queer audiences in 2005, but record companies immediately condemned this selection and claimed those songs were all about heterosexual love. A Beijing journalist voiced absurdly: 'This selection displays a wrong orientation, which does not only stain music and the entertainment circle, but also human nature and dignity'.[16] However, such fallacious condemnations do not change the reality that popular music, including its queer images and ideas, has penetrated people's daily lives. In my own research, I found that on a scale from zero to ten, the average importance of popular music in daily life is 6.1 for heterosexual people and 7.0 for queer people. A 21-year-old gay student explained to me, 'I cannot live without music. Music is like lubricant, which can make the gears of life work smoothly'. Queer people also spend more time listening to music, averaging 19.6 hours per week. To the extreme, a gay designer I interviewed plays music whenever he works, so roughly 90 hours per week. In comparison, the average time for the heterosexual people in

---

16. Hao, Xiaonan, 'the selection of pop songs welcomed by gay men by one radio station upsets other people', *Beijing Star Daily*, April 2, 2005, information is from the Internet (accessed 2 December 2010): http://ent.qq.com/music/a/20050402/000012.htm

my study is 13.0 hours. Neither group, however, thinks that Chinese popular music has contributed substantially to queer social activities and movements: the average figures of contribution are 3.0 out of 10 for heterosexual people and 3.5 for queer people. This is why the queer group is extremely frustrated and even angry: they feel that queer pop stars such as Li Yuchun and Han Hong have not spoken for queer communities in public. Even one-time national 'Golden Boy' Mao Ning, who was stabbed by a male lover and therefore exposed as gay, did not directly come out afterwards, despite the fact that many fans perceived he would have nothing to lose, as his career had begun to suffer in any case. At the same time, many others doubted his coming-out would make a difference because the Chinese government was not ready to allow the queer to be legitimately acknowledged. The queer is a serious political issue from the perspective of legitimating people's identities, but it does not often rise above the surface of people's everyday concerns.

Sex, sexuality, gender and body are highly politicised regardless of historical period, geographical location, ethnicity, social system or cultural form. In ancient China, sexual activities and political machinations were often combined in the capture of power (Goldin 2002), but in today's China, adultery is considered an issue of moral degeneracy in politics and is serious enough to have resulted in the dismissal of a large number of high-ranking communist officials.[17] In various forms of culture, sex issues are always conflicting. For example, Jia Pingwa, a well-known Chinese writer, whose controversial novel, *Fei Du* (废都 the Abandoned Capital), features a sexual pervert as its hero, explains that 'with no power, no money, no influence, sex is the only thing he can escape to from this hollow life' (quoted in Zha 1995: 150). Despite winning the *Prix Fémina* prize in France, *Fei Du* was banned in China until 17 years after its publication in 1993. Zhang Yimou, one of the most influential tastemakers in the contemporary Chinese cultural scene, takes this argument further, claiming that the relationship between sex and traditional morality can be more sensitive than politics.[18] Comparing

---

17. For example, this news report covers ten high-ranking officials who were dismissed in ten days (accessed 25 July 2014): http://news.sina.com.cn/c/2014-07-12/061330508167.shtml

18. Lin Chufang, 'Zhang Yimou is the biggest opportunist in China' (*Zhang Yimou shi zhongguo zui touji de ren*), information is from the Internet (accessed 18 September

his early to his recent films, one notices a remarkable desexualisation, a process that aligns with his ever closer relationship with the government. Sex and sexuality have become important elements to exchange for power and reward. Perhaps in one way, this is what Foucault (1978: 103) means:

Sexuality must not be described as a stubborn drive, by nature alien and of necessity disobedient to a power which exhausts itself trying to subdue it and often fails to control it entirely. It appears rather as an especially dense transfer point for relations of power... Sexuality is not the most intractable element in power relations, but rather one of those endowed with the greatest instrumentality: useful for the greatest number of manoeuvres and capable of serving as a point of support, as a linchpin, for the most varied strategies.

Because of its political and commercial significance, the queer is surely endowed with the greatest instrumentality. Popular music and the queer have become inseparable since the likes of David Bowie, Marc Bolan, Freddie Mercury, Elton John, Patti Smith, Madonna, Marilyn Manson and Lady Gaga. People can dislike these artists' queerness for different reasons, but they cannot deny the cultural influence these artists have had in the past few decades and down to the present day. Queerness can arise spontaneously from musicians' daily lives, but it can also be commercially fabricated to form an industrial product. Queerness is not only about sexuality, gender and image, but also about ideology, attitude and lifestyle. For example, Hong Kong Chinese pop superstar Faye Wong is famous for her queerness. Because she is a heterosexual woman and a mother of two, few people doubt her sexual orientation, but her uncompromising preference for alternative rock and her marriage with Dou Wei generate an unexpected gender politics in Chinese pop (Fung and Curtin 2002). Although she has distanced herself from queer communities by, for example, refusing to respond to an impersonation show dedicated to her and organised by the Beijing LGBT centre in January 2011, she remains a queer icon in Chinese pop and still influences all kinds of people across Greater China, including young Taiwanese women of all orientations (see Chou 1998).

After Zhang Huimei publically voiced her support to queer communities and, with the development of LGBT movements in Greater

2010): http://finance.jrj.com.cn/biz/2010/09/2813588247433.shtml

China, queer issues need to be handled delicately by the Chinese government in its now more subtle but nevertheless importantly political role in culture and commerce. The emergence of Lady Gaga as the new global queer icon in 2009, however, offered a practical solution. Lady Gaga is a very talented musician, but what impresses general audiences in China the most is the queerness created by the performer and her team (known as The Haus of Gaga). Under the influence of local commercial forces in China, her sophisticated ideological, political and self-identified queerness has been simplified to business strategies in relation to visuals that aim to sell fashion products or draw the attention of the public. Very often, these queer images or styles are advocated as something cool within the context of global fashion. This banalization shows up, for instance, in the way that the phrase 'Oh my God' has been changed to 'Oh my Lady Gaga' by many students at Beijing No. 171 middle-school.[19] Her songs 'Poker Face' and 'Bad Romance' became the most popular ringtone among students for a while and the queerness of Lady Gaga's image resonates with students, who revel in it as a form of rebellion. None of them could really understand what Lady Gaga is expressing in her music and videos, but the super-cool fashion images she presented were significant for their non-normativity. One student once threatened his parents, saying that he would dress up Lady-Gaga-style if they did not allow him to have a weekend trip with his friends. Students' admiration for Lady Gaga is not due to their understanding and appreciation of her music per se, but her queer image as a superbly cool and different pop star. The deliberate or accidental mix of Kuer (酷儿, queer) and Ku (酷, cool) generates two opposite effects on society and culture: the simultaneous advocacy of one form of queerness while ignoring others. On the one hand, Chinese pop becomes a platform for queer performativity; on the other hand, developing queer performativity into commercial entertainment as it moves around the globe disrupts its path and makes it into a rather mechanical performance for fun and publicity.

This paradoxical development is not solely designed, conducted and controlled by the government, but supported and challenged by the Chinese creative industries. When analysing the influence of rock music

---

19. I followed a group of students at Beijing No. 171 mid-school between 2009 and 2011.

on global pop, Regev (2002) suggests that three major characteristics cause the inevitable trend of *'pop-rockization'*[20]: a typical set of creative practices, a body of canonised albums and two logics of cultural dynamics. Avant-gardism and commercialism are the two logics. Avant-gardism refers to a cultural logic of inventiveness and commercialism refers to a cultural logic driven by market interests. Probably encouraged by Zhang Huimei and inspired by Lady Gaga, the queerness cult in Chinese pop developed rapidly. The queer became more visible in the pop scene and more gay-themed pop songs were released, a development most likely triggered for three major reasons: unknown queer musicians' bold coming-out (such as Liu Zhu's) because they had nothing to lose,[21] heterosexual musicians' (such as S.H.E.'s) support of queer communities,[22] and opportunists' (such as Huang Youjie) marketing strategies for publicity.[23] Although the Chinese government gave permission for the first gay parade in Shanghai in 2009 and has a policy of *bu zhichi, bu fandui, bu tichang* (不支持, 不反对, 不提倡 no support, no opposition and no advocacy), this does not imply that the era of queer liberation

20. Pop-rockization has dominated the development of popular music in the second half of the twentieth century in the West. Rock music has become a component used for making other popular music genres, especially mainstream pop music, and cause the once very clear border between rock music and pop music to become blurred.

21. Liu Zhu had 'nothing to lose' because he was not a successful pop star at the time, though now he is well on his way. He lost the *Super Boy* competition itself, but later, because of the attention he received on the show, he was invited to attend many other TV shows. Though certainly he had to make compromises (such as by wearing androgynous clothes rather than women's clothes) to avoid governmental intervention, he was still able to release the album *Matchless* in September 2010, and in October 2010, he had a personal concert at Chengdu stadium, demonstrating a great achievement for a university student.

22. As a very popular girl band in Greater China, S.H.E. tells a story of how three young ladies fall in love with two gay men, but when the two gay men come out to them, they not only accept the two gay men as good friends, but also help them to deal with their families in the music video *Bu Zuo Ni De Pengyou* (不作你的朋友 Not Gonna Be Your Friend).

23. In his music video *Shang Ai Zui* (伤爱罪 Hurt, Love, and Guilt), Huang claimed that he wanted to show his support to the gay communities, but the story of how a married gay man betrayed his wife and the explicit picture of male sexual intercourse in public angered the gay audiences who accused Huang of employing gay issues for publicity.

has finally arrived in China. Instead, the cult of queerness created by Lady Gaga offered a practical solution to the cultural industries and the government for the presentation and control of queerness – it could seem avant-garde while remaining commercially viable.

Genuine avant-gardism, although it is only for the minority of pop artists such as Anthony Wong, is nevertheless extremely important to minority communities. Artists like Wong are keen to express their thoughts, ideologies and attitudes related to the queer, and practice queer performativity in their music, stage performances and daily lives in order to produce their queer identity. Commercialisation is for the majority of pop stars, especially boy bands (such as A-one) that are keen to strengthen their popularity and rewards through rebellious queer performance, despite a disinterest in queer issues and politics.

In this mode of producing queerness, the Chinese government plays an often unnoticed gatekeeper role, employing its administrative power to promote or terminate projects to in a way that serves state interests. As long as pop artists are not too ideologically or politically provocative, the Chinese government will not intervene. However, when it senses something too defiant or subversive, which might transform queer entertainment into queer politics, then the government reacts quickly, demands instant changes, or suspends or terminates the production. But how much is too much? Without a clear answer, creative industries have little choice but to practice self censorship. Today, the government is experienced in controlling the dissemination of cultural products because the inability of state-owned companies to produce adequate hourly TV programmes in the 1990s made the separation between production and broadcasting possible. The government does not often intervene in production, but it maintains the final word in what is broadcast. Therefore, this twofold logic of queer politics efficiently guides governmental control. Avant-gardism likely produces queer performativity, which contributes to the development of queer politics for social movements. Although the government would not suppress it as harshly as it might have in the 1980s it will closely monitor its development and try to prevent its influence from spreading into mainstream culture. If this development cannot be prevented, the government will then try to incorporate it through commodification and ideologization, as identified by Hebdige (1979). Commercialisation surely produces queer performance, which broadens the market of queer entertainment for further commercial return. These two logics are reciprocal and maintain the balance which the government and the creative industries both need in today's China.

Conclusion

The presentation of the queer in Chinese pop in recent years does not signal the arrival of an era of better political, social and living environments in China. Yet, because of the global importance of queer cultures and images and because China arguably has millions of queer people, the government must tolerate queer-seeming performances in Chinese pop. This tolerance of image helps prevent queer performance from developing into queer performativity and from becoming a politically significant phenomenon. This demonstrates a twofold logic of control. The government monitors so-called avant-gardism to ensure it does not transmit the political value of queer performativity, while encouraging the commercialisation of a lively 'queer' performance scene and energising China's cultural economy. Because of the government's control over culture industries, queerness has generally been mediated into a kind of superficial 'weirdness' in Chinese popular culture and has become a symbol of global fashion related to entertainment, fun and 'coolness'. A small number of pop stars are trying to support queer communities through their work, but the majority are simply using the image of the queer for publicity. This does not lead to a purely pessimistic conclusion that Chinese pop cannot contribute to queer communities as some of its western counterparts have done. In fact, Chinese pop has opened up audiences to a potentially queer medium and at least broadened their tastes. But only when more thoughtful musicians who are not afraid of involving themselves with cultural activities related to queer life come to the stage will pop be truly performative and contribute to improvements in the lives of queer people.

References

Baranovitch, Nimrod (2003) *China's new Voices: Popular music, ethnicity, gender, and politics, 1978–1997*, University of California Press.

Bourdieu, Pierre (1984) *Distinction: A social critique of the judgement of taste*, London: Routledge and Kegan Paul.

Brett, Thomas and Woods (eds, 1994) *Queering the Pitch: The new gay and lesbian musicology*, London: Routledge.

Burnett, Robert (1996) *The Global Jukebox, the international music industry*, London and New York: Routledge.

Butler, Judith (1993) 'Critically Queer', *GLQ: A journal of lesbian and gay studies* vol. 1, no. 1, pp.17–32.

Chou, Ch'ien-i (1998) 'From the Star to the Fans: The formation of gender subjects in fandom and popular music' [cong wangfei dao fei mi – liuxing yinyue ouxiang chongbai zhong zhuti de tuancheng], *Mass Communication Research* (Xinwenxue yanjiu), Vol.56, pp.105–134.

De Kloet, Joroen (2001) *Red Sonic Trajectories: Popular music and youth in urban China*, University of Amsterdam.

Donald, Stephanie Hemelyrk, Michael Keane and Yin Hong (eds, 2002) *Media in China: Consumption, content, and crisis*, RoutledgeCurzon.

Foucault, Michel (1978) *The History of Sexuality, Volume I: An Introduction*, trans. Robert Hurley, New York: Pantheon Books.

Fung, Anthony and Michael Curtin (2002) 'The Anomalies of being Faye (Wong): Gender politics in Chinese popular music', *International Journal of Cultural Studies*, Vol.5, No.3, pp.263–290

Goldin, Paul Rakita (2002) *the Culture of Sex in Ancient China*, University of Hawai'i Press.

Gunter, Barrie (2002) *Media Sex: What are the issues?* New York: Lawrence Erlbaum Associates.

Hebdige, Dick (1979) *Subculture: The meaning of style*, London and New York: Routledge.

Jenkins, Henry (2006) *Convergence Culture: Where old and new media collide*, New York and London: New York University Press.

Jones, Andrew F. (1992) *Like a Knife: Ideology and genre in Chinese popular music*, Ithaca, NY: Cornell University East Asian Program.

Martin, Fran (2003a) *Situating Sexualities: Queer representation in Taiwanese fiction, film and public culture*, Hong Kong University Press.

——— (2003b) 'The Perfect Lie: Sandee Chan and lesbian representability in mandarin pop music', *Inter-Asia Cultural Studies*, Vol. 4, No. 2, pp.264–280.

Regev, Motti (2002) 'The 'Pop-rockisation' of Popular Music', in David Hesmondhalgh and Keith Negus (eds) *Popular Music Studies*, London: Arnold, pp.251–264.

Ruan, Fang-fu and Tsai, Yung-mei (1987) 'Male homosexuality in traditional Chinese literature', *Journal of Homosexuality*, Vol.14, No. 3&4, pp.21–34.

Song, Hwee Lim (2007) *Celluloid Comrades: Representations of male homosexuality in contemporary Chinese cinemas*, University of Hawai'i Press.

Waldman, Tom (2003) *We All Want to Change the World: Rock and politics from Elvis to Eminem*, Taylor Trade Publishing.sWang, Qian (2012) 'Red Songs and the Main Melody: Cultural nationalism and political propaganda in Chinese popular music', *Perfect Beat*, vol. 13, no. 2, pp. 127–146.

Whiteley, Sheila and Jennifer Rycenga (eds, 2006) *Queering the Popular Pitch*, Routledge.

Zha, Jianying (1995) *China Pop: How soap operas, tabloids, and bestsellers are transforming a culture*, New York: New Press.

CHAPTER 10

Coming Home, Coming Out
Doing Fieldwork in an Unfamiliar Homeland

Lucetta Yip Lo Kam

While flipping through piles of old photographs, I came across one that was taken in 2005 when I was attending the first *nütongzhi* (lesbian) conference in Beijing. That was the first time I participated in a *tongzhi* (LGBTQ) conference in China and it was also during the first year of my field research for my doctoral dissertation on *lala* (the local identity for lesbian, bisexual and transgender women) communities in Shanghai. It was an eye-opening experience for me to see the exploding energies of *lala* communities in China. Looking back, I realized that I had witnessed one of the most important times of *tongzhi* movement in China. In the same year, in addition to the first tongzhi conference held in Beijing, there was the birth of the first lesbian group in Shanghai and the launch of *les+*, the first queer women magazine in China.

My research project was an ethnographic study of *lala* women in Shanghai and a participatory investigation of emerging *tongzhi* politics and communities in China. It aims to look at the negotiation between the new life aspirations of *lala*-identified women and the existing heterosexual requirements imposed on them. In particular, the ways they used to cope with the pressure of marriage. In this chapter, I explore the two pairs of dual roles I played while conducting the research for this project: first, I was both a local and an outsider in Shanghai; second, I was fellow community member as well as researcher in relation to my *lala* informants.

Being an ethnic Chinese and lesbian-identified researcher when undertaking research on lesbians in China has its advantages. Travis Kong shares a similar experience of doing research among gay communities in China where he is 'one of them' (Kong 2011: 209). It is easier for a gay researcher to build rapport in the early stages and to be accepted by

179

the interviewees than it is for a straight-identified researcher. However, Kong also discusses the many possible differences between a gay researcher and his respondents, such as 'class, age, education and other socio-cultural factors' (*ibid.*). In particular, being a queer activist and researcher, I have taken many roles in the community I researched. In addition to being a researcher, I was a participant in the local lesbian communities, a co-worker in lesbian activist projects and a friend to many in the local *tongzhi* communities – including some of my informants. I shifted between roles in different occasions throughout my years in the field, seeking always to be aware of the ethical obligations of each role.

In addition, the fact that I presented myself to local *lala* communities as a fellow participant also requires me to share the same honesty with my readers. The honesty of a researcher about her personal identification should extend also to her readers (Williams 1996: 83). This is a basic ethical requirement of a field researcher. Therefore, being out in the field also includes the fact that I have to be out to my readers and the academic community. Yet, the disclosure or coming out with my queer identification also involves personal struggles, especially when being honest to my readers means that I announce my personal sexual identifications to unknown public and professional communities.

I hope the sharing of my experiences in this chapter can invite more intimate discussions of similar experiences among queer-identified researchers who are conducting fieldwork or doing LGBT research in China, or those who are doing research in their original homelands after relocating to other places for a longer period of time.

Tongzhi Communities in China

Since the late 1990s, *tongzhi* communities in China have been developing rapidly. New grassroots *tongzhi* groups have been founded every year in big and small cities, and *tongzhi* websites have multiplied. Compared to Hong Kong, *tongzhi* activists in China face much more severe forms of political intervention; the threat posed by state authorities and social control organs is ubiquitous. It is crucial for them to be fully aware of their rights and related laws to protect themselves in possible confrontations with the state authorities. They need to develop highly flexible strategies and have contingency plans in place (see chapters by Bao,

Engebretsen, Fan/Cui, Fu, Huang, and Wei in this volume for examples of regional practices).

This highly flexible nature of *tongzhi* activism is illustrated by the organization of lesbian parties in Shanghai at this time. I was curious about the 'nomadic' form of these parties when I first entered the field. Unlike those in Hong Kong, they were not attached to specific bars. Instead, Shanghai's lesbian parties were organized by a form of contractual agreement between the organisers and bar owners. The parties were then brought by the organizers to different locations. For example, a very popular lesbian party called 'the Butterfly' (*hudieba*) was active while I conducted my fieldwork. Every few months, the Butterfly landed in a new location and party-goers followed the organizer like nomadic tribes chasing after a desert oasis.

Nomadic lesbian parties and guerrilla style *tongzhi* activism have developed as a response to the volatile political environment in China. In addition to adopting flexible activist strategies and developing a comprehensive knowledge of their legal rights, *tongzhi* activists develop a sense of humour in the face of direct state interventions. A scene that well represents the confrontation between *tongzhi* activists and the force of local police intervention was documented by Elisabeth Engebretsen. Organizers of the Beijing Queer Film Festival in 2009 used humour as a form of resistance while reiterating their rights in the face of state intervention:

> Comic relief works wonders in such testy environments; at the opening screening of the 2009 festival, where I was in the audience, one of the organizers humorously addressed the 'hidden' plainclothes police in the audience, saying he hoped they would also enjoy the films. (Engebretsen 2011)

Despite these serious threats, *tongzhi* communities (both online and offline) have expanded rapidly. More and more young and passionate organizers are joining the *tongzhi* movements and creative ways of activism have been developed to combat state control.

I carried out fieldwork in Shanghai's *lala* communities between 2005 and 2010, including formal, semi-structured, recorded interviews with twenty-five self-identified *lala* women. While interacting with my informants, my primary role was as a researcher from Hong Kong with a background in local *tongzhi* activism. I also revealed to my informants that I am a Shanghai native and can speak the local dialect. Interestingly, however, many of the women who were active in the local *lala* communities were not Shanghai natives. Our common language on many occasions was mandarin or *putonghua* (standard Chinese).

The topics of family and marriage were frequently reported as major causes of stress in *lala* women's everyday lives. This was partly due to the fact that the most active and visible women in local *lala* communities were in their twenties, the so-called marital age. The intensity of this pressure led me to reflect on the social meaning of marriage in China and how marriage is understood by individuals. Rather than seeing marriage as a personal lifestyle choice and a union based on romantic love, as it is usually represented in popular culture and other public discourses, *lala* women told me different stories. To many, marriage seems to be an obligation rather than a voluntary choice. It is done to fulfil the expectation of family and society. It is done to make one look 'normal' and 'respectable'. It is done to make others recognize one's status as an adult. These cultural meanings of marriage in China enrich my understanding of *lala* women's stress of dealing with pressure to get married and also the different meanings attached to the politics of coming out in China.

The conflict between *lala* women's self-assertive *tongzhi* identification and social demands to lead a 'normal' heterosexual married life have generated a culturally specific politics of resistance. Public recognition prioritized other struggles. The recognitions range from material success and personal achievements to a so-called 'healthy' and 'sunny' *tongzhi* image and lifestyle. The compulsory nature of marriage in China leads to the practice of cooperative marriage (*hezuo hunyin* or *xingshi hunyin*), a mutually consented marriage performance between a *lala* woman and a gay man. Despite the many obvious risks and problems of the practice, it has become increasingly popular among *lalas* and gay men all over the country. This research led to my first book titled *Shanghai Lalas: Female Tongzhi Communities and Politics in Urban China* (2013) and a number of journal articles published in English and Chinese (Kam 2006; Kam 2010; Kam 2011).

Being a Native Outsider

I grew up in Shanghai in the 1970s. At that time, '*tongzhi*' was a generic identity that applied to everyone. Regardless of one's gender, age and occupation, people addressed each other by this term and everyone was assumed to be a communist comrade. I migrated to Hong Kong at an early age. Apart from short yearly visits to see my family members in Shanghai, I did not have much participation in China during the time when *tongzhi* was a communist identity. After 2000, the term has undergone a drastic change. In popular usage, it refers more to an emerging community of proud sexual and gender minorities. The new *tongzhi* communities (better to be used in plural term) are usually loosely translated as the LGBTQ communities. But 'comradeship' is ever expanding and LGBTQ is an insufficient English equivalent. In 2005, I returned to my hometown for the first time as a researcher. I started conducting field research there and was hoping to get in touch with the local *tongzhi* communities. I was amazed to see the transformation of the meaning of '*tongzhi*', which corresponded to the dramatic change in China over the years before and after its economic reform (started in the 1980s).

I started the field research of *lala* communities in Shanghai on 4 June 2005 and, from that very day, my hometown Shanghai has become a research field. The result was it turned out to be so 'unfamiliar'. After decades of rapid urban development, Shanghai has become almost an entirely new city to me. I had to carry a city map and asking for directions became a daily routine. Naturally, I asked people on the street for directions in the local dialect, in which I am still quite fluent. But after a few odd looks and suspicious gazes from people whom I stopped to ask, I realized that it was something about the dialect I used. Usually I asked for places or roads that were quite well known, such as a landmark building in the downtown area. I came to realize that, when I asked about those well-known locations in fluent Shanghainese, people would think that I was trying to cheat them as they could not understand why a 'local' did not know how to go to those easily accessible places. After that, I shifted to *putonghua* (mandarin) to ask for directions. Although people's reactions were not any friendlier than when I spoke in Shanghainese, I did not get those strange looks. Encounters like these resulted from the difference between assumptions locals made about me and what I really was. I was both an insider and outside in the city.

The idea of dual roles also applies to my relationship with the local *lala* communities. My personal engagement with them became more pronounced when I became involved in *tongzhi* activism in China. Shortly after I started field research, I became involved in a number of local lesbian activist projects. As a researcher, the *tongzhi* community was a 'field' to be studied and analysed. As an activist, it was a community that I personally identified with. There were times I needed to choose between roles and take care not to traverse the delicate line of trust.

Dual Roles

My research in Shanghai connects memories and experiences that happened in different locations and periods of time. Taking up the role as a researcher, I harnessed my academically-trained curiousity to the task of reconnecting fading memories of an older, communist Shanghai with the reality of a fast-growing, newly-marketized Shanghai that stood before me. This work allowed me to detach myself from the familiar route of family visits and venture into the new world of post-reform China. Like Alice in Wonderland, I paid attention to every possible hint of everyday norms and codes of practice. Every moment on the street, over the dinner table, or in the subway train could teach me about the environment I was studying. I had to learn how to walk safely on narrow sidewalks that pedestrians shared with cyclists. I had to learn the proper distance between bodies in different social occasions. I had to learn from others the local ways to eat and drink. I was forced to learn to be aggressive so as to catch a taxi during rush hour. I had to translate Hong Kong Chinese terms into mainland Chinese terms and learn to speak more like a local. I had to learn carefully what people expected from me and how cultural expectations varied from one sub-community to another. On top of all this, I had to learn as quickly as possible the internal codes of the local *lala* communities, such as how to address each other, what to expect in a first meeting with a new informant, how to keep in contact, and how far I could probe into personal backgrounds. I found myself shifting between the roles of insider and outsider, between terrains of familiarity and unfamiliarity. The insider/outsider tension also demanded constant management of my informants' expectations of me. For example, it might take time for some of them to realize I did not know as much about local society as they first assumed. Or, for others, I might know more than they expected about Shanghai social customs.

The notion of the inside outsider (or outside insider) role defined the relationship between myself and my informants. On the first day of field research, I went to a restaurant in downtown to meet Laoda (pseudonym) and a few of her *lala* friends. Laoda was a local *lala* community organizer and we had been in online contact before we met in person.

We were all a bit shy at the beginning. I introduced myself as a research student from the Chinese University of Hong Kong conducting a research project on *lala* communities in Shanghai. I spoke in *putonghua* with a Hong Kong accent (as others told me later). This was an obvious sign that I was not a local. I had thought about the possibility for embarrassment in the first meeting. Therefore, I did two things to help break the ice. First, I declared my identification with them in this subtle way: I wore a necklace with a female gender symbol. Also, I brought a few copies of a book on women's same-sex love that I had edited and published in Hong Kong (Kam 2001). This was a significant moment of rapport and trust building; the women were excited and started to read immediately. The second 'ice-breaking' moment was when I revealed that I was born and grew up in Shanghai. This disclosure was usually followed by a 'performance' of me speaking the local dialect. The connection between my informants and myself in terms of our multiple identifications – sexual/political and geographical as well as gender, ethnicity and age – recurred throughout the field research period. It was a necessary and productive process in building rapport. At the same time, my research also enabled me to look into the differences between various identities across space. The meanings of 'woman', a 'Chinese' and a '*tongzhi*' could be significantly different in Shanghai, compared with how these ideas are understood in Hong Kong.

As I stepped out of my home and marched into the unfamiliar field, I was confronted by a Shanghai that had transformed itself into a city of migrants. The most obvious evidence of this is everyday language. The lingua franca in restaurants, shops, government offices, workplaces, banks, offices and schools is now *putonghua*. The large-scale population movement across the country during the economic reform is reflected in the geographical origins of Shanghai's *lala*s. I estimate that half of the major organizers and active members in local communities were not locals. Most of these women were young and had come from all over China to study, work or explore new life opportunities in Shanghai. At many community gatherings, I was the only one or one of the few participants who knew how to speak Shanghainese.

My dual roles as insider and outsider to my informants raised important methodological concerns. Some of the most distinctive features of feminist methodology include an egalitarian research process that values the reciprocity and intersubjectivity between the researcher and the researched (Stacey 1988: 22). Yet, the intimate knowledge produced from intensive participatory field research also triggers many questions. Among them, the insider and outsider roles of researchers are much discussed in the feminist research tradition. For an insider researcher, which means she is studying cultures similar to her own, it is important that she engages in a constant effort to 'defamiliarize' herself from cultural practices or values that are familiar to her. In turn, an outsider researcher needs to deal with her own ignorance and unfamiliarity at the beginning of a project and, later, to maintain a sense of strangeness that might otherwise be worn off during the research process (Acker 2000: 194). This is even more complicated when a researcher is both insider and outsider to her research subjects, which is the case for me. I have had to deal with the challenges of both positions.

My strategy was to carry out cross-references between my two positions. For example, I would highlight the geo-cultural differences between myself and my informants when shared experiences such as coming out to parents were discussed. I would try to defamiliarize myself with their accounts by distinguishing them from apparently similar experiences in other societies. In this way, it was possible to find the cultural specificities of Shanghai *lalas*. On the other hand, I was also a cultural outsider to my informants regarding our regional backgrounds. In order not to let the cultural gap between us become detrimental to our interactions, I made a conscious effort to study the local society before and during field research. Taking advantage of the fact that I have local kin connections in Shanghai, I took every chance of meeting local people in an attempt to get as much insider knowledge of Shanghai as possible. For example, I learned much about Shanghai's marriage norms and culture by talking to local people in various social gatherings.

Lala individuals and communities in Shanghai were also simultaneously familiar and unfamiliar to me. At the time of starting the research project, I had already been participating in *tongzhi* communities in Hong Kong for more than ten years. Apart from the limited information and a few personal encounters with early organizers in the late 1990s, I knew very little about *tongzhi* in mainland China. This research project allowed me to connect my experiences in the *tongzhi* communities in these two locations. New insights and knowledge obtained in the field shed light on the differences and similarities between the two societies and the two *tongzhi* communities. Different trajectories of socio-political developments and systems give rise to quite different notions of 'common sense' and value systems.

One of the most telling examples is the range of views on heterosexual marriage. The social expectation of marriage is much higher in China than in Hong Kong. Marriage effectively controls everyone and defines their social positions. Women are especially vulnerable to marriage pressures as they are usually inferior in economic and social status. From the life stories of *lala* informants, I have come to understand more about how marriage affects women in China, how their social and familial statuses are tied to their marital status, and how their value is judged solely by their marriage status. This reality and these judgements have deep impacts on *lala* women's psychological and physical well-being.

The expression of social control through marriage is somewhat different in Hong Kong. Direct and compulsory intervention from senior social members such as parents, older relatives, and senior colleagues through match-making meetings, for instance, are less prevalent and less often regarded as a socially accepted practice. Social pressure is expressed more often through stigmatizing and demonizing single women; the popular media plays a major role in this process (Kam 2012). At the same time, people celebrate 'successful' single women in Hong Kong, such as female entrepreneurs, actresses and politicians. Marriage has increasingly become a lifestyle option in Hong Kong, while it is still largely held as the only recognized way of a 'normal' life in China.

Discrepancies in social values and norms give rise to different forms of activism and issues of concern in local *tongzhi* communities (Engebretsen 2013; Kam 2013; Kong 2011; Wong 2004). For instance, the notion of 'coming out' is differently understood in China and is more likely to be rejected as nonessential by mainland *tongzhi* communities. This new revelation and knowledge from the field often led me to reflect on my own assumptions and taken-for-granted views on certain issues such as coming out. The struggles of Chinese *lalas* and their lived experiences of coming out or not coming out invited me to look further into the complicated reality of Chinese families and socie-ties, and to open up my imagination of what *tongzhi* movements could be like and how discrimination against *tongzhi* is related to other forms of social inequality.

There are many advantages to having a personal involvement in the community one studies. This is especially the case when the community is a socially stigmatized one. In my experience of doing field research in China, my public self-identification as a lesbian researcher had built trust immediately. The sharing of experiences such as coming out and the day-to-day pressure of living as a lesbian in Chinese society is es-sential in rapport building; it also contributes to the self-understanding of both the researcher and the interviewees (Kong 2011). I found that gatekeepers were more willing to grant access to a lesbian-identified researcher. Most of my interviewees were eager to share their personal experiences with me. Knowing that I was part of the lesbian community in Hong Kong, some were curious to learn more about my impressions of *tongzhi* life in Hong Kong. I attribute my informants' enthusiasm to share their personal experiences to our shared sexual identification, Chinese ethnic identity and common language. It may well be easier for an openly gay researcher to obtain privileged personal information than for a straight researcher (Williams 1996: 82). On the other hand, a shared sexual identity does not mean that our representations of the *tongzhi* communities are more 'accurate' or 'authentic'. Apart from shar-ing sexual and political identity, we were different in other aspects, such as age (I was in general older than most of my *lala* informants), class, education and cultural background. We also might differ in our personal views on relationships, marriage and *tongzhi* activism. A critical reflec-tion of all these sociocultural and political differences, and how they intersect or not, is important for the researcher in order to attain new self-understandings and revise taken-for-granted cultural values.

Coming Home, Coming Out

From an unfamiliar homeland to a research field, the journey to Shanghai was one intertwined with new discoveries and old memories. Based on what I had experienced in the 1970s, I was able to understand how dramatic the changes have been over the past three decades. In the past ten years, the exchanges and collaborations between *tongzhi* activists in

Hong Kong and mainland China have intensified in both directions. In a recent Hong Kong Pride Parade, participants from China were walking with all of us on the busiest street in town. At the Queer Film Festival in Beijing, activists, directors and scholars from Hong Kong were sitting next to Chinese counterparts in the screening rooms. In the *lala* leadership training camps in China, organizers from Hong Kong, Taiwan and overseas shared experiences and built solidarity with local *lalas*. In light of all this, I took up new positions and identities as the research project proceeded. During all these years in the field, I had become a participant in the development of China's local *lala* communities in addition to using my research training to understand them. The boundary of 'insider' and 'outsider' has been blurred even further. Managing these roles remains an ongoing challenge to me as a researcher and a committed member of the *tongzhi* communities in Hong Kong and China.

My research project on *lala* communities in Shanghai has connected my memories and experiences in Hong Kong and China. Importantly, it has also provided an opportunity to come out formally to my readers and the academic community as a queer-identified researcher. This leads me, in closing, to contemplate the personal significance of conducting a queer research project to the queer-identified researcher. Such a research project not only contributes new knowledge, but it also produces a new public self and identity for the researcher herself. For the first time, I openly declare my sexual and political identity outside the *tongzhi* communities that I have been comfortably out for many years. Apart from the ethical concerns of a researcher, I believe there is a political need for me to openly announce my queer identification in the publications of this research project. The fact that this research is conducted by a lesbian has political implications for the local *tongzhi* community in China. As Harriet Evans discusses in her book *Women and Sexuality in China*, homosexuals were too often 'talked about' and constructed as the 'other' (Evans 1997). Ten years later, when I was doing my research in China, homosexuals (*tongxinglian*) were much more widely discussed and represented in local academia and the media. However, the problem of othering and stereotypical representations still persists; moralistic, heteronormative values are still taken for granted in many public discussions. I do not claim that a *tongzhi*-identified researcher can automatically produce the most authentic knowledge on *tongzhi* communities. This would be an oversimplified and overly romanticized understanding of identification. What I want to bring out, rather, is that we need community-informed knowledge and research perspectives that are developed by *tongzhi* themselves. In sum, we need more new knowledge and understandings of *tongzhi* in China that are speaking from the perspective of 'we'.

Author's Note

Many thanks to the editors for inviting me to write this chapter. I also thank Dr Eleanor Cheung for proofreading and providing feedback.

References

Acker, Sandra (2000) 'In/Out/Side: Positioning the researcher in feminist qualitative research'. *Resources for Feminist Research*, vol. 28, no. 1–2, pp. 189–208.

Engebretsen, Elisabeth L. (2011) 'Queer "Guerrilla" Activism in China: Reflections on the 10th anniversary Beijing queer film festival, 2011', *Trikster: Nordic Queer Journal Blog*, http://trikster.net/blog/?p=527&gt (Viewed 19 March 2013).

——— (2013) *Queer Women in Urban China: An ethnography*. London and New York: Routledge.

Evans, Harriet (1997) *Women and Sexuality in China: Female sexuality and gender since 1949*. New York: The Continuum Publishing Company.

Kam, Y. L. Lucetta (ed.) (2001). 月亮的騷動她她的初戀故事：我們的自述 [*Lunar Desires: Her first same-sex love in her own words*]. Hong Kong: Cultural Act Up.

——— (2006) 'Noras on the Road: Family and marriage of lesbian women in Shanghai'. *Journal of Lesbian Studies*, vol. 10, no. 3–4, pp. 87–103.

——— (2010) 'Opening Up Marriage: Married lalas in Shanghai', in Yau Ching (ed.), *As Normal As Possible: Negotiating sexuality and gender in mainland China and Hong Kong*. Hong Kong: Hong Kong University Press.

——— (2011) '表面的微笑：上海拉拉的家庭政治' [A smile on the surface: Family politics of *lala* women in Shanghai] , in Liu Jen-peng and Ding Naifei (eds.), 置疑婚姻家庭連續體 [Querying marriage-family continuum]. Taipei: Shenlou, pp. 169–192.

——— (2012) '"Leftover Women" in Hong Kong' [Bentu de sheng yu biewuxuanze]. Editorial Committee of the Journal of Local Discourse and

SynergyNet (ed.) *Journal of Local Discourse 2011: New Class Struggle in Hong Kong*. Taiwan and Hong Kong: Azoth Books Co. Ltd.

———(2013) *Shanghai Lalas: Female tongzhi communities and politics in urban China*. Hong Kong: Hong Kong University Press.

Kong, S. K. Travis (2011) *Chinese Male Homosexualities: Memba, tongzhi and golden boy*. London and New York: Routledge.

Stacey, Judith (1988) 'Can there be a Feminist Ethnography?' *Women's Studies International Forum*, vol. 11, no. 1, pp. 21–27.

Williams, Walter L. (1996) 'Being Gay and Doing Fieldwork', in Ellen Lewin and William L. Leap (eds), *Out in the Field: Reflections of lesbian and gay anthropologists*. Urbana and Chicago: University of Illinois Press.

Wong, Kit Mui Day (2004) '(Post-)identity Politics and Anti-Normalization: (Homo) sexual rights movement', in Agnes S. Ku and Ngai Pun (eds), *Remaking Citizenship in Hong Kong: Community, nation and the global city*. London and New York: Routledge.

CHAPTER 11

Queer Organizing and HIV/AIDS Activism

An ethnographic study of a local tongzhi organization in Chengdu

Wei Wei

The past decade has witnessed the rise of queer/*tongzhi activism across* China, which has contributed to the development of civil society in this country. Although it shares many commonalities with its counterparts in other societies, such as the change of socioeconomic structure, the construction of homosexual identity and the impact of HIV/AIDS epidemic, China's distinctive state–society relationships have complicated both the development paths and movement outcomes of Chinese queer/*tongzhi* activist groups. Drawing data from my fieldwork in Chengdu from 2004 to 2006,[1] this essay documents the mobilization of local *tongzhi* community around HIV/AIDS activism during the same period, with a special focus on the development of a local *tongzhi* community organization – Chengdu Gay Care Organization (CGCO). Founded in 2002, CGCO was already recognized as one of China's most successful LGBT organizations a short three years later.

This chapter aims to use ethnographic accounts of CGCO's activities to document the exciting and dynamic early days of this grassroots organization. These descriptions will then be harnessed to an analysis of the CGCO's successes as well as critical issues faced by this organization since the beginning, which have also had a deep impact on its subsequent development.

---

1. This essay is based exclusively on the data the author collected during his dissertation research in Chengdu from late 2004 to the middle of 2006. Both CGCO and its core members have experienced considerable changes since then; these changes will not be discussed here.

In December 2004, I started volunteering for CGCO and soon developed insider contacts. Through insider contacts, I identified initial participants for in-depth interviews. These men then introduced me to others in their personal networks. During my fieldwork in Chengdu, I became an active participant and observer of Chengdu's gay life: I participated in CGCO's events, visited all kinds of local gay venues and attended private gatherings. Some of the people I met through my research have become friends as well as key informants. We hung out together, met one another's friends and shared stories. As a self-conscious researcher, I often had informal conversations with these new acquaintances about their lives as gay men in Chengdu. These informal conversations brought unexpected critical insight into my study. I took field notes on all important events and everyday activities. I use pseudonyms for all informants appearing in this paper. During all phases of my research, I identified myself as an out gay man and a Ph.D. candidate writing a dissertation on the local gay community. My statuses as both 'insider' and 'outsider' have significantly shaped my research.

From Piaopiao to Tongzhi: New Identity, New Community

People in Chengdu still call homosexual men 'wandering man' (*piao piao*). *Piao* is a verb in Chinese, which means 'floating around' or 'wandering around'. It also implies a lack of root or anchor. Since old stereotypes imagined that homosexual men wandered around from one cruising place to another, they were called piao piao. This term implies that homosexual men could never settle down, but rather floated around like rootless leaves. Homosexual men also referred to one another with this term. The construction and performance of piao piao identity is closely associated with open air meeting places like streets and parks (piao chang) where piao piao find sexual gratification and build social networks. Many famous piao chang are located in local teahouses because drinking tea in teahouses has always been a cherished social custom in Chengdu. Like other residents in the city, piao piao visit teahouses to meet each other. Through word of mouth, the specific teahouses they chose to patronize became known as piao chang (Wei 2012). Although Piao piao who managed their public presence in piao chang were Chengdu's most visible homosexuals, this group was not representative of the local gay community because most gay men did not present themselves in such a public fashion. In addition to the social stigma associated with homosexuality, many did not wish to be associated with the dominant image of 'wandering men in the city'. The situation did not change until the late 1990s, when 'comrade' (tongzhi) emerged to become an identity for Chinese gay men.

The emergence of *tongzhi* identity enabled Chinese homosexuals to find something they could and would identify and connect with. First appropriated by Hong Kong gay activists in 1989, *tongzhi* soon became the indigenous gay identity term adopted by Chinese gay men across the country because of its positive connotation in the Chinese social and linguistic context (Chou 2000). Technological advancement, the internet in particular, plays a crucial role in the promulgation of *tongzhi* identity among gay men in China today, especially for the young generation who are mostly likely to use the internet. The internet not only allows new middle-class urbanites to imagine and embrace a gay identity through interaction with lesbians and gay men from other countries, but also contributes to the building of gay communities in both online and offline worlds (Chou 2000; Berry et al. 2003). In addition, many gay commercial venues started to emerge since the late 1990s under the influence of the Chinese urban consumer revolution (Davis 2000). Including bars, bathhouses, gyms, massage parlours and more, these new gay spots tended to cluster in the eastern corner of the downtown area, which created a physical, territorial base for Chengdu's *tongzhi* community (Wei 2012). Because of its glamorous drag shows as well as its owner's fame in the gay circle, Variation was the most popular gay bar in town and dominated Chengdu's gay scene for more than ten years.

Although the construction of *tongzhi* identity and the development of gay venues online and offline helped to create a sense of quasi-community, a purely indigenous, albeit limited, idea of community had already been invented. Homosexual men in Chengdu often used 'circle' (*quan zi*) to refer to the gay social network with which they were associated through sexual contact and networks of friends. My research in Chengdu shows that the term 'circle' can be used to describe different gay networks on several levels. On the micro level, circles are personal friendship networks. Most of my participants have their own small circle of gay friends with whom they regularly socialize. On the meso level, 'circle' refers to the social location shared by gay men with similar social background and lifestyle. For example, gay college students are more likely to be attracted to the 'student circle' and 'married *tongzhi circle*' consists of gay men in traditional heterosexual marriages. On the macro level, the term circle represents the gay community in general. The gay community may have geographic territory, but it exists mostly in the minds of its members. Even though the gay community is imagined, it has material and cultural effects (Weeks 2000). As indicated in my clarification of the term 'circle', its meaning is concrete when it refers to personal friendship network on the micro level, whereas the meso and macro definitions of circle are rather abstract.

Homosexual behaviour does not necessarily lead to a gay identity or to general association with gay men. Many men who have sex with other men might not recognize homosexuality as an important component of the self. They might also see no particular reason to associate with other gay men in nonsexual interaction (Murray 1991). Although all my participants have adopted *tongzhi* as individual identities, many of them have problems identifying with the gay circle – keeping a distance from it at best and rejecting association with it at worst. As several participants claimed: 'I am gay, but I don't belong to [that] "circle".' They think certain aspects of gay life in the circle, namely, casual sex and superficial friendship, represent the totality of gay experience that a larger community can offer. Consequently, many *tongzhi* do not look at the *tongzhi* circle as a community beyond personal friendship networks or systems of delivering sex. Even so, it is worth noting that, while the 'circles' definitely have more to offer gay men beyond sexual gratification and emotional support, the gay experience is never all about the life 'in the circle'.

Social constructionists argue that community should be better understood as a project for groups to engage in and a process that requires constant work to construct and maintain, rather than a social existence waiting to be apprehended (Castells 1983, Higgins 1999). Community consciousness is neither an automatic product of an abstract 'homogeneity' nor of 'common territory', but comes from a sense of participating in the same history (Murray 1979). These abstract ideas offer a good frame for understanding how new and emerging community organizations began to play a critical role in constructing a *tongzhi* community in Chengdu. These organizations sought to use resources, which were provided to address the emerging HIV/AIDS crisis, to mobilize the *tongzhi* community and challenge the existing gender order.

Confronting HIV/AIDS and the New Opportunity for Social Mobilization

There is no doubt that the outbreak, spread and subsequent government interest in HIV/AIDS created the most important opportunity for lesbian and gay activism to emerge in China (Hildebrandt 2012). In August 2001, the Chinese government finally admitted that the country was facing a serious AIDS crisis. Following a joint survey with WHO and UNAIDS in 2003, the government estimated that around 840,000 people in China were infected with HIV, including about 80,000 AIDS patients.[2] Due to a shortage of testing equipment and trained health staff, as well as the continuing stigma attached with this disease, the real numbers surely were much higher. The Chinese government recognized the urgent need to tackle the problem and set out policy objectives and strategies for AIDS prevention and control.

Funded by the UK Department of International Development, the China–UK HIV/AIDS Prevention and Care Project was launched in 2001 to help China to tackle the growing threat of the HIV epidemic. The project aimed to develop replicable models of HIV prevention, treatment and care in Sichuan and Yunnan Provinces for high-risk and vulnerable groups in order to inform and develop the national policy framework.[3] Meanwhile, the China–UK Project initiated a 'filter model', whereby international funds are directed first to the Chinese government. Government agents, usually the Center for Disease Control (CDC), then pass funds to these 'community-based' organizations. This model has been largely followed by other international funding donors in the field of HIV/AIDS prevention (Hildebrandt 2011).

Together with intravenous drug users, illegal blood donors and commercial sex workers and their clientele, homosexual men have been officially identified as a high-risk group vulnerable to AIDS infection. The social stigma surrounding homosexuality causes problems for conducting

2. Speech by Executive Vice Minister of Health, Mr. Gao Qiang, at the HIV/AIDS High-level Meeting of the UN General Assembly, 22 September 2003, http://www.china-un.ch/eng/tsjg/jgthsm/t85551.htm .

3. http://www.cnukaids.com/news_detail.asp?id=3595

effective behaviour intervention within the gay population. While many gay men, especially those with little education, experience a lack of access to HIV/AIDS information, the government faced difficulty in locating the target population, most of which hides its sexual orientation. Borrowing from international experience, the China–UK Project proposed the mobilization of self-help groups within the gay community as the resolution to the problem of behaviour intervention. Although the project did open more spaces for gay people unavailable in other regions, as I will discuss later in the article, its monetary distribution mechanism has had a deep and lasting impact on the development of local gay activism.

The China–UK Project started to look for possible collaborators from within Chengdu's the gay community. Soon, they found Xiao Zeng. He and his boyfriend, Hong Sheng, owned and managed Variation, the most famous gay bar in town. Xiao Zeng recalled his first contact with the China–UK Project in May 2002. One day some unexpected guests came to the bar. They expressed their interest in working with the gay community to cope with the emerging AIDS threat, but they needed the assistance and participation of 'insiders' like Xiao Zeng. Xiao Zeng thought it was a good idea. In addition to helping the government cope with HIV/AIDS, it would also benefit the bar business by bringing it a good public image. With the financial support of the China–UK Project, the Chengdu Gay Care Organisation was founded soon after this meeting, with Xiao Zeng, Hong Sheng and some bar staff as its founders. Self-defined as a local, non-profit gay community organization, CGCO focuses on HIV/AIDS prevention and education in the gay community under the government's guidance. It also aims to facilitate public understanding of homosexuality, increase the visibility of the gay population and, ultimately, to empower the gay community.

The appearance of HIV/AIDS in Asia provided a window of opportunity for gay organizations in countries where government and society strongly disapprove of homosexuality (Sullivan and Leong 1995). The Chinese government expressed its willingness to respond to this massive public health problem even as it acknowledged a variety of challenges to direct government action in high-risk communities. Many gay men were not willing to reveal their sexual orientation in public, which made well-meaning direct intervention difficult. The government needed 'insiders' to achieve its goal of controlling the spread of HIV/AIDS among high-risk and vulnerable groups. Further, the Chinese government expressed an interest in accepting international assistance and, as it happened, donors were also interested in using assistance to develop 'civil society' and 'community-based' approaches to development. Hence, for a few years, the interests of government and international donors both sought to create an expanded space for social organizing. The crisis generated both financial and human resources that local groups could use to get started. It seemed that the training and experience gained through work on donor-supported projects could then be used in other ways by potential community organization leaders and initiators (Howell 2004). And, in somewhat limited ways, reality reflected this vision.

Leadership and Organizational Structure of CGCO

For the development of a community organization, leadership is a crucial factor. Community organizations must mobilize resources from both inside and outside the community. In this process, organizational entrepreneurs play a significant role because, among other tasks, they can mobilize their cultural capital, social network, economic capital and personal skills to boost organization development (Yang 2005). Most of the first founders of CGCO were connected to gay commercial establishments. They were either owners of gay bars or working for these bars. After ending his eight-year relationship with Hong Sheng, Xiao Zeng devoted himself to CGCO. Another CGCO leader, Kai, was a drag show host at Variation and also well known in Chengdu's gay circle. During 2004–06, both worked full-time for CGCO. Because of their personal connections, the organization continued using Variation for its events, even though neither Xiao nor Kai retained a significant financial interest in the club.

As others have observed, it is common that group consciousness first develops and gay social networks are constructed and maintained in gay commercial establishments (Castells 1983, D'Emilio 1998, Boyd 2004). It is no wonder that CGCOs first leaders were actively involved in the gay commercial world, namely, 'celebrities' in the Chengdu gay circle (Wei 2012). They had been 'out' to the gay world for a long time, knew a lot about the gay community and, most important, had access to incomparable social networks. Among the biggest 'celebrities' in Chengdu's gay circle, both Xiao Zeng and Kai embodied these crucial qualities. The government needed the skills of Xiao Zeng and Kai to locate, and access, and mobilize the gay community in HIV/AIDS education and prevention. CGCO was thus formed as a result of a government initiative that was welcomed by prominent gay activists and personalities.

Although 'celebrities' possess social networks and cultural capital necessary for a gay organization, many gay men did not identify with these 'celebrities' (Wei 2012), so CGCO needed a diverse leadership to appeal to more gay men. Pursuing a M.D. degree and working as a medical intern in a prestigious hospital, Michael represented another type of organizational entrepreneur who combined professional prestige and a different type of cultural capital. In addition to a strong professional background that enabled him to easily claim expertise in HIV/AIDS prevention and education, Michael read extensively in western history, philosophy, politics and culture. As international organizations became more involved in HIV/AIDS prevention in China, Michael was able to use his English-language skills and westernized knowledge background to seek opportunities and resources for CGCO.

For a grassroots organization like CGCO, a community base and external resources are equally important because one provides the legitimacy of existence while the other sustains its development. Social stigma on homosexuality inhibits identification and recognition from inside and outside the community, so it was crucially important for CGCO to have charismatic leadership that could overcome the social stigma. Representing two types of leadership, Xiao/Kai and Michael embodied different flavours of charisma that appealed to different audiences. Both could mobilize the resources available to them to help the organization develop. CGCO's early success of was largely a result of cooperation between these two organizational entrepreneurs.

What about the followers? Although CGCO was open to everyone who was willing to volunteer, the organization was particularly interested in recruiting members from three groups: 'celebrities', professionals and college students. CGGO had to assure the government that it had a substantial influence over the local gay community and was, therefore, capable of communicating the importance of safe sex and regular HIV tests. 'Celebrities' were the messengers: their personal networks enabled CGCO to send these messages to different gay circles.[4] Professionals of-

---

4. '*Shiqinian tongxing fuqi shuijinhun zhenqing dongren*' [Same-Sex Lovers and Their Seventeen-Year Crystal Marriage], *Chengdu Evening Daily,* December 13, 2002

fered both concrete skills and also helped to construct a positive public image for the organization.[5] The presence of college students in CGCO was high as this group was relatively easy to mobilize. In addition to time, energy and enthusiasm the students brought to the organization, the leaders of CGCO were aware of the importance of incubating a new generation of activists.

What factors encourage or discourage participation? Research on emerging environmental NGOs in China shows that public visibility and meaningful experience for self-exploration and socializing are three major reasons that attract participation (Yang 2005). Generally speaking, public visibility is a factor that discourages rather than encourages participation in gay activism, especially among middle-class, professional and established gay men. As a group, they would like the gay community to be more visible in public, but they fear that coming out might jeopardize their careers and family ties. So, they are more likely to choose either backstage involvement in CGCO or simply 'observing'. However, socializing is certainly on the agenda when gay men volunteer or participate in CGCO events. Though there are many options available for socializing, not every gay man is into the gay scene. More importantly, many gay men put more value on the comradeship cultivated while participating in CGCO than regular gay friendship based on leisure and playing. The leaders of CGCO recognized and developed this comradeship by emphasizing that its gatherings have political implications.

If a goal of larger events was to both enable and encourage individual participants to broaden their personal circle of friends, the experiment was less than an overwhelming success. Boundaries between different circles remained quite clear in CGCO's events. People came and left with their 'own' circle of friends. I did not observe much cross-group interaction during the events and even less afterwards. Raising collective consciousness and dealing with subgroup differences were two major challenges faced by CGCO leaders in the course of mobilizing the local gay community. They needed to develop effective organizational strategies to address these challenges.

---

5. Organizations that focused on intravenous drug users and sex workers had even greater challenges in presenting their members as 'valuable contributors to society.'

Organizational Strategies within the Gay Community

Raise Community Consciousness

During my interviews, ordinary gay men in Chengdu tended to use the term 'circle' or 'group' rather than 'community' to describe gay collectivities. The notion of a common '*tongzhi community*' was not a part of their imagined existence. Recent scholarship has drawn on Anderson's (1983) concept of 'community' as an imagined but discursive reality in which people can carry an image of communion in their minds despite never having known, met or heard of each other. This particular sense of community is prominent in the western discussions of the 'the gay community' (Bell and Valentine 1994) and, in theory, it might have been relevant in China as well, resting on the idea of community as 'comradeship.' Prior to the year 2000, this idea of community did not exist in Chengdu. From a constructionist perspective, the existence of a gay community is not an automatic product of shared homosexuality; rather, it must be created through mobilizing community consciousness among gay men. Between 2004 and 2006, CGCO served as an important agency to create such a shared consciousness.

CGCO employed two strategies to facilitate the development of a positive identity and a shared community consciousness among gay men. The first was to search for 'pioneers'. Recovering a proud past is typically important in the formation of a group identity. Along with serious historical research on everyday life of oppression and on suppressed gay history, the quest for forerunner heroes was an important strategy to promote the identification of followers during the heyday of the gay movement in the US (Murray 1979). Through CGCO's successful promotion, the gay community in Chengdu discovered its own heroes: Zhao and Qian. At first glance, these appeared to be two ordinary, middle-aged men, but this couple had lived under the same roof for nearly twenty years. What makes the couple even more extraordinary is that they adopted and raised a son. Even though their relationship was well known in the gay circle, it was totally invisible to mainstream society. The life experience of Zhao and Qian poses a strong challenge to two stereotypes that have dominated public imagination of gay men in China: gay men are promiscuous by nature, so they are incapable of long-term relationships; and social pressures will eventually push gay men into heterosexual marriages. Although people may pity gay men's marginalized and stigmatized sexuality, the latter are accused of not being honest and integrated. The two stereotypes are so powerful that even gay men themselves internalize these ideas. Xiao Zeng realized the 'value' of his two long-time friends and sought to use CGCO as a platform from which Zhao and Qian could reveal their story to a homophobic and heterosexist public.

Shortly after CGCO was founded, the couple was invited to an official meeting with the local media and HIV/AIDS experts. During this meeting, the couple was interviewed and 'Same-Sex Lovers and Their Seventeen-Year Crystal Marriage' appeared in a local newspaper the next day.[6] Several months later, another local newspaper published a follow-up story on the couple, revealing more sentimental details about Zhao and Qian's struggle and their family life.[7] Although these articles touched upon the sad reality faced by gay men in present-day Chinese society, they put emphasis on the gay couple's positive outlook on life and their strong faith in a gay life choice. In June 2005, CGCO threw a twentieth anniversary ceremony for Zhao and Qian at Variation. Kai conducted a live interview with the couple on the stage. In front of hundreds of gay men from different generations, Zhao and Qian recalled the obstacles they had overcome to work out their unconventional relationship. The two storytellers were too emotional to hold back their tears. Gay men sitting in the bar were touched and inspired by their forerunners' stories. Due to CGCO's increasing fame and success over the previous three years, more and more journalists responded positively to event invitations. Zhao and Qian's story was presented by a variety of national and local media outlets. This couple became a major symbol of gay Chengdu. As one type of historical narrative, the story of Zhao and Qian serves as a rationale by an emerging gay community that seeks a sense of moral foundation and coherence: the story demonstrates that

---

6. The International Visitor Leadership Program (IVLP) is a professional exchange program funded by the U.S. Department of State Office of International Visitors in the Bureau of Educational and Cultural Affairs. The purpose of the program is to help build mutual understanding between citizens of the U.S. and other countries.

7. The International HIV/AIDS Alliance (IHAA) is a global partnership of nationally based organizations which support community organizations which promote HIV and AIDS issues in developing countries.

living an active gay life is possible despite the challenges presented by the larger society.

Constructing a positive subculture was CGCO's second major strategy. A subculture of gay men helps to create a collective consciousness and strengthen their sense of identification with a group (Murray 1979). Variation played an important role in this process. People's perception of Chengdu's gay subculture was often dominated by Variation, but its flamboyant and commercialized bar culture alienated a large number of gay men. As the owners of Variation and founders of CGCO, Xiao Zeng and Hong Sheng transformed Variation from a purely commercial venue to a cultural centre for the gay community. This shift proved to be a wise move because it not only enhanced the public image of this bar, but also boosted its commercial sales. The drag show was still the major attraction, but its host, Kai, shifted the show's tone by incorporating a stronger sense of gay consciousness. Some recent features ridicule the ignorance and prejudice of the heterosexist society; others celebrate the commitment of a gay life choice. Beyond the drag show, CGCO itself used the Variation stage for a variety cultural events, including gay film screening, gay beauty pageants, and '*Tongzhi* Knowledge Contests' that covered AIDS prevention as well as gay culture and history. CGCO worked hard to create a more diverse and inclusive image in hopes of breaking the boundaries of different gay circles.

Addressing Group Difference

The gay community consists of many 'circles' varying in age, education, occupation and marital status. Intra-group variance within the gay community can be much greater than intergroup variance. The social distance between various gay circles creates hostility that frequently threatens to shatter the cohesion of a unified *tongzhi* collective identity (Bailey 1999). In order to mobilize the whole community, CGCO had to develop its own politics to deal with internal differences. Two kinds of group differences needed to be addressed: sexual difference and class difference.

Aware of the sexual diversity within the local gay community, CGCO advocated a pluralistic sexual ethic. This proved to be a powerful way to naturalize or normalize gayness and use it as an agent of self-empowerment and sexual liberation (Seidman 1997). CGCO members were once discussing the possible tactics to tackle AIDS infection in a routine meeting. In response to one member's suggestion that CGCO should advocate monogamy in gay relationships, mediator Yu declared there was no moral hierarchy in the way people have sex. As long as sexual acts are based on consent, everybody should respect other people's choices.

Yu was a freelance writer besides volunteering for CGCO. Without any official training in sociology and queer theory, Yu demonstrated a sophisticated understanding of existing social institutions when he discussed the recent debate on gay lifestyles within the organization.

> With more new members joining CGCO, some disagreements emerge. It is about the moral standard of *tongzhi* lifestyle. For example, the debates on monogamy and multiple sexual partners … and sex trade … according to my understanding, the moral standards and values on sexuality in today's society belong to a system which is fundamentally heterosexist. They all serve the interests of heterosexist institutions. Therefore, we should not take them for granted by incorporating them into the practices of building *tongzhi* relationship. (Personal interview)

Giddens (1992) claims lesbians and gay men are 'pioneers' in 'pure relationships' and engage in a 'plastic sexuality' that is freed from the needs of reproduction. So, they stand at the forefront of the 'transformation of intimacy'. Yu had never read Giddens and yet he understood that, because gay men are pioneers in creating social relationships, they are still at the phase of exploring new models for their own lives.

> Should we just follow all these (heterosexist) ideas? Or should we explore a new moral system of *tongzhi* through our own practice? I think we are still at the phase of exploration. We should support diversity and plurality. Upon the preconditions that both individual freedom and other people's rights are fully respected, we encourage exploration and experimentation. It is not necessary to impose certain values over all of us. (Personal interview)

While the challenge of sexual differences was important, the need to address class differences in the gay community was even more pressing. Class was the major factor dividing the local gay community. *Suzhi* (quality) was a classist mark that differentiated gay men into groups who had *suzhi* i.e. being urban, middle class, well-educated and 'proper' in expressing gayness, from groups who lacked suzhi, meaning being rural, poor, little educated and 'improper' in expressing gayness such as being flamboyant and promiscuous.

The *suzhi* discourse is often associated with the 'MB' (Money Boy) phenomenon (Rofel 1999 and 2010). MBs are usually young men in their late teens or early twenties. They migrate from rural areas to cities in search of a new life but find prostitution to be the quickest way to make money (Kong 2012). Some people believed that MBs should be excluded from gay communities; some believed that MB's aren't even gay. CGCO discussed these questions and arrived at a clear decision. Kai talked about how the moral standards tied to *suzhi* obstructed the effective mobilization of the gay community in other cities.

> CGCO has been always advocating a culture of pluralism and diversity, but tongzhi organizations in other cities are different … when they recruit volunteers, some moral standards are set up. For example, you should denounce one-night-stand sex, or you cannot be a MB. Otherwise, they kick you out of their organization. I think this approach is problematic in many ways. First, it excludes a lot of people from the potential pool that can work for you; second, they don't want to work with certain types of people. If you ignore the needs of these groups among which high-risk sexual behaviours are most likely to take place, what is the point for you to do your work? (Personal interview)

As Xiao Zeng pointed out, the establishment of moral boundaries based on sexual and class difference actually imposed a new oppression over 'our own people'.

> Let's be frank. We are all repressed under today's social conditions … why would you discriminate against our own people like those being sissy or having multiple sexual partners? Why don't we help create a more relaxed environment where all of us can live with more freedom? (Personal interview)

During my interviews with these CGCO leaders, I was quite impressed by how they articulated liberal and plural values in their narratives. Being exposed to all kinds of heated debates around gender and sexual politics throughout my academic training in the US, I am familiar with this type of language but cannot help wondering what propelled CGCO to endorse these values. While some CGCO members attributed it to a relaxed local culture conductive to diversity and tolerance, a more convincing explanation might lie in the influence from training pro-grammes and workshops on advancing gender and sexual rights that have been presented in China since the late 1990s. The implementation of the China–UK Project certainly created a favourable environment for such advocacy works.

Organizational Strategies outside the Gay Community

The Claim to Expertise on AIDS Prevention

HIV/AIDS has an uneven impact on specific groups, subcultures and communities, which requires developing specific situational strategies and tactics in community-based disease control and intervention. Gay men often count on their own 'circles' for physical companionship and emotional support. 'Circles' have significant impact of gay men's everyday life. Sex is the most common subject in gay men's conversation and sex-related conversation provides an excellent opportunity for delivering knowledge on HIV/AIDS. Accordingly, CGCO has adopted 'peer education' as an effective method in the practice of HIV/AIDS education. CGCO focused on recruiting 'key persons' from the local community, providing them with training in effective communication and sexual health and encouraging them to share the knowledge with their peers.

A hotline was another important component of community intervention. In charge of answering these calls, Kai was able to provide practical and credible advice from an insider's perspective. People called the hotline for a variety of reasons, including identity struggles, relationship crises, fear of HIV/AIDS and marriage pressure. Instead of offering direct solutions to certain problems, Kai's team helped people analyse the pros and cons of each possible option and then asked them to make their own decisions. The operation of this hotline has improved gay men's sexual and mental health and bolstered their self-esteem. The government and the China–UK Project have acknowledged CGCO's achievements in HIV/AIDS intervention and education. The working model developed by CGCO was picked as the exemplary case to promote among other at-risk groups.

The fight against AIDS involves a wide range of players. Epstein (1996) documents how community-based social movements have shaped AIDS research since the early 1980s. One distinctive character of AIDS movement in the US lies in the large-scale conversion of disease 'victims' into activist-experts. The Chinese experience has been different: medical experts, relying on the authority, legitimacy, and credibility vested in them by their medical degrees, claimed a monopoly on the right to determine constitutes useful and effective HIV/AIDS prevention and education. Many doctors sometimes forgot that many gay men, to a greater extent than members of other at-risk groups like drug users and prostitutes, had education and other useful cultural capital. Many were professionals, including medical professionals like Michael. When these professionals, who were the object of HIV/AIDS related work, sought to become the subject of this work, they were typically shunned by the broader, mainstream medical and 'development' communities. Michael did not pull punches when he criticized these 'mainstream experts':

> Their ideas are not based on the needs of the community … like do something to make some difference to the community. … They often say … we have a new method of participative training, so we are going to do that. But what is the ultimate goal of such training? I have no idea. If we do something in the community, we just work on AIDS and AIDS is all we need to do. They don't pay attention to these things beyond AIDS like how to facilitate the development of the local community. Although they might mention it in their articles, it cannot be seen in their real working plans. They also implicate *tongzhi* can only work as volunteers but they cannot become experts, so they should not do something that is supposed to be done by these experts. If that is the case, what is the point to have all these programs? (Personal interview)

Michael continued his criticism by redefining the meaning of expertise.

> Do you think Xiao Zeng is an expert? I do. In terms of mobilizing community resources, or cooperating with different groups, he is an expert even though he doesn't have any advanced degree in any whatever field. For Kai, he was majoring in Chinese. But now he takes care of all the hotline calls, which makes him an expert in consulting. In my opinion, experts should be always open for learning new knowledge. Their expertise should be based on constant learning. (Personal interview)

The community's reaction to the AIDS crisis enables lay activists to claim to more, and more relevant, expertise than 'established experts' possess. Such claims are based on the fact, as Michael pointed out, that they know more about the actual needs of the community and they are more willing to revise their action plans as their understanding of these needs deepens. Too often, mainstream doctors treat HIV/AIDS as a disease the affects individuals; hence, they focus on treating individuals. Michael understood that prevention was superior to treatment and that prevention is more likely to succeed if community members were to support one another. Further, Michael understood that, in Chengdu, a community had to be created before it could be harnessed to the goal of HIV/AIDS prevention. Mainstream doctors and development professionals saw resources used for community development as 'diversion' and perhaps even 'corrupt.' Michael knew better, but the professionals wouldn't listen.

After the adjustment of official policy towards HIV/AIDS, the Chinese government has increased its spending on fighting the epidemic. In addition, many international organizations continue to be willing to provide resources to help China cope with the emerging HIV/AIDS crisis. The available resources, however, are still scarce, which leads to competition for resources among different actors. As one of the most successful local gay organizations, CGCO had gained considerable credibility in community-based HIV/AIDS intervention, but the lack of resources hindered its pursuit for further development. Hence, CGCO's challenge to these established experts and claim for expertise could be read as a necessary strategy to compete for scarce resources.

Increasing Visibility in the Media

While CGCO might not have been the first or the biggest local gay organization in China, it was definitely the most high-profile one when I conducted my research during 2004–2006. The proliferation of media coverage since the 1990s has tremendously increased the visibility of homosexuality, but it was dominated by pathologizing, sensationalist, debasing and criminalizing representation of homosexuality (Sang 2003). For CGCO and its leaders, the ideological configuration of sickness and crime had to be broken in order to change the public view of homosexuality and further alter the conditions of gay life. Therefore, CGCO prioritized a positive representation of gay men and the gay community in mainstream print and mass media in its working agenda. Under the coordination of CGCO, many local and national media outlets have presented over thirty reports on this organization as well as the gay community. Most of the media coverage documents how CGCO helps the government promote HIV/AIDS prevention and education in the gay community. CCTV's presentation of 'In the Name of Life' in August 2005 signalled a breakthrough in mainstream representation of homosexuality, and a noticeable change took place in local media coverage of gay issues. Coverage broadened from a nearly exclusive focus on AIDS activism to include issues such as gay relationships and lifestyles.

The implementation of the semi-governmental China–UK HIV/AIDS Prevention and Care Project certainly created a relatively favourable media environment. Due to the state's control over the media, the media has to cooperate with the operation of official policies. CGCO used PR strategy to attract more attention from the media by organizing and participating in many public events in accordance with the official policy on HIV/AIDS. For example, before World AIDS Day in 2004, CGCO organized a fundraising event at Variation for orphans who lost their parents to AIDS. Mr. Pu Cunxin, a well-known and respected actor and one of the image representatives of the Chinese anti-AIDS campaign, came to the bar to show his support for CGCO. Journalists were invited as well, including many who had not previously entered Variation. After this positive first contact, many journalists developed cooperative working relationships with CGCO members. These personal relationships improved both the quantity and quality of media reports. Some 'insiders' also helped to promote CGCO. One of my research participants is a gay journalist who has written several influential articles on CGCO and the gay community in Chengdu. He told me that he felt grateful to the gay community, where he found his lover and many lifelong gay friends.

Because of CGCO's success in promoting positive media coverage on gay issues and HIV/AIDS, its members were invited to join the 'AIDS and Media Coverage Workshop' sponsored by the prestigious Tsinghua University and HSBC. This workshop sought to provide journalists with training on how to cover AIDS-related news stories. CGCO members analysed concrete writing samples and suggested ways that objectivity, neutrality and depth of media coverage could be enhanced.

Media coverage of gay issues can be double-edged. While such coverage can increase gay visibility, educate the general public and facilitate the communication between the gay community and mainstream society, it can also cause trouble. The commercial press is more apt to portray gay men in a sensationalist manner or emphasize deviant behaviour, which can reinforce negative stereotypes. Although many gay men have been victimized by gay-related crimes, CGCO refused to cooperate with the media to expose these crimes because it reinforced the criminal representation of gay men and put gay men and the police in a confrontational situation. CGCO leaders were also aware of the risk that too much exposure in the mainstream media might incite a backlash from the general public as well as the government. Keeping a low profile on certain issues was necessary for survival. CGCO leaders are very concerned about media's representation on CGCO's political stance. The AIDS and Media Coverage Workshop analysed an article that had suggested CGCO was promoting legislation on gay issues. By correcting that journalist's misrepresentation, CGCO members emphasized that the organization currently only focused on assisting the government in coping with AIDS; legislation was not on CGCO's agenda. They pointed out that such misrepresentation from the media would put CGCO's political safety at stake.

Mobilizing Resources from International Agencies
In the late 1990s, many international organizations began to launch projects in China in the fields of environment, education, and health. This was particularly the case for HIV/AIDS because social taboos surrounding this disease limited government spending in this area. Therefore, almost all Chinese social organizations related to HIV/AIDS issues relied heavily upon international donors for funding (Howell 2004). CGCO succeeded in gaining social, cultural, and organizational resources from its interactions with donors. Cold hard cash, however, was hard to come by.

As a local and new gay organization, CGCO occupied a disadvantaged position drawing resources from abroad. CGCO leaders realized they first had to increase their influence in order to catch the attention of international donors. Media attention on CGCO really helped. Meanwhile, CGCO actively sought opportunities to build connections with international organizations.

Due to his professional background and language skills, Michael played a crucial role in making this happen. In March 2004, Michael applied to attend the 2004 World AIDS Conference in Thailand. He introduced CGCO's experiences on HIV/AIDS prevention, education and policy input in his application, which impressed the conference committee members, who decided to provide the funds needed for Michael and Xiao Zeng to attend the conference. The trip was a big break for CGCO. It not only increased CGCO's visibility in China but also enabled it to talk directly with (but not seek funding from) members of international organizations. This was the first of many opportunities to rub elbows with members of the international community. In February 2005, Michael came to the US as a local HIV/AIDS activist under the sponsorship of the 'International Visitor Leadership Program'.[8] During this two-week trip, he visited a variety of HIV/AIDS-related governmental institutions and social agencies in six American cities. It was an eye-opening and energizing experience for Michael, but it also made him realize the huge gap between CGCO and its American counterparts in organizational management, service delivery and community development.

In July 2005, China sent an official delegation to attend the 7th Asia-Pacific AIDS Conference in Japan. CGCO was chosen by the government to represent gay groups in China and the conference selected Xiao Zeng to give a speech at the NGO Forum. Through this conference, CGCO further strengthened its connections with other organizations, especially those with a governmental background. Michael's trip to the US and Xiao Zeng's trip to Japan are worth noting not only because both international trips have made CGCO known to a broader audience, but also because they have had a deep impact on CGCO's strategy for further development.

Along with CGCO's growing fame, its capacity of mobilizing external resources improved. The International HIV/AIDS Alliance[9] became an important funding source. Michael also successfully applied for more funding from the Swedish Embassy in 2005. In addition, private international donors such as Barry and Martin's Trust (U.K.) showed interest in supporting CGCO. The connection with international organizations helps CGCO to increase its capacity and resources, but it does not necessarily bring legitimacy to the organization in China. Extensive connections with international donors can be politically risky. As Hildebrandt (2012) eloquently argues, while LGBT activists and NGOs have benefited from transnational linkages and the fund-

---

8. The International Visitor Leadership Program (IVLP) is a professional exchange program funded by the U.S. Department of State Office of International Visitors in the Bureau of Educational and Cultural Affairs. The purpose of the program is to help build mutual understanding between citizens of the U.S. and other countries.

9. The International HIV/AIDS Alliance (IHAA) is a global partnership of nationally based organizations which support community organizations which promote HIV and AIDS issues in developing countries.

ing that accompanies them, the current political structure drives these organizations to prioritize their ties to the state over the international community. After the Chinese government changed its policy on HIV/ AIDS in 2006–2007, an increase in its financial spending was expected. Instead of focusing on international donors, CGCO shifted its major goal to secure funding from these government-sponsored programmes that it believed would boost the organization's legitimacy.

The Quest for Legitimacy

The legal status of CGCO is actually uncertain. The direct English translation of CGCO's Chinese title is 'Chengdu *Tongzhi* Care Group' instead of 'Chengdu Gay Care Organization.' For the local government, CGCO does not exist as an independent gay organization but a 'technological tool' under the sponsorship of the China–UK Project. The uncertain legal status restricts CGCO's ability to mobilize available resources. CGCO leaders realized that registering as a legal NGO would be a crucial step to sustain its growth. CGCO has been working on seeking official registration since 2004, but it did not make significant progress because of the difficulty to find a governmental sponsor under the highly restrictive legislative framework of NGO registration (Saich 2000). Potential sponsors of CGCO included the provincial Center of Disease Control, with which the China–UK Project is affiliated, and the Bureau of Civil Affairs, which is responsible for oversight of all social organizations. Neither of these, however, was willing to risk taking responsibility for CGCO due to official ambiguity regarding homosexuality. In addition to avoiding potential political risk, the local government also has a monetary incentive to keep its community partners like CGCO unregistered due to the 'filter model' that administered and distributed international funds (Hildebrandt 2011).

In the face of the registration problem, CGCO had to seek other resolutions. Like many other social organizations in China at the time, CGCO registered as a non-profit enterprise under the local Industrial and Commercial Bureau. Although this registration allowed CGCO to interact with the government and international donors as an independent legal entity, it had drawbacks because CGCO might be vulnerable to administrative interference and potential shutdown if CGCO engaged in activities beyond the formal HIV/AIDS-related scope of its 'business' .

CGCO did not give up its efforts to register as an NGO. The leaders were well aware of the importance of strong personal links in an authoritarian political structure. They spent lots of time on on building personal connections with local government officials, including inviting officials to attend CGCO's events. Their goal was both to influence government policy and to give officials a chance to see for themselves that their personal fears and prejudices regarding the gay community were unfounded.

In my view, despite all these efforts, it seems that CGCO still lacked the capacity to fully overcome the institutional restraints. In June 2005, CGCO invited government officials, HIV/AIDS experts, scholars and media personnel to attend the 'AIDS Prevention and Gay NGO Development Conference'. During that conference, the officials reiterated that the CGCO was only a 'technological tool' under the China–UK Project. This characterization frustrated CGCO leaders, who were hoping above all for official recognition of the organization's role as representative of the Chengdu gay community. Nonetheless, both Xiao and Yu thought the goal of this conference was partially achieved. First, it was a positive gesture for these officials to come to a conference organized by gay men. And second, they agreed to provide more financial support and legal legitimacy for CGCO.

This dependence on the government certainly limits CGCO's efforts in advocating interests and values that are not on the government's agenda. This could lead to the CGCO to ignore the actual needs of the gay community that they were supposed to serve, and eventually lose local gay men's support. While acknowledging that CGCO brought visibility to the gay community, many gay men I spoke with were not happy with CGCO's current work. This has disappointed middle-class and professional gay men in particular, who want CGCO to put more effort into advocating for gay rights rather than only focusing on HIV/AIDS. In the summer of 2005, CGCO hosted the 'AIDS Prevention and Gay NGO Development Conference' in order to provide a platform of dialogue between this organization and its sponsors. During the conference, a medical expert from the China–UK Project urged CGCO not to limit its vision within the gay community, but instead pay more attention to the problems faced by all people affected by HIV/AIDS. He believed that focusing only on gay issues would lead the CGCO nowhere. The expert's opinion reflected the government's expectation of CGCO. Instead of advocating the 'special interests' of the gay population, CGCO should expand its service to a broader population. Accordingly, those CGCO leaders whose main interest was fighting HIV/AIDS suggested watering down the 'gay colour' of the organization, so that the CGCO could more easily work with other disadvantaged groups such as migrant workers, who participate in the sex industry as both buyers and sellers. But for Michael, this was just another means to snatch hard-won resources away from an organization that ought to be focused on developing the gay community, with HIV/AIDS as a means to that end.

During my last meeting with Xiao Zeng in Chengdu, he talked about the organization's internal disagreements.

> I am aware of disagreements within the organization. As an NGO, we should allow people to have different voices. However, no matter whatever people do and whatever they say, we mustn't challenge the bottom line of the government and compress the current surviving space for CGCO. Strategies are very important if we want to get anything done in China. Otherwise, nothing will be accomplished. (Personal interview)

Like other NGOs in today's China, the fear of offending the government had become the major constraint in CGCO's gay advocacy work. As a result, the CGCO's role in the future would likely continue to focus on HIV/AIDS service delivery rather than on outright gay advocacy.

References

Anderson, Benedict (1983) *Imagined Communities: Reflections on the origin and spread of nationalism*. London: Verso.

Bailey, Robert W. (1999) *Gay Politics, Urban Politics: Identity and economics in the urban setting*. New York: Columbia University Press.

Bell, David and Gill Valentine (1994) *Mapping Desire: Geographies of sexualities*. New York: Routledge.

Berry, Chris, Fran Martin, and Audrey Yue (2003) *Mobile Cultures: New media in queer Asia*. Durham, NC: Duke University Press.

Boyd, Nan Alamilla (2003) *Wide-Open Town: A history of queer San Francisco to 1965*. Berkeley: University of California Press.

Castells, Manuel (1983) *The City and the Grassroots: A cross-cultural theory of urban social movements*. Berkeley: University of California Press.

Chou, Wah-shan (2000) *Tongzhi: Politics of same-sex eroticism in Chinese socie-ties*. New York: Haworth.

Davis, Deborah (2000) *The Consumer Revolution in Urban China*. Berkeley: University of California Press.

D'Emilio, John (1998) *Sexual Politics, Sexual Communities: The making of a homosexual minority in the United States, 1940–1970*. Chicago: University of Chicago Press, 2nd edition.

Epstein, Steven (1996) *Impure Science: AIDS, activism, and the politics of knowl-edge*. Berkeley: University of California Press.

Giddens, Anthony (1992) *The Transformation of Intimacy: Sexuality, love, and eroticism in modern societies. Stanford, CA: Stanford University Press.*

Higgins, Ross (1999) 'Baths, Bushes, and Belong: Public sex and gay commu-nity in pre-Stonewall Montreal', in William Leap (ed.), *Public Sex / Gay Space*. New York: Columbia University Press

Hildebrandt, Timothy (2011) 'The Political Economy of Social Organization Registration in China'. *The China Quarterly*, vol. 208, pp. 970–989.

——— (2012) 'Development and Division: The effect of transnational linkag-es and local politics on LGBT activism in China'. *Journal of Contemporary China*, vol. 21, pp. 845–862.

Howell, Jude (2004) 'New Directions in Civil Society: Organizing around mar-ginalized interests', in Jude Howell (ed.), *Governance in China*. Lanham, Maryland: Rowan & Littlefield.

Kong, Travis S.K. (2012) 'Rethinking the Self under Socialism: Migrant male sex workers ('money boys') in China'. *Critical Asian Studies*, vol. 44, no. 2, pp. 283–308.

Murray, Stephen O (1979) 'The Institutional Elaboration of a Quasi-ethnic Community'. *International Review of Modern Sociology*, vol. 9, pp. 165–77.

——— (1991)'Components of Gay Community in San Francisco'. In Gilbert Herdt (ed.), *Gay Culture in America: Essays from the field*. Boston: Beacon Press.

Rofel, Lisa (1999) 'Qualities of Desire: Imagining gay identities in China'. *GLQ: A Journal of Lesbian and Gay Studies*, vol. 5, pp. 451–474.

——— (2010) 'The Traffic in Money Boys'. *positions: east asian cultures cri-tique*, vol. 18, pp. 425–458.

Saich, Tony (2000) 'Negotiating the State: The development of social organi-zations in China'. *The China Quarterly*, vol. 161, pp. 124–141.

Sang, Tze-lan Deborah (2003) *The Emerging Lesbian: Female same-sex desire in modern China*. Chicago: University of Chicago Press.

Seidman, Steven (1997) *Difference Troubles: Queering social theory and sexual politics*. New York: Cambridge University Press.

Sullivan, Gerard and Laurence Wai-Teng Leong (1995) *Gays and Lesbians in Asian and the Pacific: Social and human services*. New York: Haworth.

Wei, Wei (2012) *Gongkai: dangdai chengdu tongzhi kongjian de xingcheng he bianqian* [Going public: The production and transformation of queer spaces in contemporary Chengdu] Shanghai: Shanghai sanlian shudian.

Weeks, Jeffrey (2000) *Making Sexual History*. London: Polity Press.

Yang, Guobin (2005) 'Environmental NGOs and Institutional Dynamics in China.' *The China Quarterly* vol. 181, pp. 146–66.

CHAPTER 12

Market Economy, Spatial Transformation, and Sexual Diversity

An Ethnographic Study of the Gay Community in Shenyang, North China

Xiaoxing Fu

Much research on homosexuality in the Chinese context has taken a historical focus, considering representations of homosexuality through the ages in literature and art rather than seeking to understand 'homosexuality' as a social identity. To some degree, there was no concept of 'sexual identity' in traditional China; gender divergence and sexual practice referred to homosexual *behaviour*. Sexuality as a specific identity that describes a subject's desires and orientation emerged only when economic reform and opening processes were implemented in the 1980s. Many scholars in the social sciences and humanities have now published important work on the emergence of self-identified Chinese gay (*tongzhi*) communities (for example, Rofel 2007; Ho 2010; Wei 2007; Kong 2011). This growing body of scholarship centrally connects homosexual men in China to a broader and dynamic context of globalization. For example, it discusses the extent to which the LGBT vocabulary, originating in Western identity politics, now travels to and resonates with contemporary Chinese culture and identity projects. Although discursive analysis across cultures has provided many insights, there is an urgent need for further empirical studies on how gay communities in various parts of China have imagined and experienced modernity, and how they seek identity in the context of thirty years of post-Mao social and economic dynamism. The presumption of a common understanding of 'the gay experience' has not yet been empirically verified – or challenged.

In this chapter, I argue that a consideration of space and social sites must be central to our understanding of gay community practices and their relation to broader social processes. In so doing I draw on important Western scholars, including Henri Lefebvre (1991) and Edward Soja (1996), who have theorized notions of power, difference and otherness by appropriating spatial analysis as a central component. I also build my argument on recent theorizing and research conducted in China. In recent years, domestic Chinese scholars have begun to employ spatial paradigms in their studies of Chinese gay communities. For example, sociologist Wei Wei has undertaken participant observation in saunas, bars and gyms in Chengdu. Based on the rich data this research generated, Wei argues that the gay community's sense of identity and production is crucially related to people's use of space and place, and especially the ways that *tongzhi* identity and subculture have evolved in an era of burgeoning consumer culture (Wei 2009; see also Wei's chapter in this volume). Using Wei as an inspiration, I harness data and insights gathered during years of research in Shenyang, Liaoning Province, to a discussion of changes in public spaces chosen by gay men for social interaction with other gay men. In the process, I evaluate how the choice of new social spaces has influenced meanings of sex, social relations and identity recognition within the gay community. To accomplish this goal, I present a three-decade genealogy of gay social spaces and their changing locations and meanings. Along with Wei, I thus contribute to creation of a richer and more nuanced map that shows similarities and diversities among contemporary Chinese gay communities.

The built environment, or the substantial expression of space, is central when considering space and modernity. Physical space serves as a carrier and a mechanism that can help us see through structural power: its social meaning, its visible physical impact, and human responses. Interestingly, socially marginalized groups such as sexual minorities sometimes occupy physically central locations. The key elements that social consciousness gives space has determined how practice of bodies, behaviours and social relations of male homosexual communities are betwixt organized, expressed and perceived, namely determines self-hide in or visible to space during interaction and negotiation with the heterosexual group.

The global prevalence of the idea that Europeans and Americans have labelled as 'gay' has already crossed the oceans and entered Asia. The trend connected to such identity communication obviously raises challenges to the ways in which we imagine and conceptualize cultural and geographical space and spatiality. However, the complexity of western and non-western cultural production, not to mention negotiation between them, has put forward tensions of carrying out spatial classification according to meaning.

Study Focus and Research Methods

Analytical framework. In this chapter, I develop the concept of 'social sites'. These are defined by both physical location and what is experienced at that location. For example, public toilets, bathhouses and bars could be social sites for urban gay men, but only if or when these sites – designed for and commonly understood as something different – are appropriated by the gay community. A complete description of 'social space' would include the following five key elements. First, it includes a physical component, possibly including buildings, rooms, trees and other natural outdoor features. Second, the social relevance of a physical space depends on how it is used. Prior to the 1980s, gay men chose physical spaces that were obscure or hidden, yet were bound by a spatial grammar that could be understood by unknown yet friendly others. There was nothing particularly 'gay' about public toilets and the more hidden areas in and near public bath houses until the gay community came to understand that these physical spaces could become social sites. Third, the appeal of a physical space as a potential social site is affected by its accessibility to all members of a social group. Every choice is the product of compromise: wealthy men might feel less comfortable at a public toilet; poor men might be excluded from a bar. Hence, limited physical choices for gay social sites might stratify an otherwise common 'gay community' into sub-communities based on differential access to proposed social sites. Social institutions, socio-economic status, and cognitive schema all affect processes of spatial stratification. Fourth, the same physical space may at the same moment play host to a variety of different – and sometimes competing – social sites. For example, the bathhouse, which elicits images of exotic passion among gay men, is defined by the Public Health Department as a high-risk behaviour site.

Finally, social sites are dynamic and evolve over time in response to social pressures, social opportunities and broader institutional evolution. A gay community can invent the idea that public toilets in general are potential social sites, which leads gay individuals to explore toilets in search of potential partners. Regular success leads particular toilets to gain particular recognition. Changing laws, norms, and values can open up new, more comfortable physical spaces to the gay community. The communication pattern starts afresh, leading to a transition time between 'current social site' to 'former social site.' Since communication among members of the gay community has been quite limited, these transitions are sometimes quite lengthy affairs.

This study adopts the analytical framework of place-space-social relations. I argue that the transformation of gay social sites in Shenyang between 1980 and 2010 was influenced by changes in economics, interpersonal relations, social networks and knowledge systems within and between groups in different physical areas. These large-scale social and cultural changes shaped and adjusted action, opinion, and value formation at local levels. However, large-scale processes leave room for local agency: the way that Shenyang's gay community transformed physical spaces into social sites involved a delicate negotiation between globally communicated opportunities and values, on the one hand, and how these were interpreted and revised in response to experiences and perceptions within the local space.[1]

Research Methods. Between 2007 and 2010 I adopted the methods of anthropological participant observation, in-depth semi-structured interviews, and focus group discussions. Early in the project, I observed a variety of 'social sites', including parks, public toilets and squares, and found that the behaviour and communication of gay communities was shaped significantly by the notion and experience of spatiality. I therefore decided to employ spatiality as a central observational perspective. To recruit interview participants, I applied the snowballing method and found ten 'older' gay men who had been active in social sites for thirty years. I interviewed each man twice. The first interview focused on spatial distribution of social sites, causes of spatial transformation, and action and communication patterns in various social sites – including

---

1. A fuller discussion of these issues can be found in my recent monograph (Fu 2012).

changes in social networking, vocabulary, nonverbal signals and social networking over time. The second interview aimed to clarify and update data from the first interview. For the focus group discussions, I recruited six 'older' gay men to assist in verifying data on the use and meaning of social sites and add data on their transformations over time. The focus group helped both to clarify apparent contradictions among individual memories and confirm variations in the lived experiences of gay men in Shenyang. This multi-layered oral history, supplemented with accounts in local newspapers, provided a robust foundation for analysis of the formation and transformation of social sites in Shenyang during the 1980s.

In the mid and late 1990s, commercial male-male sex services appeared in big cities such as Beijing, Tianjin, Shenyang, Chengdu and Xi'an, and have since developed and spread considerably. To study this aspect, I recruited fifteen male-to-male sex workers aged between 18 and 42, in home-based brothels and gay bathhouses. I also recruited ten street sex workers. The recruitment process was assisted by a local gay grassroots organization, the Shenyang Consultation Centre of AIDS Support and Health Service. These interviews focused on why sex work had been chosen; how it was carried out; relationships and coordination methods with managers and clients; social networking in work and life; discourses on ethics and values; gender performance; and health issues. Put together, this comprehensive, mixed method generated a nuanced empirical base from whence to analyse the emergence and transformation of gay male social sites in a long-term temporal perspective.[2]

The Age of Innocence: Space, Social Relations and Sex before and during the 1980s

Distribution of social sites before 1980s
My interview data suggest that social sites for gay community activities in Shenyang may trace back as far as the 1930s. The place now called Mukden No.1 Flourishing Area, on Siping Street just outside the Qing Imperial Palace, was well known as the optimal place for seeking companions. Moreover, teahouses and bathhouses were symbolically

---

2. Prior to conducting each interview, I described my study's content and purpose, obtained the informants' consent, and then conducted the interview at a convenient time and venue for the informants.

significant for male companionship in those days and became important spaces for finding same-sex recognition and communication.

> The location of Gongyu Teahouse was the only "chaotic place' of the Mukden and people of all way of life conducts activities there. Gongyu Teahouse was a small *Quyi* [Chinese folk art forms] performance theatre; there were storytelling and Peking opera and there were no big performances. It was fifty meters from the *Huilanting* (bathhouse) and there was a public toilet in the middle. I heard from the older gay men that they did not 'hang' (meet)[3] companions in the teahouse, but listened to the drama outside without buying a ticket. They hanged around outside; if encountering someone appropriate, they would 'do it' [i.e. have sex] at a deserted place outside. (FZ, homosexual worker, 51 years old, 2008)

Later on, gay male circles extended their footprints to two other districts beyond the Siping Street. One was Shenyang's new commercial street, the North Market developed by Zhang Zuolin in 1921, and its theatres, teahouses and old bathhouses were appropriated as social sites n the 1930s and 1940s. Another known gay location was at the junction of the Peking-Mukden Railway and South Manchuria Railways. The public toilet under the three-aperture bridge was a very old social site. In sum, teahouses, theatres, bathhouses and public toilets constituted the main types of social sites for gay activities before the 1980s. Throughout this long period, the same types of space were appropriated as social sites. However, the specific teahouses, theatres, bathhouses and public toilets used in this way changed over time.

Through careful analysis, I have identified three characteristics of gay social sites in China. First, they tend to be located in cities. Social networks (fragmented though they are), metropolitan anonymity and diverse lifestyles – hence a presumed openness to diverse lifestyles – all make the city an optimal location for hiding oneself. Also, a high population density enhances the possibility for gay men to find one another. In a way, then, what is often considered the most 'dangerous' place, a point to which I will return, is also the 'safest' place, even in an extreme time of politicized daily life.

Second, some cities have more – and more active – social sites than others. It turns out that cities that are transportation hubs are

---

3. In local slang, 'hang' means 'contact;' hanging people means contacting a sex partner.

more socially active. Shenyang is one such city. As early as the 1930s, railway lines intersected at Shenyang, making travel convenient both for Shenyang natives and outsiders. More interaction with a greater variety of people often leads to an openness to new ideas. It also expands the pool of potential gay partners beyond the city's population to include people moving from place to place in search of the good life. Hence, it is no surprise that the public toilet under the train bridge was a known social site.

Third, within cities, social sites tend to be concentrated in a city's central economic and political area. For example, Siping Street (mentioned above) was Shenyang's earliest political centre, from 1840 until 1898. Between 1905–1911 the North Market was the centre, after which the Huanggutun area took this role between 1911–1931.

Now that the 'where' question has been addressed, I turn to the question of 'how.' An informant in his sixties described how he and others went about seeking male companions during Mao's rule: 'Two gay men would read newspapers at the newspaper column and would glance at each other; one walked forward and gave a gesture or shook his keys rather than making eye contact, and they would hang around if they were satisfied with the companion.' I also found similar situations in my investigations in Chengdu and Xi'an in 2011. For example, two seventy-year-old men indicated that during the Cultural Revolution, one could find companions by putting hand onto someone's back, and look like not intentionally touching one another's genitals when reading the Dazibao (big character posters) in the crowd. The crowds were so tight that contact with others could not be avoided. This made intentional contact possible.

Gays used this indirect approach for a reason: homosexual behaviour was risky. Despite Mao's intention to develop 'modern' medical science, China borrowed – and retained – western medical paradigms only a few years before western countries radically revised them. Hence, Chinese experts were taught that homosexuality is a medical disease that requires treatment, and scientific scholarship remained anchored to very basic sexology ideas that western countries would soon abandon (Chou, 2001:31; Zhang, 1994). From a legal perspective, Chinese highest court appeared to be agnostic. Supreme People's Court FYZ No. 7929 in 1957 concluded that "whether adult sodomy at free will is a crime is to be solved by legislation' (Legal Daily, 2005).[4] In other words, homosexuality was not defined as a crime in criminal law. Several Supreme People's Court decisions reinforce the impression that the State had no particular intention to punish homosexual behaviour (X. Guo, 2008: 2). Nonetheless, in practice, homosexual behaviour was policed and prosecuted as one of many acts that fell under the broad category, 'hooliganism' (*liumang zui*).[5] Illegal acts and crimes would be differentiated according to the degree of lewdness.

> Being caught in homosexuality before the 1980s was handled as an offence of indecent activities. At that time, if two men were caught on-site, they would be accused for disturbance to residents. *Nantongzhi* (male comrades; meaning 'gay') hanged around by the public toilet under the three-aperture bridge; women therefore dared not go to the toilet and would call the police, accusing the *Nantongzhi* of disturbance to residents. They took us to the police station and detained us for fifteen days for the first time, and they notified our families and work unit (*danwei*). Those caught a second time would receive re-education through labour for three years. The government started loosening its control over homosexuality when the reform and opening-up program started. (LB, gay bar manager, homosexual, 51 years old, 2010)

Cases from Shenyang, Beijing, Xi'an and Chengdu show that prior to the 1980s and up until 1997, homosexual behaviour was often persecuted and punished as 'hooliganism,' but in practice, there was no ambiguity. Gays convicted for acts of sodomy were described in notifications and paraded through the streets bearing signs such as 'sodomy convict.' In the course of the interview process, I found that older men typically

---

4. I browsed issues of the 'Legal Daily' newspaper between 1980 and 2010, and discovered few reports with regard to homosexuality, among which only three are relatively in-depth reports. In existing homosexuality reports, there are few demarcations or discussions on a legal level and little contents of legal applications on homosexuality. The description focuses on homosexuality as a social phenomenon that 'undermines public morals. It is clear that the moral and legal discourses affect the social view of homosexuality.

5. In the criminal law of 1979, 'Gang war, causing disturbance, humiliating women or carrying out other hooligan activities, breaking public order and having wicked scenarios' constitute offence of indecent activities. In the specific law enforcement process, mutually agreed secret sex between adults is identified as 'other hooligan activities' which is subject to legal process and receiving the full force of penalty system. (and see Guo, 2008)

looked flustered and fearful when the topic of gay affairs back then came up. The collected cases include their own personal experiences, witness accounts and hearsay stories. Such personal narratives were constructed of nuances of intonation, verbal and bodily expressions, and modes of language, and therefore could be regarded as an event worthy of study. Their narrative mode is not autogenic but merges the narrator's perceptions of individuals and history; it carries imagination and judgment to group experience and thereby organizes the individual mode of narrating painful memories. The older generation's narratives are dominated by fear: fear of criminal punishment, administrative penalty, mutual exposure between gay partners, and notifying the work unit and family. These narratives contrast markedly with recollections of life as a homosexual after 1997, when the hooliganism law was revoked and the policy and legal environment relaxed. One wonders if descriptions of the earlier period are perhaps influenced by a 'demonizing' imagination and exaggeration.

In the hearts and minds of the older generation, the meaning of homosexuality as a 'crime' and its influence go far beyond being a 'disease'. The strength of the social fear of this 'crime' forced the gay circle to be very careful in their communication before the 1980s. This fear was embodied by the fact that they would often select concealed spots of public space to carry out communication; for example, when finding a suitable companion in social sites, they would engage in intimacy in deserted places outside the teahouse, or in the forest outside the public toilet, or in the bathhouse washing pool. On these social sites, the communication is exchanged through eye contact and not verbal language; there is no need to exchange personal information such as name, work unit, address and so forth. Informants said:

> The identification completely relies on eye expression. One follows the other, and one may stop if feeling satisfied with the other, or the other spontaneously strikes up a conversation. An eye expression shows what is going on; this kind of expression is different from that of 'normal persons' and their use of common signals. (D, unemployed homosexual, 50 years old, 2008)
>
> You sit there, I take a look at you, and look back at you in a little while, and look back at you again in a little while, and then I go out first and you follow, and we take a fancy to each other after a short conversation

or giving a light. (MT, leader of gay grassroot organization, homosexual, 42 years old, 2009)

The eye expression of a *tongzhi* upon seeing a beautiful woman is just a look, but when encountering a pleasant-looking man it will be flashing. (Ke, volunteer at gay grassroots organization, homosexual, 41 years old, 2007)

The lack of a social identity certainly underscores the importance of implicit communication in such a socio-political environment. As homosexuality was not accepted by mainstream society, individuals had little opportunity to create social networks and build resources. People could only use their own basic resources to express themselves and seek companions. In Erving Goffman's words, they were individuals with limited symbolic equipment.[6] As regular social interactive structures did not serve their needs, gay men had to generate their own social vocabulary. Eye expressions became the primary symbolic information system and, under the circumstances, was the best possible way to express one's individual self and interest. The process begins by sending out a 'flashing' look, seeking to identify a potential partner. If someone responds, then the first eye exchange establishes that both have gay desires. The second step is to discover whether attraction is mutual; continued eye contact is understood as confirmation. The third step is final consent. It is the 'I look back at you and glance and then again' as described by MT in a previous quote. If the other person still responds, it may be regarded as an invitation to the fourth step: verbal communication, intimacy and perhaps sexual contact. One person gets up and walks out, then the other follows and initiates contact by, for example, asking for the time or asking for a light. Of course, the description given here suggests more clarity than exists in the real world's the complex communication structure. In reality, such exchanges proceed in a more random order, with other modes of communication included or substituted. If both men exchanging glances this way are well aware of and experienced with gay dating culture (*wenhua chiyouzhe*), this process of negotiation and inter-

6. Goffman's notion of the limited symbol equipped individual refers to the fact that when an individual is performing on different social stages, s/he may mobilize individual resources and characterize different meanings according to factors such as stage arrangement and interacting object at the specific moment in order to make the performer and the audience both feel respectable and joyful (Goffman 2008: 19–25).

action can be rapid, without 'giving off' signs to heterosexual onlookers. Mainstream society has assigned different meanings to this vocabulary. It is for this reason that I argue that gay dating culture in urban public space is an 'invisible' form of social relationships and behaviour.

Seeking True Love: 'Men's Street' in the 1980s

In the 1980s, Chinese society turned its attention away from class struggle to focus on economic development and freeing people's mind-sets from the collective ideology of prior decades. Ideological liberation became the stuff of popular slogans and involved body liberation as well; the booming age of self-expression had begun.

Dance parties, which were regarded as 'feudalism, capitalism and revisionism' during the Cultural Revolution, once again entered people's lives. Social dance halls blossomed throughout the country. In the early 1980s, four social dance halls appeared near the City Stadium and Zhongshan Park in Shenyang; they became an oasis from the overall monotonous leisure life at that time. This area was developed on the foundations of the Japanese-built South Manchurian Railway Company's offices and warehouses, the site of Shenyang's third historical political centre (1898–1905). The gay community extended their

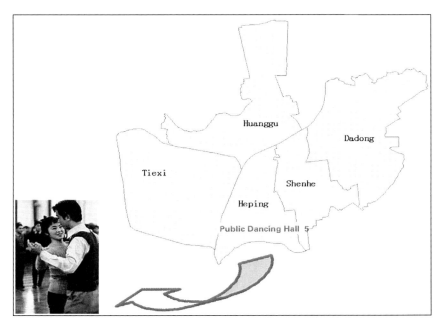

Map 12.1: Gay men's social sites in the 1980s – 5 public dancing halls

activity spaces here; in this way the scope of 'social sites' spread over the urban centre in different temporal periods.[7]

> At that time, *tongzhi* took part in dancing, hugged each other, and got to know people in the dance hall; two persons went home together if they were attracted to each other. It was safe at that time, people were nice and nobody was afraid to bring people home. The next day when you went to work, he left the key to you. To be frank, it's better to be with long-term acquaintances. (MD, yanko dancer, homosexual, 47 years old, 2008)

At this time, gay community life merged with heterosexual leisure life. For the first time they could go out to 'have a breath of fresh air' and 'release their inner torture' in a space also used by heterosexuals. The gay community also indulged in self-mockery: As someone said, 'China has carried out reform and opening up, and gay affairs are also subjected to reform and opening up.' The overall social structure in the reform transformation period began to differentiate in earnest; social status did not rely on the standard of politics and class anymore. Public awareness continuously expanded and it inspired the expression of various kinds of interests and ideas. Sexuality, once the object of public moral scrutiny, now gradually retired to the personal sphere. It was exactly this period of reform and opening up that would shape the social memory of 'Men's Street' (*nanren yitiao jie*) mourned by a generation of gays.

> When the Men's Street was in grand occasion, there were several hundred people every night, at Huanlu station across the way, sporting goods store yard in the south of the stadium. Every night there were 300~400 people which affected the whole stadium. In the street, there was a group of people every three to five steps away; people all knew each other; those who were not acquainted would get to know each other in a few days. At that time, music, modelling and dance, four people danced four cygnets, they danced 'The Red Detachment of Women' and the crowd watched. We also rehearsed 'The Top Ten Beauty in Shenyang'. Those who were not chosen got angry and they offered help as assistants. At that time, outlanders came in groups and there was communication between cities. People from Dandong would

---

7. With regard to specific distribution of 'social sites' for Shenyang's gay community activities and their space reproduction, I have appropriated Lefebvre and Soya's space theory and elaborations on body, action and social relation practice organized around the concept of social sites (Fu and Wu 2010; Fu 2012).

arrive, and locals welcomed them and provided dining. There were people from Dalian and Fushun, and from other provincial cities such as Xi'an, Hegang and Tangshan. (MD, yanko dancer, homosexual, 47 years old, 2008)

There were people appearing on the Men's Street from eight in the morning and 'there were people there almost twenty-four hours per day. We all miss that time. There were many people at that time and that was good. There were few people on the street in the morning and there were many at about 6–7 o'clock. Some people sat, stood, hanged around there, everyone was in different gestures. Some started organizing and wanted to get started. Groups of people cried uncontrollably to release their emotions and did not hide from people. (D, unemployed homosexual, 50 years old, 2008)

Men's Street was a geographic area covering a range of a square kilometre and included the four dance halls as well as many traditional social spaces for the gay community. This was by far the biggest was the main social site for gay community activities in the 1980s. Men gathered here day and night, spending their time whichever way they liked, pursuing freedom and pleasure. The train made it convenient for gay men from other towns to come and participate in this collective revelry; some would rather quit their jobs to enjoy this rare new opportunity for community and pleasure.

Still, pursuing and developing true love was what the members of the gay community truly desired. However, true love may not only be perceived to be two people's feeling of pleasure and emotions toward each other, or speak frankly together. It was also about not asking for a return or property safety. My focus group remembered the gay circle of the 1980s as 'nice' and 'simple'. This memory is embedded in the statement that one could 'go to work the next day and leave the keys to you'. This astonishing recollection symbolizes one moment in a broader process of social changes. The metaphor has a reference system; its generation is closely linked to the change of affection and concept of values in the circle of the 1990s and the early 21st century, which I discuss in the next section. In conclusion, the communication and activities of Shenyang gay community in the 1980s turned to 'public' from 'invisible' before the 1980s. Social communication and erotic passion within the gay circle became specific and visible in urban public space. At the same time, the gay community's sense of fashion and beauty began to be exhibited in public space; in this way they created visions of future lives, expressed their affections and desires in what was considered an innocent, happy and eager mentality. While there was an economic aspect to many of these activities, prices were quite low: both proprietors and customers were more interested in exploring the new openness than in exploiting economic opportunity. This would soon change.

The Commercial Age: Consumption, Identity and Desire in the 1990s

One major effect of the transition from planned economy to a socialist market economy in the 1990s was the development of a commercialized entertainment industry. According to data obtained from Shenyang industrial and commercial sector, a specific recreation and entertainment industry appeared in the 1990s. This included KTV (karaoke bars), billiards halls, chess and cards halls, game rooms, video halls, bars, coffee rooms and music cafes. Ideological change, reform of the work system (increase in holidays), and implementation of family planning policy (fertility rate falls and school enrolment approaches 100%) liberated the public from the work unit and family and provided them

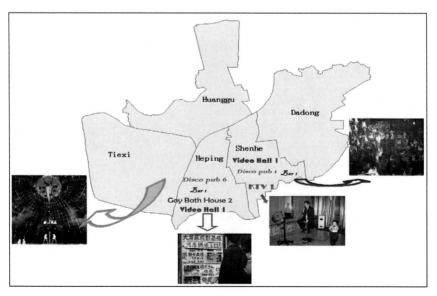

Map 12.2: Gay men's social sites in the 1990s – 7 disco pubs, 2 bars, 1 karaoke bar, 2 video halls, 2 gay bathhouses

with more leisure time. More spending money, technological innovation (development of communication and transport facilities), leisure time, and government's willingness to allow entrepreneurs to imagine and produce new services all combined to give birth to public spaces filled with diversified leisure and entertainment opportunities. As a single example, Shenyang offered 8,887 places where a person could buy drinks – tea, milk, alcohol, whatever. This figure increased to 14,217 in 1995 and to 17,368 in 1999 (Shenyang Yearbook 2001:442–443).

Compared with the 1980s, the 1990s saw the emergence of more types of social sites for the gay community. Alongside pre-existing public facilities such as traditional public toilets, parks and squares, gays stepped into the commercial spaces created by the market economy in search of relaxation and entertainment. In addition, gays started to create their own distinct social spaces.

From Cost-free to Charge in the 1990s

After the decline of Men's Street in the 1980s, Shenyang's gay community gradually moved to Zhongshan square, situated just north of Men's Street. One attraction was China Jump, a disco pub that gained considerable fame in the 1990s.

> China Jump was reconstructed from the gymnasium, and had two storeys and a big dance floor; in the southeast corner of DJ platform, gutsy gays gathered and there were thirty to fifty on Fridays and Saturdays. There were typically cross-dressing performances in the dance intervals, and the dream group of the older generation started to walk on the platform and gave fashion show. The DJ then introduced a Hong Kong performance team and their fashion model saying: this is Miss Fang Fang, nineteen years old this year; just look, no touching! (JJ, volunteer at a gay grassroots organization, homosexual, 38 years old, 2010)

The disco pub was a burgeoning entertainment industry in the 1990s. It was a trendy place for young people's recreation and entertainment in general. The gay community always had a good sense for fashion and style, and was unlikely to give up such a trendy space. The prosperity generated by the market economy expanded the communication space for the gay community and created new social sites that grew and advanced with the times. Importantly, the gay community of the 1990s had more choices; gays would shuttle between different spaces depending on changing interests and moods: a 'quiet bar' to have a chat, a noisy disco bar; an emotional release in a KTV, and partner seeking in the video hall appealed to various individuals – and to the same individual at different times. Compared with the four dance halls and the street itself in the 1980s, Shenyang's gay community constructed social sites in seven disco pubs, two bars, one KTV and two video halls in the 1990s.

This spatial expansion raises questions about the appropriation, build-up and organization of gay community space in the 1990s. Why did the gay community select the burgeoning entertainment spaces as the space for mutual recognition and communication? I suggest that there are two main factors to consider in this regard. First, in terms of official policy, the new 1997 Criminal Law deleted 'offence of indecent activities' and 'hooliganism', which had been used to punish certain forms of same-sex sexual behaviour. This change formally removed a major source of gay discrimination and fear. Second, the market-driven economy led to greater social differentiation. A consequence of this is that individuals are liberated from pressures and prejudices emanating from family and work unit (*danwei*). Greater financial independence enables individuals to participate more freely in public life. This had a dramatic impact on the way gays and lesbians could define 'self' and 'community' in the 1990s.

In addition to economic freedom, changing social values also affected how and where gays constructed social spaces. The days of 'eating bitterness' (suffering in silence) and 'complaining' (without hope for improvement) associated socialism were gone forever, replaced by the idea that personal fulfilment was a real possibility and exhibiting desires was a step toward their fulfilment. In short, the onset of the market economy and the social changes it initiated enabled new social and cultural settings that in turn helped establish distinctive and multiple community spaces for gays.

As one of my study participants explained:

> In the early 1990s, disco pubs were becoming popular; places for heterosexual socializing were becoming more appealing to us. Young people mingled with men of knowledge and pose as a lover of Culture, only wealthy people went there; in 1997, one needed to spend at least 60 to 70 yuan a night in the disco pub; a bottle of beer cost 25 yuan. The Walker Bar was at the south gate of the Medical University; that street was all quiet bars; the boss knew foreign languages and recruited some foreigners, and the foreigner played the latest foreign music. Foreigners

were open to chat with local people. (MT, leader of a gay grassroot organization, homosexual, 42 years old, 2010)

From M's narrative above, it is clear that the new characteristic of gay social sites is that of consumption, which moves away from the cost-free structures of former sites. I ask, in these new public spaces—which are defined externally by heteronormative socialization patterns—how do members of the gay community communicate with each other? JJ and M's narratives above demonstrate two major factors in new gay spatial practices. One is that the gay community normally selects and occupies one corner in an entertainment space, such as the southeast corner of China Jump's DJ platform, which serves as a gay social site. In this context, Stephan Feuchtwang has argued that place-making happens through the centring and marking of a place by the actions and constructions of people who are tracing salient parts of their daily lives as a point of reference and recognition (Feuchtwang 2004: 10). Feuchtwang also emphasizes spatial nostalgia and the continuous remaking of spatial meaning in different social structures, especially as they relate to capitalist globalization. This point relates to the creation of gay social sites in Shenyang. We have seen that despite rigorous social pressures and opposition, gay social sites have continuously developed and prospered. Whereas not everyone is satisfied anymore with the level of comfort provided in the sites of the past – indeed, some gay men seem to demand better facilities for socializing – others continue to use free spaces, such as public toilets and squares provided by the city, to pursue their identities and communicate with peers.

In short, the emphasis on performance in the 1990s is related to the spring tide of market economy, which pioneered a new spatial recognition with consumption as its foundation. All sites now cost money, but some cost more than others. While it is hard to know how many 'rich' gay men chose to include inexpensive spaces like public toilets in their repertoire of active social sites, it is certain that only relatively wealthy men (and their guests) had access to expensive alternatives. The choice by some men to express their sexuality in places from which others were economically excluded hindered the construction of an ideal 'gay community' that included all homosexual men.

In addition to economically-based distinctions within the gay community, additional tensions arose between gays and heterosexuals who sought to appropriate the same spaces at the same time. That is, both communities sought to construct specific 'spatial centres' (Feuchtwang 2004:4–12). The gay community recognized the southeast corner of China Jump's DJ platform as such a spatial centre. Feelings such as friendship, affection and erotic passion flowed here. This same space might be recognized by heterosexual in widely divergent ways. This is what Stephan Feuchtwang calls 'multi-vocality,' which describes the potential for conflict among groups sharing a space without sharing the social meanings that define the space. (Feuchtwang 2004:4–12). This triggers a new question: how do we understand how one specific stage performance speaks to different audiences: the gay contingent in the northeast corner of China Jump and the heterosexual majority in the rest of the club? Take for example the cross-dressing show with nineteen-year-old Miss Fang Fang, where the DJ shouts 'look only, no touching!' In a way, it shows a change of the gay minority community's focus, moving away from invisible 'self-entertaining' and extending its performing space to the main stage, which had been dominated by the club's heterosexual majority. The drag show was enormously popular among all audiences. The heterosexual audience may or may not have understood the drag part, that it was a male acting as a woman, but were in any case unlikely to know that was a public performance of another, gay, community. They may have interpreted the shows in the context of revolutionary operas, traditional theatre or something else. In any case, these multiple symbolic codes of cross-dressing performance is reminiscent of what James C. Scott calls a 'hidden transcript' (1990) that allows the minority group to strategically criticize inequality through performance in a specific space.[8] Such special spatial practice describes the change of social relations in the spatial setting and its influence on the gay community.

Blackmail and prostitution: The 'pollution' of social sites

In her discussion of China's socialist market economy system in the 1990s, Judith Farquhar argues that indulgence in desire becomes an important aspect of an increasingly powerful consuming nation (Farquhar 2009: 30). Farquhar also suggests that these new enjoyment techniques are unsustainable, because common people's desires change too rapidly.

---

8. 'Hidden transcript' is an analytical concept that Scott (1990) uses to describe and summarize peasant action selection and ideology characteristics.

Many became dissatisfied with their current living situation and standards and seek out any chance to make money. In the context of gay men's community, this transformation entailed a growing fixation on money, including blackmail and other illegal activities:

> Few people cared for this circle in the 1980s. At that time, gays lived simple lives without worries; we hung out in social sites and, although we might not have much money, we lived happily. Then it gradually transformed. The money issue became stronger and stronger. There were swindlers in the late 1990s; outsiders utilized gay men's weakness for blackmail. If you did not pay them, they would report you to the police and have you arrested. Swindlers especially targeted the older and timid gay men for money. (LB, gay bar manager, homosexual, 51 years old, 2010)
>
> Nobody asked for money in the 1980s; two gay men could play together at the cost of an ice lollipop. Men's Street belonged to pure gays who cared for each other and disliked women; now half of the community is there for money, it's very chaotic. Some rob, some swindle; there are all kinds of people. Now one may steal all your furniture as they did it with you. One plays with you, after you leave, he may hire a car and rob you for your furniture. (JJ, volunteer at a gay grassroots organization, homosexual, 38 years old, 2008)

According to members of the gay community, swindling activities started to appear in gay social sites in the mid- and late-1990s. The gay community was very critical of this, especially as swindlers pretended to fall in love in order to swindle the gay man's money. The emotional cheating along with the loss of money made those gays with experience of Maoist social movements lament the fast and chaotic social changes; many yearned for the age of 'pure love' before the 1990s. Furthermore, male-male prostitution appeared at this time; young men were selling sex in the disco pubs and their number was increasing quickly.

> After the reform and opening-up, and the planned economy transformed into market economy, sex work subsequently appeared. About eighty per cent of them were not tongzhi; they did it only for the money. (L, unemployed homosexual, 53 years old, 2007)

Some gays blamed and criticized the market economy. Some interpreted this as an older generation that was confused by the emergent diversification of values and desires. In their eyes, mainstream ethics were dissolving in the rush to put money above all.[9] In turn, old values of control and stability were weakening, and younger people's excessive pursuit of material values violated the basic principle of honesty. In this context, 'homosexuality' had become a kind of emotion capital and a major means of making a living. Survival and emotion, then, were thereby held together tightly by money. This perception increasingly guided choices and actions, especially among younger people. This was a heavy blow for the older generation, which believed that society had become loose and that gay social sites were now polluted as a result of the commodification of emotion and sex.

The High Risk Age: Disease, Sexual Networks and 'Quality' in the 21st Century

In the 21st century, consumer demand for public recreation and entertainment has continued to expand. The diversification of the entertainment industry, including sites and venues, has developed along with it. The scope of gay social sites and activities continuously expands in turn, transforming from only occupying one corner of mainstream, public spaces to constructing exclusive spaces of their own. In this final section, I discuss some key factors in the creation of exclusive gay space, before I consider the issue of health risks, especially as they relate to HIV/AIDS.

Bathhouse, Bar and Brothel: The Establishment of Exclusive Gay Space
In the discussion so far I have shown that, prior to the mid-1990s the gay community mostly occupied a secret, small corner of urban public space and tacitly interacted in such space to establish contacts and communicate, for example by observing others washing up in a public bathhouse, latrine, or in a public toilet without partition walls. Then, as society gradually began to tolerate gays and their behaviour, gay community culture became semi-public. Subsequently, the gay community has developed a desire for its own, exclusive space. In Shenyang, two gay-owned bathhouses for men (*tongzhi yuchi*) and their 'circle' emerged in 1998. *Tongzhi* bars (*jiuba*) were an even more popular space after the first was opened in 2000. By 2012, Shengyang boasted at least six gay bathhouses and twenty-two gay bars.

---

9. These men were lamenting a change in business ethics. However, before people could use dishonesty to make money from the gay community, they had to acknowledge the existence of this community.

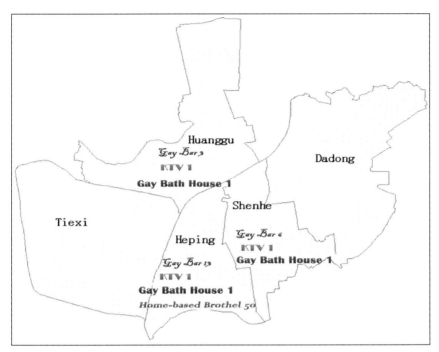

Map 12.3: Men's social sites in the 2000s – 22 gay bars, 50 home-based brothels, 6 gay bathhouses, 3 karaoke bars

The emergence of specifically gay bathhouses and bars illustrate the spatial transition from behaviour to identity. Establishing exclusively gay spaces facilitates gay entertainment and communication; more importantly, it helps the gay community construct itself as a spatial and social presence. Development of a market economy has made this spatial development possible. However, two gay-bar managers, LB and M, explained that gay men Shenyang do not engage sufficiently in 'bar consumption' to keep the business viable. As a result, the lifespan of gay bars was often short. In order to survive and stimulate consumption, LB and M started another kind of industry, providing money boys, or in local parlance, 'selling children' (*mai haizi*).[10]

To operate bars and expand the operation, more and more customers and children come; at the same time, bars can be a shield and the busi-

10. 'Children' (*haizi*) does not point to age specific difference per se, but rather to a lower status socially; it can also be an affectionate term to denote intimacy. More generally, the term 'money boy' (MB) is used to define a male person providing sex service to other males for a charge.

ness is good. There are about 10 to 15 children in each bar. The number of children in home-based brothels is almost the same. The advantage of bars is that they have fixed locations; out-of-towners may come to the bars as they are unable to find entertainment area; it's more convenient to find some children to drink with. (LB, gay bar manager, homosexual, 51 years old, 2010)

Gay bathhouses and bars came into being due to the need for recognition of gay identity and community. Aided by the emergent market economy and consumer culture, more gay-exclusive and diverse spaces could develop and gain popularity. These exclusive spaces catered to variegated needs and desires, including business objectives (making money) community needs (making friends, meeting lovers).

Underground sexual networks, 'quality', and HIV/AIDS risks

The commercial factor has further contributed to developing a male-male sex industry based in gay bathhouses and bars as well as home-based brothels.[11] Whereas prostitution was rare until the late 1990s, it developed on a large scale after 2000. In just one decade, at least fifty home-based brothels have emerged in Shenyang. The industry is supported by male-male sex workers, entertainment venue managers and clients, who together form a kind of 'triangle' of interested parties.

A notable aspect of the male-male sex industry is that many male-male sex workers are not gay. Most heterosexual ('straight') male-male sex workers are introduced and employed through encountering coded job advertisements in the media, such as newspaper ads for male PR person or bathhouse massage therapist, or via employment agencies. Others have encountered male gay clients in a generic service job, where they were offered too much money to resist in exchange for sexual favours. Gradually, these men become seduced by the cash and they begin to market their services. Bodies are becoming commodities. Male-male sexual transactions emerge as a practice not only within the gay community, but also among straight and bisexual people. The straight male-male sex workers I interviewed did not feel morally repulsed by their

---

11. Home-based brothel: male-male sex service operators purchase or rent an apartment by themselves, live and work with employed male-male sex workers; build up family atmosphere in internal management and external service. This is separate from male-male sex services offered and provided in parks or squares. Analysis of such services is beyond the scope of this chapter.

work. Still, and similar to female sex workers, they would conceal their actual occupation from parents in the countryside, and they acknowledged that some requested sexual practices were difficult in the beginning. In choosing this special industry, male-male sex workers use their own bodies as capital in order to obtain urban citizenship and economic returns as quickly as possible (Kong 2011: 175–193).

The sex industry has complicated the development of a gay community by reducing trust and dividing potential members among four groups: sex workers whose sexual identity is uncertain; gays who are willing to pay for sex, gays who had been willing to pay for sex under the guise of relationship-building, but were then both heartbroken and economically damaged when their potential lover was revealed as a fraud; and gays who wanted economics to be completely separated from sexuality. For better or worse, the blame for these divisions has been placed squarely on the sex workers. Not only are some of them the individuals who cause the problems, but most of them are recent migrants from rural areas. In addition to the stigma of being a sex worker, they also carry the negative 'rural, uneducated, unsophisticated' stereotype which is especially appalling to many gays in Shenyang, who like to imagine themselves as among the most urbane members of the population. Several authors use 'quality' (*suzhi*) to have discussed this double discrimination sex workers face from the very community they exist to serve (see Rofel 2007; Ho 2010; Kong 2011).

Sex work is also problematic in relation to health risks, especially HIV/AIDS. As the male-male sex work industry expanded, so did the prevalence of HIV/AIDS infections. In the first decade of the 21st century, the infection rate of HIV/AIDS in the gay community increased from 1.5 in 2001 to 5.3 per cent in 2009 (E. P. Chow, et.al 2011:845). The HIV/AIDS infection rate in the male-male sex worker community was 5.1 per cent, which was similar with the gay community.[12] However, the internal heterogeneity of this community made them fall into a more complicated high-risk condition. I investigated the HIV/AIDS risks in

---

12. At present, there is no official data of AIDS infection rate with regard to male-male sex workers. 5.1% is obtained through mean value calculation by adopting meta-analysis statistics method, searching and screening relevant references from domestic CNKI, Wanfang, Cqvip database and abroad PubMed and Embase database and finally determining 20 Chinese references and 9 English references.

different spatial settings and found striking contrasts, but also overlaps. In four entertainment venues, the number of straight sex workers was greater than fifty per cent. Often they are more popular with gay clients because they are perceived to be more masculine and, hence, virile. In the sexual encounter, the straight sex workers were mostly passive (being anally penetrated), except from when complying with the client's request for 'play'.

However, the passive recipient in anal sex has a higher risk of infection than has the active partner. In the entertainment venues, younger sex workers lack sexual health and self-protection awareness and engage in high-risk sex more often than older men with more experience. Sex workers in public parks and squares are in a much more inferior position to the sex workers of entertainment venues in terms of sanitary conditions, health knowledge and condom use. Because this community is highly mobile and invisible, it is hard for support organizations to find them and offer systemic outreach intervention services. The situation of the cross-dressing money boys is even more worrying. In my investigation in 2009, I found that, among the thirty-four men I had identified as transgender money boys, four were confirmed HIV positive.[13] Three of these four told me that they practically never used condoms when having sex with migrant worker clients; this greatly increases the risk of contracting HIV.

The prevalence of HIV/AIDS has added health risks to multiple types of social sites in the 21st century, also beyond the gay-identified ones. This is because anyone who engages in unsafe sex with gay community participants in each metropolis across the country can contract the virus, including rural wives and female partners of male migrant workers. In addition, the popularization of another important space – the Internet in the gay community – enables sex work to develop from traditional face-to-face networks of acquaintances to the more secret, rapid and low-cost online communication. The health risks are invisible in the virtual space but keep on expanding as more men are introduced to one another online. Meanwhile, the growing use of drugs in leisure

---

13. Since 2007, a new type of prostitution practice has begun to appear in urban parks. Some male-male sex workers cross-dress by wearing wigs, makeup and female attire to pass as female sex workers to solicit business at night. Most of their clients are migrant workers coming from other places to work in Shenyang.

spaces exacerbates high-risk behaviour and further inhibits control and outreach.

Conclusion

This chapter has explored the characteristics and emerging trends of Shenyang's gay male community through the three post-Mao decades, which I have conceptualized as the innocent age, the commercial age, and most recently, the high risk age. The genealogy of the changing desires and practices through these periods is clearly presented through the mapping of gay spatial transformation, as well as the following changes of identity, human capital, sexuality, values, and diseases.

Spatial transformation. I have shown that, in the 1980s, when people began their liberation from the oppression of the Maoist era, men revelled in the ability to engage in male-male passions. In this period, gays participated in the few mainstream entertainment spaces available, such as dance halls, and otherwise connected in urban public spaces, such as Men's Street. The relationships were characterized by sincerity and true love. When the market economy began in earnest in the 1990s, socialist ideals and norms waned 'market citizenship' became the new norm (Kong 2011: 169). The spatial construction and practice of the gay community also started to associate with the global capitalist system. The ever-increasing entertainment and service industry created new types of consumption-driven social sites, such as disco pubs, bars and KTV. This type of space also became a standard for the gay community and led to greater internal stratification. The consumption emphasis expanded in the 21st century and enabled exclusively gay spaces to emerge, including bathhouses, bars, and home-based brothels. This development also points to the new aspect of gay identity discourses and increasing demands for social recognition. These changes moreover, fostered the emergence of male-male sex work, or a sense of 'masculine consumption', in gay exclusive spaces. The male-male sex industry in Shenyang developed rapidly and extended connections to gay communities in major cities across China. In sum, the introduction of the market economy enabled many developments in gay community space and practice.

Emotions and desires. Expression of emotions and desires has travelled a long road. In the 1980s, people who had denied their identity and repressed their desires began to open themselves to the possibility of pursuing pure love. This type of precious sincerity, however, was transient; the older gay population was unprepared for the more commercialized era to come, with its sex work and deceptive liaisons. This population believed the new consumptive practices and ideals were polluting gay community space. I have discussed two major aspects of this transition. First, the changes mean that older moral norms are deconstructed, multiple desires emerge to challenge the true love focus of the 1980s, and gay community spaces and possibilities expand and become somewhat accepted. Second, when considering the male-male sex work phenomenon from the perspective of the discourse of quality(*suzhi*), it is important to connect this with the expanding urban-rural division within the gay community. In other words, factors such as rural background, different sexual orientation (including heterosexual, bisexual, and transgender) in the male-male sex work industry, have come to indicate low quality among men in the gay community. The rise of sex work simultaneously shows that sex, as human capital, has become an important variable affecting men seeking employment. By contrast, variables such as sexual orientation, sexual desire and sexual pleasure are less important.

Identity construction and recognition. I have shown that spatial flows of behaviour, relationships and information necessitate a comparison of mainland gay identity in relation to their global context. The transnational concept of 'gay' identity and recognition certainly has shaped the sense of cultural citizenship and 'do-it-yourself citizenship' of the Chinese gay community, representing a kind of neoliberal subject of the post-Mao age (Rofel 2007: 94–97; Kong 2011:169–179). However, the local appropriations of transnational concepts can vary significantly, especially for older generations who developed their own vocabulary before being presented with international alternatives. For this reason, the ideas of 'gay' and 'community' in Shenyang are perceived and interpreted quite differently by this city's older and younger generations. In this chapter, I have shown that the intertwining factors of 'older,' understood both as age/generation and space-time variation, have undergone considerable changes in the reform and opening up period. In the hearts of gay men of the older generation, the notion of 'gay', similar to that of 'the West' is a useful noun, which reflects the space time persistence inscribed by the official institutions, history and culture. I would therefore argue that this shows that the articulation of 'gay' and '*tongzhi*' is a product of economic reform but 'with Chinese characteristics'.

From sharing free urban public space, to occupying and charging for the participation in commercial space, then to establishing consumerist exclusive space, the gay community of Shenyang has experienced and imagined a sense of deferred identity endowed to them by broader forces of modernization, while being in the process of persistently constructing their own exclusive space in the city.

As a telling example of the processes I have discussed in this Chapter, one of the men I interviewed, F, sighed with emotion and said: '*Tongzhi* are more oppressed than people of all levels in the society; when other people started to make money, we began to make contact with the society.' We have seen that the gay spaces brought by the market economy have become increasingly abundant in the new millennium, and have in turn provided a platform connecting gays with the mainstream world, in the process enabling the development of a specific gay identity, terminology and discourse.

References

Byron, Reginald (2005) 'Identity'. In Alan Barnard and Jonathan Spencer (eds), *Encyclopedia of Social and Cultural Anthropology*. New York: Routledge.

Chou, E.P., D.P. Wilson, et al. (2011) 'Human Immunodeficiency Virus Prevalence is Increasing among Men Who Have Sex with Men in China: Findings from a review and meta-analysis' *Sexually Transmitted Diseases* 38(9): 845–857.

Chou, Wah-Shan (2001) 'Homosexuality and the Cultural Politics of *Tongzhi* in Chinese Societies'. In Peter A. Jackson, et al. (eds), *Gay and Lesbian Asia: Culture, identity, community*. New York: Haworth Press.

Farquhar, Judith (2009) *Taotie zhi Yu:dangdai Zhongguo de shi yu se* [Appetites: Food and sex in post-socialist China], trans. Guo Yiyao et al. Nanjing: Jiangsu People's Publishing House.

Feuchtwang, Stephan (2004) 'Theorising place'. In Stephan Feuchtwang (ed.), *Making Place: State projects, globalisation and local responses in China*. London: UCL Press.

Fu, Xiaoxing (2012) *Kongjian, Wenhua, Biaoyan: Dongbei a shi nantongxinglian qunti de renleixue guancha* [Space, culture, performance: An anthropologicalstudy of gay male communities in a city in China's northeast]. Beijing: Guangming Ribao Chubanshe.

Fu, Xiaoxing and Wu Zhen (2010) 'Urban Space Distribution and Cultural Production of the Gay Community: An example from Shenyang'. *Gongcheng Yanjiu: Kuaxueke shiyezhong de gongcheng* [Engineering study: engineering in the interdisciplinary visual field] vol. 2, no. 1, pp. 38–52.

Goffman, Ervin (2008) *Richang Shenghuozhong de Ziwo Chengxian* [The presentation of self in everyday life), trans. Feng Gang. Beijing: Beijing University Press.

Guo,Xiaofei (2008) 'Legal Environment of the Chinese *Tongzhi* Community'. In Tongge, et. al. (eds), *Zhongguo Tongzhi Renqun Shengtai Baogao (I)* [Ecological report (I) of the Chinese *tongzhi* community] .Beijing: Ji'an De Information Center.

Ho, Loretta W. W. (2010) *Gay and Lesbian Subculture in Urban China*. London: Routledge.

Knopp, Lawrence (2006) 'Sexuality and Urban Space: A framework for analysis'. In David Bell and Gill Valentine (eds), *Mapping Desire: Geographies of sexualities*. New York: Routledge.

Kong, Travis (2011) *Chinese Male Homosexualities: Memba, tongzhi and golden boy*. London: Routledge.

Lefebvre, Henri (1991) *The Production of Space*. Oxford: Blackwell Publishers.

Ren Yixiao (2005) 'Gay Behavior Right or Wrong Requires Legal Explanation'. *Fazhi Ribao* [Legal Daily], 27 October.

Rofel, Lisa (2007) *Desiring China: Experiments in neoliberalism, sexuality, and public culture*. Durham, NC: Duke University Press.

Scott, James (1990) *Domination and the Arts of Resistance: Hidden transcripts*. New Haven: Yale University Press.

Shenyang Yearbook editorial committee (2001) *Shenyang Nianjian* [Shenyang Yearbook). Beijing: Chinese Statistics Publishing House.

Soja, Edward (1996) *Thirdspace: Journeys to Los Angeles and other real-and -imagined places*. Malden (Mass.): Blackwell.

Wei, Wei (2009) 'Consumerism and Queer/*Tongzhi* Space: A map of Alternative Desire in Urban Life'. *Shehui* [Society], vol. 29, no. 4, pp. 79–106.

Zhang, Beichuan (1994) *Tong Xing Ai* [Same Sex Love]. Jinan: Shandong Science and Technology Publishing House.

CHAPTER 13

Interview with Cui Zi'en

Popo Fan[1]

Editorial Note

Cui Zi'en (崔子恩) is a prolific novelist, screenwriter, director, and open *tongzhi* activist based in Beijing. His films include *Enter the Clowns* (《丑角登场》, 2002), *The Old Testament* (《旧约》, 2002), *Feeding Boys, Ayaya* (《哎呀呀，去哺乳》, 2003), *My Fair Son* (《我如花似玉的儿子》, 2007), and *Queer China, Comrade China* (《誌同志》, 2009). Cui's works have been presented at the Flanders International Film Festival, Vancouver International Film Festival, Hong Kong International Film Festival, London Film Festival, Berlin Internationale Filmfestspiele, Pusan International Film Festival, and many universities in the USA. He has been the recipient of several awards, including the 2002 Felipa de Souza Award from the International Gay and Lesbian Human Rights Commission, honoring his outspokenness on *tongzhi* issues in Chinese society. He is a research fellow at the Beijing Film Academy, where Popo Fan was his student.

The following is a redacted translation of an interview that was completed on 18 December 2011 at Fan's home for a special issue of the *Youth Film Handbook* (《青年电影手册——华语同志电影特辑》) on Sinophone *tongzhi* films. We acknowledge the generous permission of the publishers for Fan to use the material in this book

At that time, Fan and Cui both had been participating to different degrees in internet debates about queer theory and identity politics, what China's relevant historical experience had been, what kind of movement was needed, and what kinds of connections and gaps existed between

---

1. Interview translated by William F. Schroeder.

women's rights, '*tongzhi*', and the queer. Cui (C) and Fan (F) engaged in a dialog about these and other themes.

ᙯ

F: Which side are you on in terms of '*tongzhi*' and '*queer*'?[2] Where do you think you stand vis-à-vis these concepts? Do you disassociate yourself from one, or do you feel like you understand them both well?

C: Personally, I got involved in making moving images[3] because of the *tongzhi* movement. But I have a background in queer theory. These two things are actually on separate tracks. They are non-linear. I'm not sure if they intersect at any point. Some editing could be done to achieve that, but I have no idea how to do this kind of editing.

For example, in my observation, I would say those widely discussed commercial works such as *Milk* are very *tongzhi*. It was a very *tongzhi* picture. The *Philadelphia Story* is another one I consider very *tongzhi*.[4] If you were to compare, the larger an audience a work has and the more commercial it is, the more it could be linked to the concept of *tongzhi*. Otherwise, the smaller the audience a work has, the less it is talked about, the fewer people see it, the more '*queer*' there is in it.

F: You have mentioned a few very *tongzhi* films, can you name some very queer films as well?

C: Besides myself, I think Cheng Yusu has some very queer works, such as *Shanghai Panic* and *Welcome to Destination Shanghai*. Some young directors also have a very queer approach in their work. Chen Han is an example. Some of his pieces are quite *tongzhi*, but some others

---

2. Cui and Fan make a distinction here and throughout between the English-derived *ku'er* (酷儿), translated here as '*queer*', and *tongzhi* (同志), which simply has been transliterated to recognize that most Chinese speakers do not hear the word as foreign.

3. The translator has used the term 'moving image' here and elsewhere to capture Cui's sense of rejecting the specificity of 'film' when referring to movies that are made using digital video instead of celluloid or acetate reels. The nuance cannot quite be expressed in English, which does not interchange its range of words for film/movie/motion picture/moving image as often as Chinese does.

4. *Milk* is a 2008 biographical film about American gay rights activist Harvey Milk. *Philadelphia Story* is a 1993 American drama film and one of the first mainstream Hollywood films to acknowledge HIV/AIDS, homosexuality, and homophobia.

are, consciously or unconsciously, very queer. Popo Fan's works are very *tongzhi*, so are Kit Hong's. This is how I feel about my director friends around me. Lots of these works are shown in film exhibitions too. The two directions are also quite distinct in the pictures in the Beijing Queer Film Festival. Using traditional film categorizations, queer works would tend to fall into the category of the experimental or have an experimental quality to them. They break the style of the linear narrative, and in breaking that linear narrative, they smash our sense of rational truth, our perception of movement. I think this is the difference [between queer and *tongzhi* works]. It's a small difference, but I think the nuance is critical.

F: So, do you prefer the queer part of you or the *tongzhi* part?

C: My moving images are not very *tongzhi*. If anything, my documentary is more *tongzhi*, such as *Queer China, Comrade China*, where obviously *tongzhi* [comrade] is in the title. Most of my moving images are more queer than *tongzhi*; in other words, more queer-oriented. They need to be explored – even I need to explore them. That is, even after they've been finished, I still carry on probing them. What is it that happened when I shot this thing, what is it that happened in this piece? When it's finished, after a certain period of time, what then happens again with it? It's something that keeps on developing. But the *tongzhi* aspect would be fixed in time and shape.

Queer China, Comrade China, produced in 2009, was essentially a piece about 2009. It could not have included anything from 2010 or 2011, not even a concept. For example, concerning the concept LGBTQ, now we have the addition of an 'I', but that idea didn't even exist at the time. There wasn't much of a queer part to the work, as it dealt more with the movement. The queer part was more complicated – more complicated in terms of the structure of movement. Or put another way, basically in line with this kind of thinking, perhaps the most influential idea would be that homosexuality is a prison – this kind of thinking would have the most influence. But once such ideas were put into a piece like that, it would cease to make sense, and become itself a cage. In fact my separating these two concepts is strategic. We still need time to make sense of them in the context of the Sinophone.

F: You are actually quite creative in many areas, including novels, films and screenplays. Later you started organizing events. It gives you an opportunity to deal with different people in different areas. Do you think your versatility resulted from a detailed plan for yourself or it was simply a coincidence?

C: Writing and making pictures were both planned. Other things just came along. Speaking of organizing activities, a lot of media found me because I came out in public very early. So naturally I became a kind of contact person. Ten years ago I was basically a go-between for the media. They came to me for everything, mostly phone numbers and interviewees. It's like I was a kind of hub. Sometimes I think this is our choice – it's our choice how we plan our history. But sometimes we are chosen by time. The work of organizing film festivals belongs to the latter. When I was cooperating with Yang Yang,[5] I didn't belong to any exhibition groups. I was simply pulled into their group and helped them with the planning. And I just slowly, slowly, slowly kept going. The same thing happened in my cooperation with Zhu Rikun and Fanhall Studio.[6] They were hosting an event in Huangtingzi when I lived in the Film Academy. Something just clicked between us. In terms of *tongzhi* movements, it was the same with Wu Chunsheng, Wan Yanhai,[7] and Susie Jolly[8] – it just felt right. I lived very far away at that time, but Chunsheng didn't mind and went all the way there to find me. The link was all there was. Come to think of it, there wasn't anything logical in there, let alone an intentional choice.

CB

F: In your works of that period – novels, film reviews, and the like – was that *tongzhi* desire embedded consciously or unconsciously?

C: How can I describe it? My narratives were always in the first person. There were always multiple 'I's telling the story. My background in literature is fairly rich. An advantage of this narrative method is that

---

5. 杨洋, Co-founder of Beijing Queer Film Festival.
6. 现象工作室 Xianxiang Gongzuoshi, a very important independent film organization since 2002.
7. 吴春生, 万延海, LGBTQ activists since the very early stages of the movement in mainland China.
8. Susie Jolly is a programme officer for the Ford Foundation in Beijing.

it can disrupt any kind of mode. So if you're talking about normative, theoretical, cognitive, or physical modes, I don't think these are enough – they're all needed, but they're not enough. The physical, philosophical, political, or activist modes are all expressed in those different 'I's. But each of them is not singular, or I can't choose a singular one. But I was never really satisfied with that—that is, with singularity – and each time I finished a book, I thought of it as belonging to the uniqueness of that period. Even if I could use some so-called modernist literary or post-modernist literary methods to make it not unique or illogical, I would still think it had a temporality, during which there was what might be called a core – a nucleus to that especially spiritual life. I always felt that nucleus, that pit, was very hard, so I always thought I needed to write another book to say goodbye to that core. Then I would write another one to say goodbye to another one. And again and again. I was incessantly saying goodbye to these cores, and it wasn't until after I started to make movies that I felt the core was gone.

F: When a lot of people compare your films to your writing, they say that your writing is more acceptable to most people, more modern, while your films are more post-modern and hard to understand. But in my mind, your writing and your filmmaking are very consistent – they're both destructive in a way. What's your opinion?

C: I agree. I was just using different methods of destruction. Literature has this thing called narrative. Without narrative, it's not literature. Essays are something else of course. But to me, that norm still exists, so it was in all the literary approaches I used in my writing, including in the recently published *The Big Dipper Has 7 Stars* 《北斗有七星》. That literary vein ran through all the books. That literary vein isn't mine – doesn't belong to me – but belongs to all humanity. But I was responsible for replacing its blood with my own, for replacing the old blood. This was in fact the literary effort – the destruction you were just talking about, it was a replacement of the old blood with the new. But that flow was still there, it was just renewed.

But in terms of making moving images, I would say that the destruction is on the whole Jesus-like, as if demolishing the temple – to destroy something and rebuild it within three days, that kind of feeling. Actually, the act of demolition is far more important than the act of rebuilding.

Changing blood is different from all this. In changing blood, you still recognize the vein, as it were – fundamentally I was still endorsing that literary vein. But in making moving images, instead of endorsing the vein, I completely demolished it.

As a matter of fact, anyone who has ever picked up a camera to shoot a film would know that – that indeed from the very emergence of moving pictures themselves – film has always had a relationship with capital. If you want to become part of a blue-blooded literary lineage, you might not require capital. All you have to do is start reading from an early age or spend a lot of time reflecting on things. Or basically you can surround yourself with the trappings of a blue blood – you could call this the art of becoming a yuppy.[9] But making moving images is totally different. You cannot disguise yourself. You cannot pretend to be something else.

My destruction in making moving images is thorough and embedded. As soon as I start shooting, I find that all the connections, at least all the connections that a film critic would make – the blood vessels – are completely no good, useless. They're completely restrictive, complete rubbish. If you want to use them as a reference point – stay within those blood vessels, as it were – in making your moving image, then you're just heading towards a dead end. Especially if you're making so-called independent, or even, especially, queer material in China. If you go that route, it's as if you've stripped naked to sell your body, but nobody's buying. It's basically like that.

When I realized these things, when I was making my first picture, I started to understand that I would be resolute in rejecting this path, that I wouldn't submit to capital and tradition, including European art-house or commercial traditions.

F: So you started with literature. What was your break into filmmaking like? Did it have to do with being involved in the film *Men and Women* (《男男女女》)?

---

9. In Chinese, 小资 (petty bourgeoisie, yuppy), the word Cui uses here, suggests the trappings of a certain 'tasteful' lifestyle, which could be affected. This word can be used as a verb in contemporary slang usage, as in '今晚咱们去小资一回', or 'Let's go *xiaozi* tonight', suggesting that one go with one's friends perhaps to a western-style café or bar to 'hang out'.

250

C: No, because I had been writing scripts before *Men and Women*. When I got involved with *Men and Women*, it looked like an independent production, but it was shot on film, which meant it identified with thinking that wasn't really me. I didn't see much good in that. When DV [digital video] came out, I thought this thing would no longer require a big crew. It would be just like several good friends getting together to make something. It was at that stage that I got into it. I thought I could use this method of expression, and that it wasn't the same as filmmaking. So whenever I'm having discussions with independent filmmakers, I always think it's a bit annoying that everyone uses the word 'film', because I'd rather use 'independent moving image' [独立影像] or something – I think that summarizes it better.

F: Yes, so do I actually. I feel that, especially sometimes when people say *tongzhi*, what they really want to say is 'homosexual', or after it they add all sorts of extra words. Actually, 'queer' and 'film' are two complementary words – they don't have such clear borders. But in any case could we say that *Men and Women* was the beginning of your *tongzhi*-related image production, regardless of what form it took?

C: Let me think about it. No, actually. Because *Men and Women* was just something that was cobbled into a movie. I had written many *tongzhi* scripts before. But I was writing about a lot of things at that time. My novels had bits of stage play and bits of film, but at that time they all took the form of a screenplay. At a very early stage I wrote a children's queer screenplay called *A Very Long Game* (《长长的游戏》), which was published later as a novel. It was one of my earliest works in the 90s, about middle school students. I had been writing things like that up until *Men and Women*. *Men and Women*, as soon as it came together as a so-called 'movie', it was screened at festivals and made public. So everyone thought Cui Zi'en had started to write *tongzhi* scripts. A lot of people also thought this was when I started making moving images, but I personally don't think so. Actually, as far as the script for *Men and Women* goes, it wasn't as if after I finished writing it, it was then shot. There was already a script and I was to play a character. But when I went and saw the script, I said, I'm not going to act that, I'm not going to act out that terrible script. Then they said, well, you write one. So I spent three days writing one. That was the situation.

F: We've also had an interview with Simon Chung.[10] He said he actually liked the screenplay. He felt that the complicated relationships in it were worth figuring out. So then how did you go about creating such a thing in three days?

C: Because I had written many things like that before, things that were far, far more complicated than that. I had written a lot of – not necessarily things of literary merit – but so many things. So, to me, it wasn't much of anything, it was simple. I would say it was a fairly ready-made thing, something I could just pick up without putting in much time or energy.

F: You had written so many things before that. Have you ever thought of shooting those pieces?

C: Not at all. That is, I've never stopped to think about it. Because later when I started making my own moving images, I've always thought of my creations as doing and thinking at the same time. I couldn't complete a script and then go shoot it. Since I started making moving images, none of them have been made with a completed screenplay in advance. They were all made on site with a concept and a rough outline, according to the resources we had available and the composition of the crew. So, for example, whether we shot for three days or five, what sort of location we used, all was *ad hoc*, and the dialog was improvised. Or on a morning I would write an approximation for the daytime actors and then send them off to find their own method of dialog, and shoot it that way. No piece I've shot has relied mechanically on a script.

F: Has it been like this since *The Old Testament*?

C: Yes, but *The Old Testament* was the most scripted because it was an extract from one of my novels. In that novel there was also a part from *Enter the Clowns*. People were watching a movie called *The Old Testament*. There were three stories involved. The actors were acting in a stage play, which was a part of *Enter the Clowns* that I filmed later. They had roles in many areas, including films. The actors also had lives of their own. It was all interwoven with many fragments. So in *The Old Testament* the three stories were quite clear from the beginning. One of the stories was from the 80s, which I learned from Zhen Li. It was based

---

10. 钟德胜 (Zhong Desheng), Hong Kong film director.

on a true story. But when I shot it, I couldn't find actors old enough to play dad and mom, so I found a man and a wife and turned it into a story in which they had started looking after each other in their youth.

F: What is your system of production like?

C: It's quite varied. Sometimes a friend will tell me I can shoot in his place for two days and eat anything in the fridge, use what I want. Sometimes another friend will give me 5,000 *yuan*. Some will treat us for a meal, or treat the crew to a couple of meals. Some will provide cameras. The cast and crew naturally feel like they're just coming to a party[11] and wouldn't think about what rewards they can gain – they're just coming to have fun. It's basically like that. This is my production system. In terms of production systems, actually, I don't think it really resembles one – it's more like a system of getting together.

F: But that sounds a little like a communist troupe.

C: A little bit, a little bit. This comes out of my ten years' experience with filmmaking. Actually – like when you and I went to Copenhagen – I tend to think those anarchist-type places are charming. Capitalism is continuously corroding contemporary China, which makes me feel that humanity really must find a new ideal that comes closer to Utopianism, or communism, or heaven and the like, than capitalism.

F: Are these ideas reflected in your films?

C: Yes, they must be. Quite a few international film critics have taken an interest in what I call the proletariat, or people who have nothing at all. Actually they are not necessarily proletarian but are people with absolutely nothing. For example, in *Refrain*, there are two parentless brothers who have nothing at all. The younger brother must sing to support his older brother with learning disabilities. The younger brother also worries that if he dies the older brother will not be able to survive. So he wants the older brother to commit suicide with him. In international critics' observations, they all thought this had to do with a concern for the extremely poor, but at the time, I didn't think about whether they were poor or not. When I was choosing my characters, whether it was experimental or what, I wanted them to have a feeling of being stripped down or bare.

---

11. Cui uses the English word 'party' here.

Many commercial directors consider nudity a tool for provocation, while I would rather present it as exactly what it is. So, many viewers, if they were exposed to nudity from start to finish in my films, would get no erections from it, even if the actors were all good-looking. That's because my orientation wouldn't at all be towards sex as a provocation, or sex for consumption. There are some people who say that actually the class of people I'm concerned with in my films would not watch my films. Some people have said that. I say, really? I haven't thought about it before. I can't remember which critics have discussed this with me.

F: What's your opinion about that? Do you wish that they could see those films? Do you wish that they could understand what is expressed in your films?

C: From a very basic perspective, I think that the second-generation wealthy[12] also have absolutely nothing. I have many such friends, such as Wang Sijia. They are people with nothing at all. In a manner of speaking, we are all poverty-stricken, we all find ourselves impoverished. In terms of our lives, they have limits, they will forever have limits. When it's over, it's over; when it's let go, it's let go; it's gone. I think that no matter what kind of people see my pieces, they could be that impoverished person, but they might not think they are. But my emphasis isn't on class, it isn't on whether you are a pauper or not – I don't think that's what I want to focus on. But I'll always choose the situation of poverty, or bare, stark nudity, to present my understandings of the world.

F: I remember in *Feeding Boys, Ayaya* you asked why when the water flows downwards, people struggle upwards. Is that the kind of thing you're talking about, does that have to do with your overall way of thinking?

C: Correct. This is a very important idea. But this idea is about power, and not primarily about class. It's not about materialism, not about socialism or socialist observations or interpersonal relations or whatever – that standpoint is a bit different, because it's concerned with the distribution of wealth. In terms of socialism, at that level, you'd be concerned with

---

12. Cui uses the term 富二代 here, an expression referring to the children of entrepreneurs who profited from the economic opening and other reforms Deng Xiaoping initiated. The term has a mildly pejorative sense, suggesting that this generation is over-privileged.

what kind of person you are, whether you're middle class or whatever – because the basic principle comes from the idea of proletarian revolution. But my basic thinking comes from a perspective that seriously considers the recognition of power. In other words, why do all people want to become successful people – actually, fundamentally, why do you want to become a success, why do you want to hew towards that political core, why do you want to become the kind of person whose content is determined by that political core? Especially in this visual era we're now living in, why do you want to become that glittering image, constantly making yourself up, constantly disguising yourself, and constantly concealing your real identity? Why is that the thing you want to affirm, when in the end you've negated your most authentic, original face? Why do you want to continuously be scrubbing [off your makeup]? Actually, the more you scrub, the duller you become – it's that simple. Why do people always face the wrong direction and strive to go in it?

This is what it deals with, including the question of sex, because *Feeding Boys* basically talks about someone whose interest in sex is fading. Because in terms of sex, why would a child of a wealthy household, a kid who is in the middle class at the time, why would he be a 'money boy' of his own volition? So really it's dealing with that kind of stable, frightening, stultified human relation – a human relation that you'd think was secure. But what is security? This security sits on a foundation that floats, constantly floating up and up and up. For example, since that period – I filmed it in 2003 – it's been nearly ten years, and that era's middle class has floated up to be this era's wealthy class. Basically, that's how society gets divided.

F: Are these thoughts all your personal observations? Or have you also learned them from reading western ideas?

C: Yes, it's from reading, but also not. Sometimes it's an observation of the west, an observation of western art and literature. I think so-called good western art and literature, including good film, even masterpieces of film – because at a time I had written almost an entire book on the films of the masters, and I held them in extraordinarily high esteem – but then I discovered that the so-called great masters' films were all built on a foundation of capitalism.

♋

F: Your new film has received a fair amount of investment. Have you changed? Or is this a new kind of self-destruction?

C: I haven't really. Actually, this so-called investment, if nothing else, will simply extend the period of filming. It will extend the period of getting together. For example, we used to have only five or six days ...

F: But it's still a social gathering, right?

C: Right, but this time the gathering took place in a villa, and we could all eat well. Transportation was covered for everybody. It was basically a middle-class gathering. That's where the investment went. But it was a lower middle-class gathering to be exact. There were no fancy dinners, no parties, no big show of it. We didn't have a dance party, there was no waltz. Actually, it was a little different, a little bit – actually this time it was because among the participants there were some people who themselves had a middle-class identity, and because we used HD equipment. I think it was a little odd, it would count as a little odd. The good thing was that this odd method had an odd end – we weren't able to show the film.

☙

F: A few films you shot before, in terms of form and content, had quite a destructiveness in them. But there have also been some comparatively milder ones, such as *Withered Lads in a Blooming Season* and *The Old Testament*, which we mentioned earlier. What is the relationship between these creative works and your others? Why did you shoot those kinds of things at those moments?

C: Actually it was quite by chance. For example, I could use only three rooms for *The Old Testament*. So if I could use only three places, the feeling could be like three eras, those three stories. It's just like how in my world there are infinite concepts, and there's a big radar that goes out into the universe. I've got a lot of planets and stars in my mind, a lot of concepts are there – that is, a lot of scripts. I just have to scan along, and when I'm finished – for example, now I'm at your house, I'd want to focus in on shooting a piece at your place – I just use that radar to beam and beam until I beam down that star to here, until I call it down to here. Then I start to shoot – I take that star's ideas and things and put them in here. It's that sort of process.

F: The site comes before the concept?

C: Yes, what kind of site, what kind of people and equipment we're going to use. And even including, for example, our cinematographer, what kind of personality he or she has, what the actors are like. It's basically like that, because then – for example around the time of *The Old Testament*, we often had to change actors for different stories. The reason was that we had too many actors around, too many actors who could act, but none could pull it off entirely. At that time we were all unoccupied, so for different stories we could use a couple extra actors. It was like that, so at that time Menghao and Xiaogang were both in there. Because they were actors in *Men and Women*, I don't know why, but after we finished that piece, I felt that I owed them something. It was strange – I wasn't even the director, but I thought, if I shoot a new story, I definitely want to invite them to be in it. This was because of the disorganization of *Men and Women*.

F: That's like, *Withered Lads in a Blooming Season*, that's part of the 'Breaking Ethics Trilogy'.

C: Right.

F: You had a very strong view of ethics in China at that time. What made you do this 'Breaking Ethics Trilogy'? From the sound of it, it was quite conceptual. It doesn't feel much like an idea popping up based on a house or the kind of camera you had. Or did it come after shooting?

C: The so-called 'Breaking Ethics Trilogy' was actually a bit ironic, because a lot of directors like this idea of a trilogy, but I think trilogies are quite affected. By coincidence all three films had something to do with ethical relations, or with breaking relational ethics. So I came up with this idea of the 'Breaking Ethics Trilogy' to satirize those people with trilogy addictions. Actually that's what it was about, so it was a name given afterwards. But the so-called 'Breaking Ethics Trilogy' has a narrative feeling, and they have similarities. That is, they all have to do with family, fairly straightforwardly to do with family. At that time – it was 2005 or 2006 – the assemblage I had in my mind was that I felt Chinese society was precisely one of those particular ones that started to go bad from the family. At that time, that aspect of the narrative was quite strong, it was quite strong in all three parts of the trilogy. The dramatics behind it was quite strong, and against that dramatics – that pronounced narrative – I used a destructive method to realize the whole thing. One of the reasons is also because we used extremely inferior products, and because when our crew was working together, everyone appreciated using what looked like an especially good, especially tight, markedly narrative script. We brought it out in an entirely different way in terms of image, because there was something experimental about our entire crew as well.

CB

F: You're someone with a lot of theories. But I'm not sure, I wonder, in the end, what role do you think theories have played in your creative work? Is your work guided by theory? Or do you use a freer method?

C: Theories, to me, are a kind of utter emancipation. You can be very carefree in shooting since you already know where it's coming from and where it's going. For example, if we talk about the masters, if you say, I want to shoot a masterful film, well, you're dead in the water. Why? Because it's very clear where that master is coming from, or where those so-called masterpieces are coming from – what their economic, cultural, political backgrounds are like. And I know very clearly what my own economic, cultural, and political background is. So I can't just rewrite that person's history – I can't. For example, everybody always puts me together with Fassbinder, Almodóvar, even Godard – international film critics like to compare me to them. But I don't have their political, cultural, economic – physical – background at all. My background is something else. If my theory is strong, I'll know what my background is – I use my background, or my abilities, to make my moving images. I don't have to think about anything else – I have that confidence. But people without theory might think, oh I've not done this well. I've not shot this well enough, my technique isn't good, I haven't achieved this and that, the lighting and sound were bad, the actors didn't perform well – this whole range of things, because to begin with, the person has taken this other thing as an example, as a model. But for me, I don't have models – or, models are there for me to reference, to destroy. They're not there to condition me.

And then if you're talking about [what happens] after a film, this problem becomes important to me, actually to all filmmakers. If your theory is strong, you don't need to wait for reviews. I've never waited around for reviews after I finished shooting a picture, never waited for somebody to tell me so-and-so wrote this, or somebody criticized me as this or that kind of person. When somebody reviews me, as soon as I see what kind of review it is, I think, well, that's what kind of review it is. I won't go looking for the ultimate reason why the reviewer didn't go deeper, or why didn't the reviewer capture the essential points in the criticism, because I know that in terms of all that, a review has just stopped at a place for ten minutes, has used a certain bit of energy, or just prepared only that little bit for reviewing your work. And the reviewer's whole background is just like that, so I never think about the problem of how I've been reviewed or received. Because, if I were to go criticize someone else – someone else's work, or if I were to be a so-called director – the way I'd have prepared my lessons, as it were, would be like that, because it's what's called special academism, that kind of preparation. But all preparations have their limits.

F: I talked to Ivan from Spain a few days ago. He said you're the Chinese Almodóvar, and in Germany they call you the Chinese Fassbinder. Then I read in Wang Xiaolu's article how it compared you to Andy Warhol.[13] You've been in some fairly high-profile Western film festivals, and your pictures have these kinds of reactions, so how do you feel about that? How do you think they've understood your pieces?

C: I think the most important thing – for example, in the western world, and actually in Asia, for example in Hong Kong, South Korea, Taipei, those kinds of places – is that they don't especially look at me as a Chinese director. I think this aspect makes me quite happy. They use their own film-viewing platform, their own cultural platform to discuss my moving images. They don't say, this is a Chinese social phenomenon, but when they're categorizing things they will place me in the 'Chinese queer' category. They're quite willing to talk about my queer activities in China, that I'm an activist, that I participate in the movement, or even that I'm an organizer – that I'm one of those people – not that I do that in

---

13. In his book 《电影与时代病——独立电影文化评价与见证》 (Film and epochal problems: critiquing and witnessing independent film culture, 2008, 花城出版社/Huacheng Press), film critic and curator 王小鲁 (Wang Xiaolu) compares Cui with Andy Warhol.

a Chinese way or in a Chinese person's way, that I'm part of a collection in a cabinet, someone who purports to speak for *tongzhi*, not that kind of person. So I think their observations are quite sharp. Of course, not everybody understands my situation or my background. But they can immediately see very clearly that, whether it's moving pictures, activism, moving-picture activism, that he's integrated into a globalistic philosophy or movement, or parallel with it, in step. That's the feeling I have.

F: So they don't approach you with an ingrained orientalist aesthetics? They don't say, I want to go see something oriental, an oriental boy, the oriental proletariat? Is there anything like that?

C: Not very much, not very much. But there are a few people, because when you put on a moving image, they do know it's a Chinese moving image. Of course, people who are concerned with China or Asia would come to see it. But for the most part they wouldn't find the sexualized aesthetic they're after in my pieces.

F: [This is a combination of several related but incomplete questions.] There's another question about something you said this year, about China having three imports from the west. Not long ago you had an argument with Hao Jian about how *tongzhi* was an import. Can you elaborate on your point of view, especially the idea that *tongzhi* is an import?

C: Yes. I said China had three imports – one is Marxism, one is Christianity, and one is the homosexual movement. These three imports – with the exception of Marxism having been accepted as orthodoxy – the other two have been forced underground, or reduced to unconventional status, or they've been turned into illegal situations. The way that Christianity and homosexuality have been persecuted is basically quite similar. It's just that the manner in which they've been persecuted and their historicity are not the same. Christian persecution takes on a bit of a saintly aspect, that feeling of being martyred for one's religion, but homosexuals who have been persecuted have sacrificed their sexualities instead of their religion – they've been turned into jokes, into laughingstocks. But that history is slowly being rewritten; history is slowly changing. And the acceptance of orthodox Marxism is also now very, very slowly being turned into a bit of a laughingstock by history. Christianity is being recognized anew, the homosexual movement is rising, both are readjusting history's colors to the way they are supposed to be. That is, every color scheme should be on equal footing – Christianity's white, homosexuality's rainbow, Marxism's red. These colors all should emerge in this place as they are – you can't take something and make it into black and white, you just can't. I think this is a change that's happening at the level of the contemporary Chinese spirit, or at the level of Chinese culture.

Sometimes people despair about Chinese society. The reason I don't despair is that I see these kinds of changes, even if society has become more centralized and more monopolized by capital. But I think it's good that we now have a globalized backdrop that can bring out all the colors. The hegemony of the monochrome is being rejected by the whole world.

F: I've heard it said that the reason the Communist Party now does not hate the *tongzhi* movement as much is that they hope the *tongzhi* movement and the Christian movement will suppress each other. So the most dangerous thing about putting the two together is the frightening power they would have. As a religious person yourself, and an open *tongzhi*, do you feel any contradiction between these two aspects, or what's the result of them coming together in you?

C: Actually I might be drifting from both of them, or actually from all three. For one thing, we're all being suppressed in this system of centralized society, but we're also breaking out every day. Doing this work of breaking out, striving to break out every day, none of us belongs to that group of people who don't. This is the first thing. We're all being besieged in a red city, but each day we break that siege. In striving to break that siege, we hope to break down that surrounding wall, hope that that temple will topple over, hope to rebuild it in three days. Actually, each of us in this centralized polity are doing this kind of work, this work of digging out or destruction.

And as for the *tongzhi* movement, we are also breaking out, just like I always feel I'm breaking out. And I'm also breaking out of Christianity. I don't think I belong to Christianity, and I don't think I belong to the *tongzhi* movement. I think I'm somebody who is constantly trying to break out of Christianity, constantly trying to break out of the *tongzhi* movement. I almost feel like I'm this sort of person, more disposed to breaking out of the *tongzhi* movement and Christianity. For example, regarding Christianity, I once had a conversation with my mother. She said you have to observe all the regulations of the church. I said the church is my alma mater, and you can graduate from your alma mater. I've graduated.

This is breaking out. I've already determined that I'm breaking out, but this doesn't mean you can really break out – all that Christianity enshrouds you. The process is a relatively endless one. So I slowly make sense of the scriptures by myself. For example, Protestantism has removed seven chapters of the Catholic Bible. If I go back to the scriptures again and again and again, there will only be a few chapters left. And then when I'm finished, on to the rituals and their meanings. For example, the trinity – the church determines that it's three beings in one. And making the sign of the cross, this ritual is just a cultural tradition to me. I can make the sign of the cross, but I can say 'in the name of the son, and of the son, and of the holy son' – what I've said is all 'sons', there's no father, no spirit. It's that simple. I can make the sign of the cross, but for me, there's only the kind of god who has sacrificed himself for the world, not the kind who rules the world. For me, there's no god who rules the world, and no spiritual church. In any case, I've used these methods to express a cultural inheritance, while at the same time negating religion – that is, it's a negation of that type of all-encompassing religion for humanity.

Regarding breaking out of the *tongzhi* movement, there's always this talk about *tongzhi* pride because of the movement, but I think this pride is a strategic discourse. You can't say that because of your *tongzhi* pride you've become a privileged person or a privileged gender, or that you are part of a so-called group with special rights. For example, when we were talking about bisexuality in Copenhagen. That is, your pride is just like Christianity – you're god, and if you're god you should sacrifice yourself all the more, and this is not about realizing your own spirituality, it's about sacrificing your life, without reservation. So if you're really a privileged person, if you really have a privileged gender, if you're really that valiant, what are you still doing depriving other people? What are you still doing exerting your authority over those who are socially weaker than you – for example, the ugly, the old, the sick, women? How is this any different from people who amass power? So I'm trying to break out of this kind of thing, very consciously, very theoretically.

☙

F: In China now there are some arguments between the *tongzhi* movement and queer theory. How do you think we should understand the relationship between these two things? Or is there no relationship at all between the two?

C: I think the arguments should happen within the two different areas – queer theorists should argue with queer theorists, and people in the *tongzhi* movement should argue with people in the *tongzhi* movement. I think that's the only way to get results, and queer theory will advance. If queer theorists go and argue with people in the *tongzhi* movement, it would be to absolutely no avail.

F: Doesn't the most basic mistake lie in queer theorists' participating in the *tongzhi* movement, and people from the *tongzhi* movement studying queer theory – this is the reason they would cross over with each other?

C: I really don't know how it practically should be done, but I think it's nearly the same in the west. Keen queer theorists don't especially participate in the movement, and keen activists don't pay much attention to queer theory. But in America it's different. I think they do both at the same time. The best few queer theorists among them now take these very concrete topics like masculinity, or female masculinity and that type of thing – the way they set up, research, and complete these projects ties in especially closely to the movement and activism. It hasn't just stopped at Foucault and that era, just with the very sober observation that it's limiting, that the *tongzhi* movement is limiting.

I think contemporary queer theory in the United States has seen some new developments. This isn't necessarily the case in Europe, but in America there's been a completely new shift. Queer theory there has completely broken through the boundary between itself and activism or the movement. That boundary isn't there anymore. For example, take any sexual preference – take SM, or foot fetishism – they could write a book about the queerness of it, but at the same time it would be part of a movement, it would affirm the rights of foot fetishists. It's not alienating anymore, it doesn't say if you love feet you're this and that kind of minority, you're a something-or-other. It's not at that level anymore. But as to whether we have this kind of research here in China, it doesn't seem so.

F: Perhaps there will be in the future.

C: There will be.

F: What's your outlook on censorship in China? Do you think that after a while, film censors will allow *tongzhi* movies to exist?

C: The amendment made today removed that stipulation saying homosexuality was unacceptable.

F: Really?

C: Yes, yes, yes.

F: No, they just discussed a few lines.

C: The document has grown, but the wording of 'homosexuality' isn't there. I've seen it, but it's not necessarily the final version – I don't know what they released today, I saw what came out yesterday. It was what was discussed. But I think it's reverted to a pre-1997 type of situation, in the way that they used to use 'the crime of hooliganism' as a sanctioning measure or a way to cast judgment.

[The new wording] is meant to address the problem of minors or something. It will certainly say that sexually explicit content is harmful to minors or something like that, and because there are no ratings in place, homosexuality will be considered harmful to minors – it has a clause that especially emphasizes minors. I think that's been put in as a way to censor things. This rhetoric of minors and the lack of ratings functions like the rhetoric of hooliganism – they'll just sanction you for harming minors.

But I think this amendment will be around for a while. It's a bit like changing the soup but not changing the medicine.[14] That's why Zhang Ming said in his blog that in the current situation there's absolutely no sense in discussing a ratings system for China, because even with such a system, your film wouldn't pass, or you could be rated as a level 1 film but you'd never be able to show a level 1 film, so what do you do, right?

---

14. Cui uses the phrase '换汤不换药' here, referring to the requirement in Chinese medicine that prescribed herbs be boiled down to make a viscous kind of soup. If one changes only the water (the 'soup') one really has not changed the essential qualities of the medicine. Cui means here that in reality nothing has really changed in this law, despite its alteration of some of the language.

They could very well assign a level but still say you can't show it, that you can't show your film in cinemas.

☙

F: Finally, let's talk about your new book. What is *The Big Dipper Has 7 Stars* about? What was the writing process like?

C: *The Big Dipper Has 7 Stars* is a book that I spent years writing. All in all it must have taken me about ten years to write it – in the ten years I've been making moving images, I haven't written much apart from screenplays, but on and off I wrote this book. I approached it piecemeal at the beginning, just using singular memories to write it, and then afterwards I turned it little by little into a book.

Basically, it's a retrospective on my family's story. As I wrote it, I had quite a strong utilitarian goal in mind – I wanted the story of my family to influence Chinese people. My family was quite special, like a family of castaways all alone on a desert island – that sort of feeling. We didn't live together with my grandparents' generation. It was just us two generations – father, mother, and brothers and sisters. There were no friends or relatives around. It was very different from most of Chinese society, which has very strong kin ties and where the power of the extended family supports this kind of lifestyle. I just wanted primarily to share this kind of family, this family story, with everybody. And what's more, my family was Catholic, and we lived confidently as Catholics in Chinese society, so I thought I should relate that kind of power, and what that force we had was like. Also, my father was a doctor, with a particular attitude towards the body and towards life, and our family was a bit different from other households in terms of the way we saw these things. For example, I remember from a young age that our family discussed death and illness – that is, we had a profound acknowledgment of these things, what was sickness and what wasn't. The standards were set by my father. The only kind of illness that mattered was the illness that killed you; otherwise, an illness wasn't really an illness. So therefore you'd always think you were quite healthy, even if others thought you had some sort of malady – we'd think, what malady? From a very young age, I remember we were critical of those kinds of hypochondriacs. These are the kinds of things I really wanted to bring out in this book.

☙

F: I wish you great success with your new book!

C: OK, thanks, thanks.

Index

267